Teaching Poetry Now

Teaching Poetry Now

Edited by
CAROLINE GELMI and LIZZY LeRUD

Published by State University of New York Press, Albany

© 2026 State University of New York

All rights reserved

Printed in the United States of America

No part of this book may be used or reproduced in any manner whatsoever without written permission. No part of this book may be stored in a retrieval system or transmitted in any form or by any means including electronic, electrostatic, magnetic tape, mechanical, photocopying, recording, or otherwise without the prior permission in writing of the publisher.

Links to third-party websites are provided as a convenience and for informational purposes only. They do not constitute an endorsement or an approval of any of the products, services, or opinions of the organization, companies, or individuals. SUNY Press bears no responsibility for the accuracy, legality, or content of a URL, the external website, or for that of subsequent websites.

EU GPSR Authorised Representative:
Logos Europe, 9 rue Nicolas Poussin, 17000, La Rochelle, France
contact@logoseurope.eu

For information, contact State University of New York Press, Albany, NY
www.sunypress.edu

Library of Congress Cataloging-in-Publication Data

Names: Gelmi, Caroline, 1984– editor. | LeRud, Lizzy, 1985– editor.
Title: Teaching poetry now / edited by Caroline Gelmi and Lizzy LeRud.
Description: Albany : State University of New York Press, [2026]. | Includes bibliographical references and index.
Identifiers: LCCN 2025029154 | ISBN 9798855805666 (hardcover : alk. paper) | ISBN 9798855806977 (epub) | ISBN 9798855805680 (PDF) | ISBN 9798855805673 (pbk. : alk. paper)
Subjects: LCSH: Poetry—Study and teaching.
Classification: LCC PN1101 .T44 2025
LC record available at https://lccn.loc.gov/2025029154

To poetry teachers everywhere.

Contents

List of Illustrations	xi
Preface: Editors' Note on the Now	xiii
Acknowledgments	xv
Introduction *Caroline Gelmi and Lizzy LeRud*	1

Part 1: How We Think About Poems

1. A Conversation on Dinétics *Esther G. Belin and Jake Skeets*	13
2. Post-Craft *Michael Leong*	23
3. Unsettling Modernist Poetry *Erin Kappeler*	31

4. Legacies of Empire in the Western Poetic Line:
    The Problem of Caesura
    Heather H. Yeung
	39

5. Unpacking the Interpretive Toolbox: Historical Poetics
    in Introductory Courses
    Caroline Gelmi
	47

6. "I hear it now"; or, Teaching Students to Read Poems in Novels 55
    Annelise Chick and Gabrielle Stecher Woodward

7. Moving "Rooms" Across Borders: Putting Pressure on the Stanza 63
    Reem Abbas and Heather H. Yeung

8. Under the Sonnet's Menace: Helping Students Navigate Race, Constraint, and Rage in the Post-Romantic Sonnet 71
    Anton Vander Zee

9. Rawest Radical Material: Teaching Poetry's Diction 79
    William Fogarty

10. Reading, Misreading, and Rereading "We Real Cool" 87
    Mike Chasar

Part 1 Cluster: Ideas on Teaching Lyric

11. Retheorizing Lyric via the Pedagogy of Eighteenth-Century Antislavery Poetry 95
    Chris Chan

12. Lyric Borders: Reading and Writing with Gloria Anzaldúa's New Mestiza 103
    Leah Huizar

13. Lorenzo Thomas's Griot Lyric: Reading Persona and Race in the Digital Age 111
    Lukas Moe

14. Lyric After Lyricization: Learning and Unlearning the Lyric *I* in the Activist Classroom 117
    Anastasia Nikolis

Part 2: What We Do With Poems

15. Poetry as Empathetic Praxis: Black Poetics and the Creative Writing Classroom 127
Monique-Adelle Callahan D.

16. Performing Desire: Collaborating with Sex Worker Poets in the Composition Classroom 135
Philippa Chun

17. Oral Poetries Are (Not) Lost to Us: Ethnopoetics in the Digital Age 145
Kenneth Sherwood

18. Against Mastery: Working Through the Desire for Order in Teaching M. NourbeSe Philip's *Zong!* 157
Jess A. Goldberg

19. Future-Facing Archives: Phillis Wheatley Peters and the Intertextual Poetic Past 167
Sarah Nance

20. Cultivating a Culture of Enjoyment in the Poetry Classroom 173
Rachel B. Griffis

21. Reframing Modernism: Creative Composition and the Analysis of Modernist Poetry at an HBCU 179
Candis Pizzetta

22. Whose Voice Matters? Reading Aloud Across Language and Ability 187
Eileen Sperry

23. Reimagining the Poet's Procedure: Imitation as Literary Analysis 195
Lizzy LeRud

24. From Stifling to Expansive: Reimagining Poetry Teaching and Learning with *The South African Poetry Project* 203
    Sooriagandhi Naidoo, Toni Gennrich, and Eunice Phiri

25. Transgressive Teaching and Subverting Censorship in the Dual-Credit Classroom 209
    Ronnie K. Stephens

26. The Florence Poetry Collective: Death Row as a Site of Poetic Production and Expressive Sovereignty 217
    Joe Lockard

Part 2 Cluster: Project-Based Learning

27. Engaging Poetry: The Review as Critique and Conversation 227
    Victoria Chang and Dean Rader

28. City, State, and Self: A Collaborative Book Project 237
    James Innis McDougall

29. Experimental Indexes: Quantifying Poetic Patterns and Project-Based Reading 245
    Nick Sturm

30. Teaching Anti-Racist Research Practices Beyond Research Papers: Emma Lazarus, Esther Schor, and My First-Year Composition Students 253
    Mollie Barnes

31. Student Research, Digital Humanities, and Cross-Campus Collaboration: Building *Mina Loy: Navigating the Avant-Garde* 265
    Susan Rosenbaum, Suzanne W. Churchill, and Linda A. Kinnahan

List of Contributors 275

Index 283

Illustrations

Figure 28.1 An entry for the letter *F* by Wanyu Gan. 240

Figure 29.1 Data visualization from nonhuman index by Joshua, Tova, Hannah, Josh, and Leah. 249

Figure 29.2 Excerpt from nonhuman index by Joshua, Tova, Hannah, Josh, and Leah. 250

Figure 30.1 Screencap of interactive edition. 254

Figure 30.2 Early advertisement showing architectural scaffolding. 258

Figure 30.3 An example annotation that I teach students to revise for clearer/stronger interpretation. 259

Figure 30.4 Interactive edition assignment sheet. 260

Figure 30.5 Interactive edition pre-proposal assignment sheet. 262

Preface

A Note on the Now

We developed the idea for this volume in the spring of 2021, deep within the COVID-19 pandemic and in the wake of a global movement that brought antiracism into mainstream public discourse. The essays in this volume, including the introduction, were written and revised over the course of 2022 to 2024. As we write this preface in early 2025, we face a backlash against racial justice movements, threats to higher education, and the continued erosion of democracy in the United States and abroad. We don't pretend to know what "now" will look like when you read this book. But we hope that its focus on anti-oppressive teaching, questioning the status quo, and effecting change through concrete actions will make all future moments rich with possibility.

Acknowledgments

We would like to thank the University of Massachusetts, Dartmouth, Minot State University, and the University of Oregon for the many ways that they supported this project. A special thank you to the Provost's Office at UMass Dartmouth for a fellowship that bolstered this work in its early stages and to Laurel Hankins for her insights on a draft of the introduction. We also wish to thank the University of Oregon and the Office of the Dean of the College of Arts and Sciences at UMass Dartmouth for providing subvention funding in the final stages, which helped make this book possible. Rebecca Colesworthy and the staff of SUNY Press have guided this book in crucial ways, and we are grateful to four anonymous readers whose feedback helped us clarify our approach. Céline Parent provided expert indexing services and finally got to index the word *index*. This book exists because of our students, and we thank them for every generous, open, thought-provoking conversation. What a privilege to work with the contributors in these pages, who have taught us so much. To our families, our deepest gratitude. And everything always to Bill and Audrey, Ben and Thaddeus.

Permissions

Nezhukumatathil, Aimee. "Self Portrait as Scallop" and "On Listening to Your Teacher Take Attendance" are published in *Oceanic* (Copper Canyon, 2018). Used by permission of the author and Copper Canyon Press. This poem appears in "Lyric After Lyricization: Learning and Unlearning the Lyric *I* in the Activist Classroom" by Anastasia Nikolis.

Philip, M. NourbeSe. "Zong #11" and "Ventus" are published in *Zong!* (Wesleyan UP, 2008). Used by permission of the author. This poem appears in "Against Mastery: Working Through the Desire for Order in Teaching M. NourbeSe Philip's *Zong!*" by Jess A. Goldberg.

Schor, Esther. " 'The New Colossus' by Emma Lazarus, An Interactive Poem Annotated by Esther Schor" (Nextbook Press, 2015). Used by permission of the author. This interactive poem appears in "Teaching Anti-Racist Research Practices Beyond Research Papers: Emma Lazarus, Esther Schor, and My First-Year Composition Students" by Mollie Barnes.

Permission to include the poem "Plastic Beauty Floats through Frustrated Days" was given by James McDougall's student, Wanyu Gan. The poem appears in McDougall's essay "City, State, and Self: A Collaborative Book Project."

Permissions to include student examples from Nick Sturm's course, "The Poetics of Sustainability: The Environment and Race," have been granted by the individual students involved. Forrest Crayford, Jayden Kimbro, and Aditi Shekhar granted permission to use a quotation from the collaboratively written introduction to their group's experimental index. John Beavers, Lora Tomova, Leah Tuck, and Hannah Wagner granted permission to use images of the pie chart and one page from their group's collaboratively made index. Ryan Schumann granted permission for the quotation from his reflective essay. Joshua Braun granted permission for a quotation from his reflective essay, an image of his group's collaboratively made pie chart, and an image of a page from his group's collaboratively made index. Rachel Germany granted permission for a brief excerpt from her end-of-semester reflective essay and a quotation from the collaboratively written introduction to her group's experimental index. These examples appear in Sturm's essay, "Experimental Indexes: Quantifying Poetic Patterns and Project-Based Reading."

Introduction

CAROLINE GELMI AND LIZZY LERUD

As any poetry teacher knows, the best ideas about poems are built with students, shaped by their skepticism, pragmatism, creativity, questions, and joy. The most innovative research in poetry—especially work that interrogates what's otherwise held sacrosanct—grows out of diverse educational communities: classrooms with people from a range of racial and ethnic backgrounds, with different sexual and gender identities, abilities, ages, economic classes, life experiences, ethical frameworks, and beliefs. Teachers who operate within such communities benefit from a productive feedback loop. Partnering with their students to identify calcified, outmoded techniques, they develop activities and assignments that, in turn, spark new ways of writing and studying poems.

But there have been precious few forums for sharing these approaches. Opportunities for rigorous conversation about teaching poetry are sporadic, taking place in ephemeral venues, like conferences, where audiences are limited and there are few avenues for sustained engagement. Only rarely do these conversations get recorded or published. Integral changes taking place in any one classroom remain isolated there, shared only among a small group at best. As a result, instructors who aren't poetry specialists but who teach poetry—the novelist who handles entry-level Creative Writing courses, say, or the Gender Studies scholar teaching Black Feminist poets—have nothing but outdated guidebooks ready at hand. In literature classrooms, the available textbooks focus myopically on close reading and analytical essay assignments, even though the New Critical canon of modernist poets who sparked such methods are no longer at the heart of poetry curricula. Likewise, in mainstream handbooks on creative writing, the workshop model and concepts of craft still predominate, despite prominent critiques of the ways that poets of color are systematically excluded from these frameworks. Those willing to hunt may glean a helpful chapter or two from a flourishing crop of generalist's handbooks for anti-racist, socially just teaching (for some of these titles, see our list of "Further Reading" below). But even then, interested teachers of poetry must always toggle between collections focused either on writing texts or analyzing them, a disciplinary divide between literature courses and creative writing that is itself in need of rethinking.

This book aims to jumpstart a larger, public conversation about teaching poetry now, grounded in the following premises. First, conversations on teaching poetry now are necessarily situated in the contexts of our classrooms, responsive to the needs of diverse student populations across a range of instructional settings, and ever impacted by shifting local and global circumstances. Second, these conversations question norms. Just as more recent scholarship in poetry studies challenges naturalized methods for reading and writing poems, so too does current poetry pedagogy interrogate received methods of instruction, addressing what might need to be revised or altogether discarded and exploring new possibilities. Finally, discussions of teaching poetry have broader disciplinary implications. They have the potential to reshape and complicate how we think about fields like literary studies, creative writing, and more.

This book offers a decentralized approach to revising poetry pedagogy. We sought out poetry scholars with expertise and experience in a wide range of different fields: postcolonialism, ecocriticism, feminist, queer, and gender studies, critical race theories, disability studies, and more, with scholars working in Anglophone poetry across temporal and geographical boundaries. We looked for poetry scholars with expertise in creative writing as much as in literary studies, including practicing poets as well as poetry critics, historians, and theorists. In selecting essays, we aimed for broad pedagogical coverage rather than coverage of particular periods, movements, or poets. You will find essays that take up many different elements of pedagogy, including course design, learning theories, assignments, in-class activities, digital and analog tools, and assessment ecologies. Ultimately, this volume is about *how* to teach, not *what* to teach.

How We Organized This Book

Essays in this book are organized into two parts. Part 1, "How We Think About Poems," questions traditional frameworks for engaging poems in classroom settings, inviting readers to rethink longstanding concepts, terms, methods, theories, and histories in poetry studies while offering new ways to approach poems with students. Part 2, "What We Do With Poems," considers new ways of applying those concepts, terms, methods, theories, and histories. While essays in both sections emphasize practical applications, part 2 focuses especially on activities, assignments, and assessment strategies for poetry classrooms. Within each part, a cluster of essays highlights larger topics relevant to today's conversations about poetry and teaching. Part 1 features a cluster entitled "Ideas on Teaching Lyric," and the cluster in part 2 is on "Project-Based Learning."

Part 1 begins by reminding us that countering patterns of oppression requires more than just replacing something old with something new: in their conversation about Diné poetics and the erasure of Indigenous cultures, Esther G. Belin and Jake Skeets observe that anti-colonial pedagogy must always acknowledge what it opposes. Speaking specifically of the ways Black and Brown people are excluded from classrooms, Skeets puts it this way: "no amount of undoing or revising can truly remove the DNA of erasure. Instead of trying to remove it, there should be honest and vulnerable gathering around the fact. Those are the kinds of spaces rich and dense with creativity." Michael Leong builds from here, pointing out that seemingly neutral terms and concepts can be implicated in oppressive pedagogies "contaminated by years of exclusionary teaching practices." His essay, "Post-Craft," demonstrates how to redress our most damaging pieties and myths to expose their latent pitfalls, starting with one of the most crucial terms in poetry studies, *craft*. Essays by Erin Kappeler and Heather Yeung similarly consider the colonialist contexts of poetry instruction. Kappeler addresses ways to disrupt the myth of free verse as an innovative break with tradition and to instead help students to understand free verse as a racial formation of whiteness. Yeung considers what it means to resist the imperialist legacies of caesura.

Further in part 1, essays by Caroline Gelmi, Annelise Chick and Gabrielle Stecher Woodward, Reem Abbas and Heather Yeung, Anton Vander Zee, William Fogarty, and Mike Chasar all consider afresh some of the most normative elements of poetry instruction, weighing the pros and cons of each while also offering alternatives for interested teachers to explore. Gelmi makes the broader case for using historical poetics in introductory courses to complicate received definitions, narratives, and reading practices. The five essays that follow each take up various ways to rethink more specific terms, narratives, and practices. Chick and Woodward explain how to help students see the value of reading verse embedded in novels and offer teaching strategies for reading versiprose. Abbas and Yeung highlight the unexamined Western dominance of the stanza as a formal descriptor and suggest ways to counteract that dominance. Anton Vander Zee thinks about modes for decentering racial and imperial superiority in the sonnet tradition by teaching the sonnets of Black poets like Claude McKay and Terrance Hayes. William Fogarty argues for an approach to teaching diction as more than the seemingly neutral concept of *word choice* and instead as a "multidimensional formal element with the capacity to unite aesthetic and social spheres." Lastly, rather than taking up a particular literary historical narrative, formal feature, or generic convention, Mike Chasar's essay poses a trenchant critique of normative readings of Gwendolyn Brooks's "We Real Cool," a popular poem for teaching close reading in literature classrooms, and suggests an alternative reading that ties Brooks's work more closely to the Black Lives Matter movement.

The cluster "Ideas on Teaching Lyric" rounds out part 1 by focusing on the genre that has become so central to contemporary scholars and poets, especially in the wake of New Lyric Studies and its call for a historical poetics that troubles ideas of lyric universality. Starting by examining lyric's historical roots, Chris Chan uses eighteenth-century antislavery verse to puncture assumptions about the lyric. Next, Leah Huizar's work takes up a similar set of concerns as Chan's but focuses on the creative writing classroom, drawing on Gloria Anzaldúa's concept of the "new mestiza" to develop writing prompts that challenge the racial and imperial dominance of the lyric. Lukas Moe finds a potent alternative to lyric pedagogy in the concept of a griot poetics drawn from the Panamanian American poet Lorenzo Thomas. Finally, Anastasia Nikolis makes a case for the political value of teaching students the lyric "I" while working to dismantle their assumptions about it.

Part 2's focus on applied teaching methods prioritizes students' processes over production, with Monique-Adelle Callahan D. reminding us to ground learning processes in empathy. Poetry classrooms can "promote the ability to effectively read our world and write about it, most importantly the world of people, all of whom are at once the same and different from one another," she writes. Essays by Philippa Chun and Kenneth Sherwood show Callahan D.'s approach in action. In "Performing Desire: Collaborating with Sex Worker Poets in the Composition Classroom," Chun explains how she team-teaches with sex worker poets, disrupting damaging social stereotypes while encouraging critical thinking about marginalization. Kenneth Sherwood describes how he guides English-speaking students to approach poetry from non-English global and Indigenous cultures, using audio recordings and transcription methods to encourage students to listen for paralinguistic features beyond content. Similarly, Jess Goldberg also focuses on pushing students beyond conventional reading strategies, and their essay, "Against Mastery: Working Through the Desire for Order in Teaching M. NourbeSe Philip's *Zong!*," uses for its example Philip's experimental book-length poem, a text which confronts the horrifying history of the transatlantic slave trade. Goldberg's essay shares with Sarah Nance's—and Chris Chan's in part 1—a focus on teaching the legacies of chattel slavery; where Chan focuses on historical texts and Goldberg takes on a contemporary one, Nance's approach shows how teachers can productively use recent poetry about eighteenth-century Black poet Phillis Wheatley Peters to help students engage Wheatley Peters's own writing. Nance's close reading and research activities guide students to build their own sense of poetic lineages and cultural narratives, connecting their lives and experiences to the long history of systemic racism.

As part 2 continues, four essays introducing anti-oppressive, norm-breaking classroom activities carry on from Nance's essay. Rachel B. Griffis offers an array of short assignments that cultivate humor, joy, and admiration to counteract white supremacist tendencies toward objectivity and seriousness. Candis Pizzetta guides her students at an HBCU to create found poetry out of white modernist texts, thereby empowering these students of color to develop their own interpretive framework for white writers. Eileen Sperry transforms oral recitation exercises to avoid displacing non-English speakers and Deaf students, and Lizzy LeRud centers creative writing in her literary studies courses through a guided imitation activity, prompting groups of students to write their own "American Sonnets" after the experimental poet Wanda Coleman's. Next, three essays push beyond the bounds of traditional higher education spaces to unsettle assumptions about who belongs in our classrooms. Sooriagandhi Naidoo, Toni Gennrich, and Eunice Phiri describe ways of incorporating English First Additional teachers and learners in South African poetry classrooms by encouraging these populations to draw on non-English African cultural experiences. Ronnie Stephens points out the powerful ways poetry instruction can subvert the politicized curriculum requirements of United States secondary education, preparing dual-credit students for complicated conversations about social justice. Lastly, Joe Lockard's essay is a primer on teaching poetry to people who are incarcerated, drawing on his experience conducting the Florence Poetry Collective Workshop at the Death Row Unit of Florence State Prison.

Part 2 concludes with a cluster on "Project-Based Learning," exploring how the affordances of this broader pedagogical method intersect with poetry instruction. Essays in this cluster emphasize collaboration and large-scale assignments, moving beyond traditional essays and portfolios. In "Engaging Poetry: The Review as Critique and Conversation," Victoria Chang and Dean Rader discuss the pedagogical applications of their popular collaborative review column for the *Los Angeles Review of Books*, and James McDougall's essay follows with another group assignment that results in a multiauthored book project. Next, essays by Nick Sturm and Mollie Barnes both introduce poetry-centered multimodal assignments for first-year writing classrooms, demonstrating how the interdisciplinary elements of poetry cultures are ready materials for teaching entry-level research skills. In the cluster's final essay, Suzanne Churchill, Linda Kinnahan, and Susan Rosenbaum narrate the process of launching a website, *Mina Loy: Navigating the Avant-Garde*, coordinating with multiple student groups across three different campuses to build and maintain this scholarly resource.

You will notice that we have not grouped these essays along disciplinary lines, that pieces on teaching poetry in literature courses, creative writing workshops, and first-year composition classrooms all appear beside one another. This structure aims to rethink boundaries between creative writing, rhetoric and composition, and literary studies, an aim shared by several of the essays within the volume. By placing essays from different disciplines in conversation with one another, we hope to further shake up the commonplaces of poetry instruction and highlight throughlines between approaches in this collection.

But while these writers may hail from different disciplines, each essay shares a similar basic format. All essays introduce classroom-tested methods and concrete ideas for teachers seeking to retool their pedagogy, and all are short, designed to be easily digestible by busy teachers maximizing a brief course-planning session. Contributors are explicit about the material circumstances of their classrooms so that readers will be able to anticipate differences when they adapt new methods. In addition, each essay features a "Further Reading" section that helps to make the work's array of interlocutors more accessible, offering interested readers ways to move forward discursively with a given essay's approach.

A Few Definitions

As you enter this conversation, you'll notice that many of the essays share key lines of inquiry, some of which might feel unfamiliar to newcomers to poetry studies, so we'd like to offer some brief, grounding definitions. Several writers refer to New Criticism, a mid-twentieth-century approach to literary criticism that foregrounds the text itself, even—oftentimes—apart from its context. For New Critics, the text was an autonomous object that could be interpreted through the practice of close reading. Historically, many New Critics were themselves poets, and adherents to this school of criticism often used poems as exemplars for their methods. As a result, their methods maintain a strong hold in poetry studies—even though vanishingly few scholars and poets would identify as New Critics—and many of the essays in this volume seek to explore and evaluate that legacy, offering alternative practices where necessary. In addition, several essays respond to the New Lyric Studies, a more recent set of critical approaches that emerged in the early 2000s, which some view as itself a response to New Critical methods. Work in this field seeks to understand lyric less as a self-evident genre and more as a formation of particular reading practices. In this way, New Lyric Studies challenges received definitions of lyric by investigating its complex historical and political dimensions. Those seeking to better understand these literary theories will find numerous helpful resources in the "Further Reading" sections of the essays here.

In a book like this that aims to open up conversations about teaching poetry, it's no coincidence that many of the essays are themselves collaborative, demonstrating the kinds of dialogues we hope to provoke: this introduction is, of course, co-written, as are contributions by Belin and Skeets, Chick and Woodward, Abbas and Yeung, Chang and Rader, plus Naidoo, Gennrich, and Phiri, and Churchill, Kinnahan, and Rosenbaum. Ultimately, our goal to inspire further dialogue is best evident in the "now" of this book's title. While it may seem like we're pointing out the obvious, we want to underscore the fact that "now" presupposes "later," a time with different—and perhaps even better—ideas about teaching poetry than what you'll find in this book. For too long, poetry studies tried to get at what's timeless and fixed about poems, overlooking the dynamic ways that poetry interfaces with its surroundings, changing our world and being changed by it, too. There's always more to talk about when we talk about teaching poetry, and that's a good thing. We welcome you warmly to our conversation.

Further Reading

We would first like to acknowledge, and encourage you to read, the work that has informed the structure, format, and philosophy of this volume. Our book is modeled after *Bad Ideas About Writing*, edited by Cheryl E. Ball and Drew M. Loewe (West Virginia UP, 2017). The conceit of writing against particular norms and assumptions, as well as the structure of the "Further Reading" section, come from this important and endlessly useful book.

The thinking in this introduction and in this volume is also deeply indebted to decades of work on anti-oppressive pedagogy. A comprehensive list of titles is (fortunately) too extensive to include here, so ours is just a selection of works particularly resonant with our teaching practices, organized by publication date: *Teaching to Transgress* by bell hooks (Routledge, 1994); *Performing Antiracist Pedagogy in Rhetoric, Writing, and Communication*, edited by Frankie Condon and Vershawn Ashanti Young (CSU Open Press, 2016); the special issue of *MELUS*, "Teaching Multi-Ethnic Literatures of the United States: Pedagogy in Anxious Times" (vol. 42, no. 4, Winter 2017); *Teaching Race: How to Help Students Challenge and Unmask Racism*, edited by Stephen D. Brookfield (Jossey-Bass, 2018); *Teaching With Tension: Race, Resistance, and Reality in the Classroom*, edited by Philathia Bolton, Cassander L. Smith, and Lee Bebout (Northwestern UP, 2019); and *Letting Go of Literary Whiteness: Antiracist Instruction for White Students* by Carlin Borsheim-Black and Sophia Tatiana Sarigianides (Teachers College Press, 2019). There are also numerous digital archives with resources on anti-oppressive pedagogy, including San Francisco State University's "Anti-Oppressive Teaching Resources" (ceetl.sfsu.edu/all-anti-oppressive-teaching-resources) and Bryn Mawr's "Anti-Oppression Resources for Learning, Reflection, and Action" (www.brynmawr.edu/inside/offices-services/career-civic-engagement-center/civic-engagement/anti-oppression-resources-learning-reflection-action). In addition, we wish to highlight a selection of titles that emphasize social justice in poetry writing workshops, including Crystal Leigh Endsley, *The Fifth Element: Social Justice Pedagogy Through Spoken Word Poetry* (SUNY Press, 2016); *The Anti-Racist Writing Workshop: How to Decolonize the Creative Writing Classroom* by Felicia Rose Chavez (Haymarket Books, 2021), and Bloomsbury's series on research in creative writing (www.bloomsbury.com/us/series/research-in-creative-writing).

Part 1

How We Think About Poems

1

A Conversation on Dinétics

ESTHER G. BELIN AND JAKE SKEETS

Poets Esther Belin and Jake Skeets are citizens of the Navajo Nation, and members of Saad Bee Hózhǫ́: Diné Writers' Collective. They both have led poetry workshops at the Emerging Diné Writers' Institute. They conducted the following conversation via e-mail in the spring of 2023 and developed its framing questions together. In spring 2024, they returned to the conversation and made some small revisions and additions.

What about Diné poetics challenges current methods of poetry pedagogy?

ESTHER: Diné poetics, or as Jake has coined, *Dinétics*, combines poetics and aesthetics which aligns with hózhǫ́, in particular how we see the world through relationships. Diné poetic devices make language more communicative in ways that confirm relationality. Combining that thought with aesthetic generally means to add beauty—something beautiful to say or hear. In this case, I would say that Dinétics is a pure form of Indigenous pedagogy as it uses the Navajo language and the cultural context of people in relationship to their homeland, place, other living beings, and deities. The challenging component is that it uses relationality first—a demonstration of how writers relate to the blank page, to the silence or white space, to the sound/rhythm/meter—and then present the poetics in an order that is beautiful—creating balance. Another way it is challenging is because it also confirms an Indigenous intellect, countering the stereotypes of primitivism, savagism, and other racialized metrics that justified Indigenous genocide and erasure. While Dinétics embraces the more common poetic devices that chisel out structural, grammatical, rhythmic, metrical, verbal, and visual tools to create rhythm, enhance meaning, and intensify a mood or feeling, I feel its potency lies in confirming meaning and intensifying feelingness to land. Land could be a device but I think land commands the ways we use language.

JAKE: Through Dinétics, we can learn a more intentional way to relate to language in the art of writing and teaching poetry. If poetry is an organic structure—and we know this because of the way Indigenous poets and poets from marginalized communities continue to illuminate deeper engagements with language within US poetics—the ways in which we quantify its existence should also be organic. I agree that land as a device can be a way to render ways of seeing and thinking. For example, if I asked the question, "What are the purpose of grades in a poetry classroom?" From a Diné perspective, assessment takes form in real time and in the field as opposed to arbitrary percentages. "Assessment" might have occurred quite literally in the pasture or on the range. In our community, the occasion of losing one of your sheep while sheepherding is often the precise moment you self-assess (that is, when finding yourself in very deep trouble). Of course poetry is a field where risks are not as tactile (but not less urgent in some cases), so how can one self-assess when it cannot be felt? Poetry itself remains an unquantifiable act. However, classrooms continue to use common US systems of grading to measure the success of students learning how to write and read poetry. Poetry is antithetical to such neat ways of assessment. Land as a device within a Diné poetics can help move pedagogies away from arbitrary systems of assessment to more intentional ways of documenting the journey we take through poetry. One way students receive real-time and real-world assessment is through in-class and public presentations of their work where they are met with live audiences and reactions. I've had students plan and organize zine fairs and public poetry readings, for instance. In class, students present their work in mock gallery walks where half the class walks through the classroom as if it is a gallery and the other stands by their work and answers questions. At the end of the assignment, the thing submitted to me then is not the actual assignment itself because that is what is being presented. Instead, the self-assessments and self-reflections become the deliverable (as they say) that is used to satisfy institutional requirements for assessment.

ESTHER: Yes—yes, grading and assessment is another component of the challenge. You and I have been talking about freeing ourselves from grading—yet part of that process requires agency from the student to differentiate levels of mastery—what qualities should be mastered? Even those words *master* and *mastery* are unsettling to use. So much of the English language is unsettling to Indigenous ears and the ways we listen. And now we intersect into Indigenous sound studies! Yet going back to your idea of poetry risks and the unquantifiability of it—this is where I pause and introduce the functionality of language, digging into the tangible qualities of individual uses, styles and attachment to sound—absence of sound. That relational quality we have to sound and use of sound in poetics. I often initiate student conversations about sound and sound symbolism—how attachment is created to familiar sounds and the relationality of sounds in the poem, and then how does that revert back to the land.

JAKE: I agree, we highlighted two aspects of poetry pedagogy: craft and assessment. Conversation can both be a tool for teaching craft and assessing student learning. For me, pedagogy involves every part of its processes and the contextualization and conditions of those processes. We are not separate from the world. Pedagogy is embodied because it involves an interiority necessary for teaching and learning. Pedagogy cannot exist in a vacuum, right? Dinétics and other alternative ways of knowing and living across the globe understand the ways in which language is related to the interior spaces of the body (emotion, memory, experience) and are felt through exterior motions such as sound, movement, and other sensory details. Poetry also understands this. However, the colonial constructions of English disembody language and its grammars are ones rooted in a kind of erasure. I think of the prose poetry by Diné poet Paige Buffington that takes the shape of normative prose and its formatting but compresses layers of ancestry, family, and language within those containers. The prose itself, then, molds and shapes to that content. Poetry repatriates embodiment.

How would you define what it means to teach poetry now?

ESTHER: I feel that there is an interdisciplinary creative process occurring—and I love that idea because that is reflective of Indigenous knowledge systems. This freedom from genre is welcome and adaptive, especially useful when re-narrating history. My storytelling as a woman of color, an (educated) Indigenous person, an asdzáán Diné mother of four unsettles US society. More precisely, my thoughts, my writing, the mere space I position myself in challenges everything the US believes in, the entirety of federal Indian policy, all the legislative efforts to wipe out Indian people. I tell this to my Indigenous students all the time—that their presence in the classroom unsettles—and is a practice of decolonization . . . and that I still practice ways to reconcile with some of the colonial parts of teaching and existing as an Indigenous poet. And poetry is a great vehicle for all that (big smile).

JAKE: Poetry is an organic structure and its filtering through higher education (for example, the MFA) does attempt to industrialize the process of writing poetry. Poets know, however, that writing workshops are almost a phenomena in that it's hard to replicate a standard experience every semester. Our workshops rather are designed with the purpose of cultivating creative spaces. However, as higher education continues to raise tuition for profit, the necessity to quantify the utility and tangibility of the writing workshop is increasing because students need high-paying jobs to pay for the high cost of attending university in the first place. Writing and teaching poetry, then, continues to attempt standardization for the sake of industry: write an hour every day, read all the poems before workshop, write letters to your peers, revise, revise, revise. So I agree that the poetry classroom itself can be a site for unsettling because it is already in opposition to a standardized education. Poetry and other art forms remind us of our humanity: its messiness. What you and I both know of settler colonialism is the attempt to tame the "savage frontier" of the so-called United States. Standardizing pedagogy shares a lineage with this manifested belief that what is not considered "civil" is considered something "wild." The strength and breadth of poetry, though, is in its wildness, its inability to be tamed. Pedagogies should reflect that. Pedagogies should unsettle and work to decolonize that.

ESTHER: I like what you are saying here, the organic nature is dynamic not only with the writing of poetics but also with the institutions poets are affiliated with or receive funding from—and the institutional anchor shapes direction, movement.

JAKE: The pedagogy settles into the shape of the institutional power to prove it is not radical or counter to the project of the institution itself. Poetry, though, is inherently counter because it requires a consideration of language and fires back at the consumptive pressures of literature and media. We can look to Diné poets writing in English as an unsettling because the very project of assimilation was to "kill the Indian, save the man." However, Diné poets continue to write from ancestral lineages while incorporating Western poetics and tactics. I think of a poem written by a boarding school student that is included in the introduction to *The Diné Reader*. Poetry, I assume, was a key pedagogy of settler teachers in an attempt to teach English to Diné children ripped from their home communities. Instead, those children drew from the power of their homelands to write into the record a desire to return home, to be Diné. "If I were a pony," the child wrote,

> I would run away from school,
> And I'd gallop on the mesa
> And I'd eat on the mesa,
> And I'd sleep on the mesa,
> And I'd never think of school. (qtd. in Belin et al. 5)

ESTHER: Yes, yes—this poem also speaks to the erroneous settler stance—that Indigenous people lacked intellect and required civilization from primitive thought. This anonymous Diné primary school-aged student not only completed the assignment while innately incorporating Dinétics, they received publication in federal government propaganda for an assignment meant to be an example of successful acculturation!

JAKE: Unsettling poetry pedagogy, then, is not simply returning to its original intention because that intention, too, takes the shape of institutional powers, that is, it can still be erasure. Instead, the pedagogy should actively unsettle the ways in which voices were erased in the first place. This means cultivating spaces with intentional inclusion of voices and the origins of those voices.

ESTHER: Both the Emerging Diné Writers Institute (EDWI) and the Indigenous Nations Poets (In-Na-Po) summer writing workshops are doing groundbreaking steps to raise up the next generation of writers. EDWI focuses on Diné writers, while In-Na-Po is open to all Indigenous writers. We are experiencing a revitalization of Indigenous writers—just within the boundaries of the United States, there are over five hundred different nations—and while Indigenizing spaces needs to occur, we also rely on allies who are willing to assist in decolonizing. Creating equity and inclusion is everyone's job.

How does Dinétics support community-engaged pedagogy?

ESTHER: Dinétics is a way to cultivate space for the Navajo people and language. There are many examples of usage, and since our foundation is in oral storytelling, community engagement assists in building and structuring the craft of story. Storytellers are keen in the craft of Dinétics. The practice of telling stories at the community level strengthens the story and the craft. More known Diné poetics devices are the lyric where a call and response relationship is present between the storyteller/speaker and listener; onomatopoeia, punning; pause, pitch, stress; continuum, on-going, sequencing; repetition (verbs); sonical rhythm; and an overall dynamic symmetry.

JAKE: Dinétics is rooted in beauty. And by beauty we don't mean a cosmetic beauty but a way of life oriented toward hope and kinship. The Irish poet John O'Donohue described beauty as a substantial way of becoming, a forever unfolding of our lives. We enter our communities with the intention of hope and kinship. We are nurtured by those around us and we seek to reciprocate that nurture. The individualizing of existence removed us from ourselves and our networks of belonging. Diné poetry reminds us that we are connected to lineages and our future is inherently entangled with our pasts. Dinétics are anti-capital, a true ecopoetics, and call on its readers to dwell in what O'Donohue calls a pedagogy of interiority.

ESTHER: I love the idea of anti-capital, countering accumulation for personal gain, and seeking kinship first. And ecopoetics makes so much sense because we get so much of our language—its sounds and rhythms from the land—so when we storytell we give back to the land—the land wants to hear us using and delighting in its sounds and what we create with its sounds.

JAKE: Yes, language is a gift from the land. The ability to communicate came from sounds existing in the world around us and Diné poets like Sherwin Bitsui and Orlando White show us the ways Diné words mirror the sounds of things like water, horses, and mud. The land also gave us the written word and art in general. Our books are printed on paper and that paper required a process of manufacturing the land.

ESTHER: That is a tough one—I love printed books. One way to reconcile that process requires us to be attentive listeners and storytellers, to utilize the orality within our cultures.

JAKE: Earlier, I mentioned cultivating spaces for intentional inclusion of voices and the origins of those voices. I think now is a good time to share concrete practices that teachers can do in their classrooms to cultivate these spaces. For one, I always start with my grading policy and the language around other course policies listed on my syllabus. I look to scholars like Dr. Jesse Stommel who have been leading conversations around the idea of *ungrading* that asks teachers to revisit their classrooms with a serious kind of intention with regard to the conditions of our reality. Perhaps teachers teaching poetry writing should be clear and intentional about how a poem earns an A or B. But I think teachers should be honest that a poem could earn neither of those grades because poetry is the unquantifiable thing here that cannot be assessed neatly. Instead, I've relied heavily on self-assessment and self-reflections that ask students to track the journey of their poems from first draft to last draft (and removing words like *final draft* in the process). As a result, I hope my students are less concerned about earning the highest grade or simply getting a passing grade and instead focused on the content of the class in a community of learners. Dinétics supports this because it again asks us to consider the intentionality of the language we use. Language becomes a fluid almost when looked at through a Dinétic lens. It has a taste, a texture, a pressure, and an impact on the human body. So if a student asks for an extension, maybe the answer shouldn't be to point to a deadline. Instead, perhaps there could be a way to think through the values and tenets of the community.

ESTHER: I like to incorporate the use of context into assignments. I have been fascinated with the concept of pre-work. Asking "what needs to happen before this work can be created?" I tend to frame the creation of work with the Diné philosophy—Sa'ąh Naaghái Bik'eh Hózhǫ́ (SNBH) to inform the consciousness of self, relative, ancestor, and community. This enforces another Diné concept: k'é, a kinship term that helps us embody love and compassion for self and others while helping us see how things are related (human and nonhuman beings). This is where sound symbolism is introduced, and the societal constructed hierarchy of sounds. The SNBH framework consists of four parts: Nitsahakees (think relationally, interior and exterior), Nahat'a (gather your thoughts and make them tangible), Iina (utilizing emotions/thoughts as a device), Siihasin (reflective creative act inspired by the knowledge gained so far).

What are some approaches to teaching Dinétics as a genre?

ESTHER: After establishing a structure with the SNBH model, I generally introduce Dinétics using the history of American Indian education practices in the United States. The coercive and restrictive methods used when Indigenous people were taught the English language becomes an illustration of acculturation and assimilation while simultaneously highlighting integral components of Dinétics. By revealing the sacred qualities of language and sound unique to Diné thought and intellect, the tortuous learning methods used in federally run Indian boarding schools shape-shifts into savagism. Diné philosophy teaches us that sound and breath is the vehicle driving thought and intellect—thus language has the power to curse and to bless—and humans control that power. The racist and traumatizing methods implemented in boarding schools taught Navajo students that the English language is brutal, that it can be butchered, or heaped into a globby mess like glutinous boiled oats pasting the insides of one's mouth. Part of Dinétics is folding back into using our mouth cavity and breath to re-territorialize the sounds of Diné bizaad—which over the centuries we have been led to believe is foreign. I emphasize the sonic aspects of language—the breath.

JAKE: It starts with the breath and a sunrise. The spark of life. An orientation toward morning is necessary in teaching Dinétics as a genre. Its pedagogical constructions are idiosyncratic and rely on community to define what that orientation might look like in the classroom and in the world. If I can offer any advice on approaching a pedagogy inclusive of Dinétics and similar ontological and linguistic ancestries across the world it would be this: the classroom is a colonial invention meant to erase Black and Brown people from the United States. The very methods of instruction today share a lineage with those origins. While education today looks very different and is actively trying to revise itself for more inclusivity, the shape it takes is still informed by its pasts. It is an inherited trait and requires intentional undoing to correct but no amount of undoing and revising can truly remove the DNA of erasure. Instead of trying to remove it, there should be honest and vulnerable gathering around the fact. Those are the kinds of spaces rich and dense with creativity. I'm happy you brought up SNBH as a kind of map that allows learning to take place organically and with intention. I think teachers can learn from the model in approaching their own classrooms. I'll add to your translations of Nistahakees, Nahat'a, Iina, and Siihasin, the translations of Dr. Vincent Werito, from his essay "Understanding Hózhǫ́ to Achieve Critical Consciousness: A Contemporary Diné Interpretation of the Philosophical Principles of Hózhǫ́." He translates the values of SNBH into the words Conceptualization, Actualization, Action, and Reflection. Our classrooms fail to deepen these values because of the industrialization of education in general. You mention context as a way to conceptualize and actualize an assignment and I talked about ungrading as a way of Reflection. I think teachers can start there.

Further Reading

The Diné Reader, edited by Esther G. Belin, Jeff Berglund, Connie A. Jacobs, and Anthony K. Webster (U of Arizona P, 2021), is the ideal entry point to Dinétics, and readers will also find work by Paige Buffington, Sherwin Bitsui, Orlando White, and others in the *Reader*. For more poetry, see especially *Flood Song* by Sherwin Bitsui (Copper Canyon Press, 2009) and *Bone Light* by Orlando White (Red Hen Press, 2009). See also *From the Belly of My Beauty* (U of Arizona P, 2021) and *Of Cartography* (U of Arizona P, 2017) by Esther G. Belin and *Eyes Bottle Dark with a Mouthful of Flowers* by Jake Skeets (Milkweed Editions, 2019). To begin exploring John O'Donohue's ideas about beauty and interiority, check out his interview with Krista Tippett of the podcast *On Being*, "The Inner Landscape of Beauty" (originally aired on February 28, 2008, and updated on February 10, 2022).

Works Cited

Belin, Esther G., Jeff Berglund, Connie A. Jacobs, and Anthony K. Webster. Introduction. *The Diné Reader: an Anthology of Navajo Literature*, edited by Esther G. Belin, Jeff Berglund, Connie A. Jacobs, and Anthony K. Webster, U of Arizona P, 2021.

2

Post-Craft

MICHAEL LEONG

Not expecting the word would be controversial, I improvised the term *post-craft* while on a virtual roundtable ("American Poetry in the Twenty-First Century: New Approaches") for the 2022 MLA convention. I wanted to explain what it was like to teach in a particular MFA program at an art school, which I did from 2019 to 2022. Speaking off the cuff, I meant the term *post-craft* to be historically descriptive, to indicate a departure from the Iowa workshop model that had come to dominate decades of writing instruction. Moreover, I meant to indicate a repudiation of the way mainstream literary culture makes recourse to "craft" in order to disguise a white poetics as an objective set of techniques. My usage of *post-craft* was met with both confusion and belittlement. In the chat box, an audience member asked—perhaps influenced by the fact that I was on the roundtable to talk about Asian American poetry—if we only did "identity politics" in our program, as if identity politics were the obvious other of well-crafted writing. I responded that the term *craft* had become contaminated by years of exclusionary teaching practices.

To quote Matthew Salesses's *Craft in the Real World* (2021), the prefix *post-* in post-craft is meant "to open up craft to writers beyond the cis, straight, white, able, middle-class (etc.) literary establishment" (15). Post-craft doesn't imply that *poiēsis* is possible without *technē*. In fact, the naysayer at the MLA might be surprised to hear that in my MFA classes it would not be uncommon for us to talk about, say, parataxis or paratexts;

serifs or caesurae; analepsis or allegory; and when discussions of politics would occur, they would often be more coalitional than identity based. A post-craft approach abandons the myth that craft is a neutral category unmoored from cultural contexts. Salesses's book has done much to correct this misapprehension for fiction writers by reexamining a range of common craft terms, such as tone, plot, and conflict, that can perpetuate what he calls "literary imperialism" (5–6). Similar effort is crucial in the poetry world—especially in quarters that conflate a white, plainspoken lyricism with universal experience.

I am not interested in "distort[ing] by exerting [. . .] pressure to read some abjected texts lyrically and with shame" (White 16) but in identifying racist assumptions that constrain the possibilities of poetry writing pedagogy. Privileging, for example, the mainstream "voice poem" can denigrate nonwhite bodies, voices, and cultural practices. In the video "Is Hip Hop Poetry?" (2018) Robert Pinsky opines that poetry "is written for anybody's voice in a culture in which we worship performers." His smug formulation "I write with my voice, for your voice" is an example of Pinsky reading himself lyrically according to New Critical ideals; it not only devalues the embodied performance of poetry but also supports the inequalities of the bourgeois public sphere, that, as Michael Warner has argued, "has been structured from the outset by a logic of abstraction that provides a privilege for unmarked identities: the male, the white, the middle class, the normal" (167). This logic of abstraction allows the conversion of Pinsky's voice into the common currency of "anybody's voice," thereby making it interchangeable with the "voice" of the reader. Such deference to poetry's printed voice ("anybody's voice") over and against the any number of approaches a writer might take towards textuality, discourse, and performativity privileges a plainspoken style and an unmarked lyric identity. Projecting oneself into "anybody's voice" allows one, in turn, to playact as anybody, which might explain the prevalence of racial masquerade in popular white poetry. Billy Collins begins his poem "Ignorance" by contrasting the "naked existence" of dwelling mundanely in American suburbia with an antipodal Asian exoticism: "It's only a cold, cloud-hooded weekday / in the middle of winter, / but I am sitting up in my body / like a man riding an elephant / draped with a carpet of red and gold, / his turban askew, / singing a song about the return of the cranes" (84). Collins's casual brownface via simile anxiously pushes against the limits of white writing that represses textual adornment and depends upon an abstracted voice and identity.

According to Herbert Tucker, the fiction that a poem has a speaker, and by extension a voice, is motivated by a "thirst for intersubjective confirmation of the self" as well as "an anxiety of textuality"; thus, poetry is "[t]extuality a speaker owns" (242). For Robert Pinsky, there is an anxiety of textuality in addition to the anxiety of marked—which is to say racialized—bodies that disrupt the convenient fiction that the ownership of universal experience can be intimately exchanged. In *The Sounds of Poetry* (1998), Pinsky sidesteps the fact that his medium—and the medium of most mainstream poetry—is printed text: "there is a special intimacy to poetry because [. . .] the medium is not an expert's body, as when one goes to the ballet: in poetry, the medium is the audience's body" (8). There is little room in Pinsky's definition for, say, Tracie Morris's expert sound poetry, delivered in her voice, or Douglas Kearney's visual poetry arranged through expert design. What Pinsky calls "the audience's body" has, in fact, no body at all; it is a discursive construction that indicates the predominantly white print culture of the US.

Occasionally, I have students who, like Pinsky, equate poetry with the decontextualized voice poem—who, indeed, want to "bracket [. . .] the larger problem of context" and "remove [. . .] from the study of poetry the burden, and the dignity, of establishing contact with history," which is what believing in the fiction of a poem's speaker encourages (Tucker 241–2). I met one such student—who once called the study of history "elitist"—in a class I had designed on debut books. I began the semester with Robin Coste Lewis's *Voyage of the Sable Venus and Other Poems* (2015) precisely to counter the fact that the field of contemporary poetry is "too often parceled into 'lyric' and 'antilyric,' or 'avant-garde' and 'mainstream'" (White 16). While the centerpiece of Lewis's *Voyage* is a long collage poem whose reading does not depend on the phenomenalization of voice, there are, in other sections of the collection, numerous voice-based poems that may be legible as lyric. In contrast, the title poem, "Voyage of the Sable Venus," which stretches across eighty pages, appropriates words from titles, catalog entries, or exhibit descriptions of Western art objects, from antiquity to the present, that depict Black women.

Divided into chronological clusters that Lewis calls "Catalogs," "Voyage" is an (art-) historical epic that depends on the remixing of preexisting texts. As a text made of intertexts, "Voyage" requires researching and understanding various historical contexts to interpret it; this is to say it is difficult to receive "Voyage," à la John Stewart Mill, as an intimate lyric voice overheard. The student in question vigorously rejected "Voyage" on the grounds of craft, favoring Lewis's first-person lyric poems, which, he thought, had more artistic value.

To be fair, "Voyage" is not an easy read; a highly allusive (and elusive) work, it functions by an accumulation of often traumatic material. The third section of "Catalog I: Ancient Greece and Ancient Rome" begins,

> Heraldic Lion Holding
> Between His Paws the Head
>
> of a Kneeling Black Captive
> Statuette of a Negro Captive Kneeling
>
> Hands Bound Behind Back
> Negro Youth Struggling
>
> with a Crocodile (51)

There is, of course, nothing inherently wrong about preferring one type of poetry over another. Nevertheless, favoring Robin Coste Lewis's voice-based poetry over her more experimental documental work risks perpetuating "the falsity of the assumed opposition between singing and signing in both Africa and America" (Nielson 36). It is also important to note that this student is white and had told me in a private meeting after class that he had signed up for my course to learn about poetry and not about race, perhaps concerned by the fact that mostly women of color were on the syllabus. In other words, this student only wanted to learn about craft.

Since poetry is an inter-discipline, there is no such thing as "craft itself." Despite efforts by New Critical thinking to isolate the specific nature of poetic technique, it is not possible to speak of poetry as a discrete discipline with an essential core. Early twentieth-century advocates of institutionalized creative writing conceived of craft as a portable and teachable set of disciplinary skills, in part, because they were assuming a certain cultural homogeneity in their student body. According to Wilbur Schramm, the founding director of the Iowa Writers' Workshop, creative writing students should "read other men's work with the intelligent understanding of a fellow craftsman, in order to see how others have met the common problems of the craft and to estimate the effectiveness of their solution" (195). But, as Laura Riding sensibly observes, "workmanship is as various and contradictory as the number of workmen" (59); "common problems" can rigidify into problems for white (male) writers. As student populations become increasingly diverse, we need to keep the permeable boundary between poetry and not-poetry as open as possible so as to admit the widest possible range of cultural practices. We need to break down the received categories of poetry, fiction, creative nonfiction, and criticism that segregate interdisciplinary ways of knowing and making. Any given conception of poetic craft can stem from any extraliterary field or practice.[1] Langston Hughes aimed for his poems, as he said in 1926, "to grasp and hold some of the meanings and rhythms of jazz" (58). Muriel Rukeyser theorized how film and science can enrich poetry as "a meeting-place between all the kinds of imagination" (xi). For Robin Coste Lewis, "Voyage" became an interdisciplinary meeting-place for nonwhite innovation across the visual and performing arts.

What I wanted to convey in my last class session on *Voyage* was that poetry can perform many different types of work and that many different types of work can go into the making of poetry. After presenting a crash course in contemporary Black poetry studies, from Eugene Redmond's *Drumvoices: The Mission of Afro-American Poetry, A Critical History* (Anchor Press/Doubleday, 1976) to Evie Shockley's *Renegade Poetics: Black Aesthetics and Formal Innovation in African American Poetry* (U of Iowa P, 2011), I emphasized an important wrinkle that Lewis had added to the procedural constraints of "Voyage." In the poem's prologue, she explains, "As an homage, I decided to include titles of art *by* black women curators and artists, whether the art included a black female figure or not [. . .] I also included work by black queer artists, regardless of gender, because this body of work has made consistently some of the richest, most elegant, least pretentious contributions to Western art interrogations of gender and race" (35). Lewis's inclusive gestures of homage are on full display in the final section of "Catalog 7: Modern Post":

> Paris is burning the white to be angry, Anonymous.
> Your *kunst* is your *waffen*, Anonymous.
> Untitled tongues untied, Untitled American
> Gothic marginal eyes, still/here, looking
> for Langston. The Black Birds on a steamboat,
> Guardians of Desire, the singing head:
> *Where Do We Come From—What Are We—*
> *Where Are We Going?—*Blues. (107)

According to Sara Ahmed, "[c]itation is how we acknowledge our debt to those who came before" (15). Surely there is, across these four couplets, an acknowledgement of Ela Troyano (*Carmelita Tropicana: Your Kunst is Your Waffen*), Marlon T. Riggs (*Tongues Untied*), and Gordon Parks (*American Gothic*), among many others, in an honoring of intersectional memory, yet the epistrophic repetition of "Anonymous," which acts as a counterpoint to the anaphoric repetition of "Untitled," acknowledges the unacknowledged and exposes the limits of documentality. At the same time, Lewis's dazzling display of technique often depends on the reader's recognition of how she has manipulated her diverse source materials. To understand that she is bringing together titles by Jennie Livingston and Vaginal Davis in the syntactically coherent phrase "Paris is burning the white to be angry" is to appreciate the shade being thrown at rightwing white supremacy. So too does Lewis's phrase "marginal eyes, still/here, looking // for Langston," which mashes up titles from Osa Hidalgo de la Riva, Bill T. Jones, and Isaac Julien, indicate an enduring (and what José Esteban Muñoz might call a "disidentificatory") search for Latina and Black queerness from the Harlem Renaissance through the AIDS epidemic. In the last sentence above, there is a radical recontextualization of Paul Gauguin's *D'où venons-nous? Que sommes-nous? Où allons-nous?* (1897–98), which, as with many of his other paintings, exoticizes and eroticizes Polynesian women. Lewis astonishingly turns Gauguin's title into a "Blues" lyric "sung" by an assortment of entities that have a ritualistic presence. Her tricolon "The Black Birds on a steamboat, / Guardians of Desire, the singing head" allegorizes Black female artistry in a calculated response to Gauguin's tripartite title; my suspicion is that "the singing head" refers to Elizabeth Catlett's sculpture *Singing Head* (1980), "Guardians of Desire" refers to Betye Saar's assemblage *Guardian of Desires* (1988), and "The Black Birds" refers to a 1930s photograph, from the Hulton-Deutsch Collection, of a line of showgirls in costume.

The point is that one needn't have interpretive mastery over the text, as if that were even desirable, in order to grasp Lewis's desire to decolonize Gauguin and establish questions of lineage, identity, and futurity outside of European modernity. The point is that rather than appealing to transcendental criteria (that is, "the common problems" of "craft"), we need to sufficiently research the relevant historical and cultural contexts embedded within the text. If I were to teach "Voyage" again, I would have small groups of students choose particular passages from "Catalog 7: Modern Post" and attempt to track down and explore that passage's various intertexts. I'd have those groups present their findings—their discoveries and frustrations—and talk about how the activity of making "contact with history" helped them appreciate Lewis's historical poetics.

After I taught "Voyage of the Sable Venus," I received an email from another student; the message began, "Thank you so much for introducing [Robin] Coste Lewis' work to the class and for so effectively scaffolding the prowess of the work for those [. . .] who, for some strange reason, were unable to fully see it." I was concerned as well about this "strange reason," which made that semester one of the most challenging of my career. Nevertheless, I was glad that someone appreciated the "prowess" of Lewis's "Voyage"—and was able to say so without using the word *craft*.

Notes

1. John Kinsella argues that in contrast to the "cultural purity" of a "'craft'-emphasis," "*all* 'crafts' from *all* cultural spaces should be acknowledged" (160). For Kinsella, "Craft doesn't need quarantine, but it does need leavening—to open itself, flip its lid like a eucalypt fruit. Craft growing through anti-craft" (161). What I am calling a post-craft approach of making and interpreting is meant to honor within pedagogical contexts traditions and counter-traditions of anti-craft practitioners, who have resisted what Kinsella calls the "fetishized production values" of a craft-based poetics (159).

Works Cited

Ahmed, Sara. *Living a Feminist Life*. Duke UP, 2017.
Collins, Billy. *Nine Horses: Poems*. Random House, 2002.
Hughes, Langston. "The Negro Artist and the Racial Mountain." *Within the Circle: An Anthology of African American Literary Criticism from the Harlem Renaissance to the Present*, edited by Angelyn Mitchell, Duke UP, 1994, pp. 55–59.
Kinsella, John. *Polysituatedness: A Poetics of Displacement*. Manchester UP, 2017.
Lewis, Robin Coste. *Voyage of the Sable Venus and Other Poems*. Knopf, 2015.
Muñoz, José Esteban. *Disidentifications: Queers of Color and the Performance of Politics*. U of Minnesota P, 1999.
Nielsen, Aldon Lynn. *Black Chant: Languages of African-American Postmodernism*. Cambridge UP, 1997.
Pinsky, Robert. *The Sounds of Poetry: A Brief Guide*. FSG, 1998.
———. "Video: Is Hip-Hop Poetry?" *Robert Pinsky*, 19 June 2018, robertpinskypoet.com/is-hip-hop-poetry.

Riding, Laura. *Contemporaries and Snobs*. Edited by Laura Heffernan and Jane Malcolm, U of Alabama P, 2014.

Rukeyser, Muriel, *The Life of Poetry*. Paris Press, 1996.

Salesses, Matthew. *Craft in the Real World: Rethinking Fiction Writing and Workshopping*. Catapult, 2021.

Schramm, Wilbur. "Imaginative Writing." *Literary Scholarship: Its Aims and Methods*, edited by Norman Foerster, North Carolina UP, 1941, pp. 177–213.

Tucker, Herbert F. "Dramatic Monologue and the Overhearing of Lyric." *Lyric Poetry: Beyond New Criticism*, edited by Chaviva Hošek and Patricia Parker, Cornell UP, 1985, pp. 226–43.

Warner, Michael. *Publics and Counterpublics*. Zone Books, 2005.

White, Gillian. *Lyric Shame: The "Lyric" Subject of Contemporary Poetry*. Harvard UP, 2014.

3

Unsettling Modernist Poetry

ERIN KAPPELER

If you teach free verse poetry, particularly if you teach free verse poetry in classes that discuss literary modernism or twentieth-century literature, chances are that at some point you have explained to your students that free verse marked a break with traditional or conventional poetry. You may have talked about the democratization of form or about the idea that conventional meters kept poets tied to outmoded ideals of history and nation and genre. This essay has two simple goals: (1) to show that this narrative of free verse as break or innovation covers over the racialization of the form in the early twentieth century and (2) to provide other ways of talking with undergraduate students about free verse and modernist poetics more generally—namely, to discuss them as racial formations of whiteness.

It is important to note from the outset that I am making this intervention as an Americanist, based on my research about the early twentieth-century American academy and the way ideas about literary form and racialization moved from the academy into American little magazines and poetry anthologies. There are other stories to be told about poetic form and racialization, but I've spent my career thus far researching this one in part because of how frequently it is disregarded, particularly in teaching texts aimed at undergraduates. In what follows, I provide a brief overview of how free verse was racialized as a white form in the United States in the 1910s and 1920s before turning to a description of some of the ways

I have altered my teaching to help students understand how discussions of poetic form and ideas about racialization have been linked, and how that linkage should unsettle us. I focus primarily on course sequencing in survey courses and text pairings in special topics seminars.

The Whiteness of Free Verse

As I argue elsewhere, academics, critics, and editors in the early twentieth century consistently and vociferously argued that free verse was a return to Anglo-Saxon rhythms, and that it marked the ongoing ascension of the supposedly world-conquering Aryan race.[1] Philologically trained scholars in newly created departments of English in this era offered accounts of poetic evolution that tied the racial traits of Anglo-Saxons to the metrical forms of English verse, quickly cementing an association between whiteness and experimental, "free" poetic forms (blank verse, free verse). Indeed, these scholars often used the biological term *plasticity*, which Kyla Schuller and Jules Gill-Peterson define as "the capacity of a given body or system to generate new form" (1) to describe both the imagined racial plasticity of Anglo-Saxons (the ability to evolve progressively as a race) and the imagined plasticity of literary form that was seen to be generated from this racial plasticity. Free verse was, in other words, very explicitly understood to be a form generated by whiteness.

The idea that Anglo-Saxons had a greater degree of plasticity than other racialized groups was an idea that subtended much of the culturally appropriative primitivist poetry of white authors in this era. For instance, *Poetry* magazine editors Harriet Monroe and Alice Corbin Henderson argued repeatedly that white poets had made better, more innovative use of African American folk materials such as spirituals than had any Black poets of the era due to the superior flexibility and assimilative powers of white Americans, who were imagined to be more capable of shaping "raw" folk materials into polished aesthetic forms. Critic and author Mary Austin followed a similar logic to imagine free verse as a technology that could turn Native American oral expressions into the raw materials out of which white authors could make modern poetry—a logic that materialized in popular anthologies like *The Path on the Rainbow* (1918). In these anthologies, free verse poetic interpretations of ethnographic texts by white authors were presented as the aesthetic culmination of Native American poetry. Introductory and concluding essays in *The Path on the Rainbow* made this idea explicit, arguing that white poets had given properly literary form (free verse) to the natural but unshaped poetic impulses of Native American groups who were supposedly vanishing into the historical past.[2] For many white critics in the early twentieth century, free verse functioned as a gatekeeping mechanism that could allow non-white cultural materials like African American spirituals and Native American oral art into a white literary tradition without actually letting any African American or Native American authors into that tradition. Teaching free verse as a rupture or a salutary break with nineteenth-century poetic conventions ignores that free verse was explicitly racialized as a white form by academics and critics in the early twentieth century. So how can we unsettle the way we teach free verse and modernist poetic experimentation more broadly?

Two Approaches to Unsettling Free Verse

As my work on the racialization of free verse has developed, so too has my teaching. From 2016 to 2019, I taught at Missouri State University, a large, predominantly white, public institution. There I had frequent opportunities to teach the second half of the American literature survey (1865 to present). Particularly the first time I taught the survey, when I was prepping three new courses simultaneously, I found it helpful to teach from *The Norton Anthology of American Literature*, but I was also mindful of the way this anthology reinforces the narrative of modernist rupture (especially in the explanatory headnotes and contextualizing essays) that has helped to make the racialization of free verse as a white form illegible for so long. In order to work against the presentation of modernism as rupture in the anthology, I stacked the deck by beginning the course with a unit on American poetry after the Civil War, with a focus on the selections of texts by Walt Whitman, Emily Dickinson, and Paul Laurence Dunbar made available to us in the *Norton Anthology*. In each case I offered readings of their works that went against student expectations (students tended to have a passing familiarity with at least Whitman and Dickinson). We talked about the affordances and limits of Whitman's queer stranger intimacy (particularly when it came to his portrayal of enslaved individuals), about Dickinson as a Civil War poet, and about Dunbar as a master of dialect conventions who illuminated the highly mediated, textualized nature of dialect poetry. These discussions primed students to understand both formally "experimental" poetry (Whitman's free verse) and formally "conventional" poetry (Dickinson and Dunbar's ballad meters) as deeply, complexly engaged with the politics of their time.

When we reached our unit on modernism, many students were quick to see how the narrative of modernist rupture enabled the fascist aesthetics and identity politics of F. T. Marinetti and Ezra Pound—the violence of "making it new"—and to unpack the formal and political complexity of sonnets by Claude McKay and blues poetry by Langston Hughes. Some white students in the class balked at the idea that Dunbar, McKay, and Hughes were experimental poets in the same way that Whitman, Dickinson, and Pound were, which led to intense debates about what it meant for a text to be "about identity" as opposed to purely about formal experimentation. Though not all students were convinced, we began to get at the idea, expressed so succinctly by Natalia Cecire, that "[e]xperimental writing is a white recovery project" (34), thereby pushing against the idea many white students have that experimental writing by white authors cannot be about whiteness. This, then, is one way to unsettle common approaches to free verse: sequencing course readings in such a way that free verse does not appear to be a significant rupture or an entirely unprecedented mode of poetic experimentation. Ideally, such an approach allows students to read free verse by white poets as another form of writing about identity, and to see how the formal elements of a poem can be deployed to diverse political ends.

Since 2019 I have taught at Tulane, a small, private, predominantly white university. At Tulane I am lucky to have many opportunities to teach seminars specifically focused on modernist literature. This is a field that I have increasingly approached through the lens of work produced within Native American and Indigenous Studies (NAIS), which poses important challenges to the framing of modernism as an exciting, generative period of literary experimentation. As Cherokee scholar Kirby Brown argued in 2017, modernist studies continues to struggle with an "Indian problem" (289)—a problem evident in the volume of the Norton anthology that covers American literature from 1914 to 1945, which contains no writing by Native American authors. I have taken seriously Brown's call to rethink modernism not only by including Native American authors in courses on modernism, but to fundamentally restructure my courses to center writing by Indigenous authors who wrote in the early twentieth century. I am especially interested in teaching early twentieth-century poetry by Indigenous authors because it is so often overlooked in favor of more readily accessible texts such as novels and plays (much of this poetry was published in periodicals and was until recently uncollected).

In the first iterations of my restructured modernism seminars, I paired poems by Indigenous authors with more well-known texts by white modernist authors in order to highlight how Indigenous literary works challenge common literary historical narratives about modernism—particularly the tacit association of poetic experimentation with white authors. One set of paired readings I have found particularly helpful is Cherokee author Too-qua-stee/De Witt Clinton Duncan's 1899 poem "A Vision of the End," collected in Robert Dale Parker's anthology *Changing is Not Vanishing*, and T. S. Eliot's 1922 poem *The Waste Land*. Students in specialized seminars are often familiar with *The Waste Land* and with the narrative of historical and formal rupture that is so often used to introduce students to this text as paradigmatic of modernism. In using free verse to characterize modernity as a kind of full-scale cosmic breakdown, *The Waste Land* bolsters the sense that something radical did in fact change about human experiences and their literary representations after 1910, as Virginia Woolf quipped. Too-qua-stee's poem, on the other hand, helps to remind students that there had already been any number of violent cultural and epistemological ruptures prior to 1910, particularly for colonized peoples. Although "A Vision of the End" is written in the prophetic mode of a jeremiad, it also roots its vision of apocalypse in a material analysis of the major forces of modernity: capitalism and colonization. While it is beyond the scope of this essay to offer an in-depth reading of "A Vision of the End," I want to highlight the radical, jarring vision of modernity that Too-qua-stee offers and that resonates strongly with students navigating the environmental catastrophes they have inherited.

"A Vision of the End" is written in ballad meter with one stanza shifting to heroic couplets toward the end—formal choices that may at first glance seem to be antiquated or antithetical to modernist experimentation. But the vision the poem presents is arresting. Too-qua-stee's poem envisions "the end of time" as the stoppage of the stream of years that creates "a filthy sea" of "reeking waste." Within the waters floats everything white colonizers valued—the military, the university, the state, and capitalism. A personified capitalism is the only entity left alive in the wrecked landscape of the poem, and it continues to devour oil, coal, land, and "anything the Indian asked to have." In other words, rather than offering a narrative of civilizational collapse due to cosmic spiritual decay, as *The Waste Land* does, Too-qua-stee offers a materialist analysis of capitalist colonization as the force that will destroy the planet and the people inhabiting it if left unchecked. This textual pairing thus helps to drive home the lesson that poetry did not suddenly become politically radical or experimental or avant-garde in the twentieth century, and that many Indigenous poets of the era used so-called traditional poetic forms to challenge settler historiography and narratives of progress.

This is another key way to unsettle pedagogical approaches to free verse and modernist poetry: not by including more Indigenous authors in courses that continue to valorize experiment and modernity, but to center texts that radically question the value of modernity and the politics of formal innovation. White modernist aesthetics were often part of settler colonialism in the United States, making it crucial to turn students on to authors such as Too-qua-stee who used "conventional" poetic forms to challenge imperial aesthetics and politics. The narrative of revolution and rupture that has shaped the way so many of us teach free verse poetry and modernism to undergraduates for so long has made it difficult to see the overt racialization of modernist poetic forms, but making this racialization visible to students is one way to do the unsettling work of anti-racist teaching.

Further Reading

For more on the racialization of avant-garde literary forms, see: Cathy Park Hong, "Delusions of Whiteness in the Avant-Garde" (*Lana Turner*, no. 7, 2014, pp. 248–53); Fred Moten, *In the Break* (U of Minnesota P, 2003); Anthony Reed, *Freedom Time* (Johns Hopkins UP, 2014); Evie Shockley, *Renegade Poetics* (U of Iowa P, 2011); Dorothy Wang, *Thinking Its Presence* (Stanford UP, 2013); Timothy Yu, *Race and the Avant-Garde* (Stanford UP, 2009).

For more on the conceptual challenges NAIS poses to modernist studies, see: Kirby Brown, editor, "Cluster: Indigenous Modernities" (*Modernism/modernity Print Plus*, vol. 5, cycle 4, 21 Mar. 2021); Ben Conisbee Baer, *Indigenous Vanguards: Education, National Liberation, and the Limits of Modernism* (Columbia UP, 2019); Elizabeth Harney and Ruth B. Phillips, editors, *Mapping Modernisms: Art, Indigeneity, Colonialism* (Duke UP, 2019); and Adam Spry, *Our War Paint is Writers' Ink: Anishinaabe Literary Transnationalism* (SUNY UP, 2018).

For resources on teaching Indigenous literature as a settler scholar, see: Daniela Bascuñán, Shawna M. Carroll, Mark Sinke, and Jean-Paul Restoule, "Teaching as Trespass: Avoiding Places of Innocence" (*Equity and Excellence in Education*, 2022, doi.org/10.1080/10665684.2021.199 3112); Channette Romero, "Teaching Native Literature Responsibly in a Multiethnic Course" (*The Oxford Handbook of Indigenous American Literature*, edited by James H. Cox and Daniel Heath Justice, Oxford UP, 2014, pp. 433–40); and Eve Tuck and K. Wayne Yang, "Decolonization is Not a Metaphor" (*Decolonization: Indigeneity, Education and Society*, 1.1, 2012, pp. 1–40).

Notes

1. This argument is most fully developed in my book manuscript in progress, but an early version can be seen in "Constructing Walt Whitman: Literary History and the Histories of Rhythm," *Critical Rhythm*, edited by Jonathan Culler and Ben Glaser, Fordham UP, 2019, pp. 128–50.

2. I explore Austin's understanding of free verse in "Free Verse, Historical Poetics, and Settler Time," *Literature Compass*, vol. 17, no. 7, July 2020.

Works Cited

Brown, Kirby. "American Indian Modernities and New Modernist Studies' 'Indian Problem.'" *Texas Studies in Literature and Language*, vol. 59, no. 3, 2017, pp. 287–318.

Cecire, Natalia. *Experimental: American Literature and the Aesthetics of Knowledge*. Johns Hopkins UP, 2019.

Schuller, Kyla and Jules Gill-Peterson, "Introduction: Race, the State, and the Malleable Body." *Social Text*, vol. 38, no. 2, 2020, pp. 1–17.

4

Legacies of Empire in the Western Poetic Line
The Problem of Caesura

HEATHER H. YEUNG

> It matters where the line breaks
>
> —Zaffar Kunial

> These other stories . . . can teach us how to keep living.
>
> —Julietta Singh

Caesura is unsettling. But caesura also marks settling. It is perhaps one of the oddest of poetic figures in Western poetics, one which is the least transmuted in translation, and also one which carries with it the heaviest and most difficult burden. Caesura, césure, Zäsur—this figure that divides is a figure that is also divisive, double-edged. It is a figure that splits into two, but is invisible—a figure that comes into form from a space in-between things. And it is a figure that actively overwrites its point of origin, so much so that we sometimes forget about it, noting more obvious poetic "breaks"—the line-break, the stanza-break—as those which bear a clearer task of violence and formation. In contrast, caesura is made invisible, being more difficult to clearly identify even as traditional metrical rules attempt a law of the effective cut. Against those other more obvious breaks, caesura is assumed to be a slighter, smaller, form. Caesura's difficulties are often forgotten, hidden under forms of close reading where the caesura in the poetic line is something to be pinpointed, a simple moment where a term might be applied and an effect analyzed. This essay seeks to speak to these breaks, whilst also making them visible formally, syntactically, in its progress between paragraphs and across the edges and center points of the sentence or line.

       Caesura:
              a breathing-space,
         a moment of pause,
    a breach,
  gap,
countercurrent.
    Between the words a space   a poetico-rhythmic effect.
      Is it this simple?

    Trauma speaks through the breaks in the line. Caesura's intimacy is at one with its violence; its aesthetics intimately bound to its politics. The rules of caesura are an attempt only to naturalize caesura within the rules of scansion in a hierarchy of formal effect, to paper over the raw history of these breaks and the stories they tell. Caesura has for a long time been overwritten by its masks and other more vulgar materialisms of the line's breaks; it has been metaphorized by thinkers who have forgotten its difficult beginning into a marker of difference, of change; in itself, caesura is not visible, so open to such refashioning. What is it, though, that has been refashioned? Poetry holds its resonances tight, and does not give them up quickly. We must begin by looking back, and see how far we have come without noticing. What do we mobilize when we mobilize caesura? What prehistories do caesuras carry with them? How might the breaks speak back? This move is a part of a wager of mine, as poet, as critic, as teacher. I wager that with closer attention to caesura we might begin to encounter differently the burden that any poem carries, to approach more clearly difficult poetic histories, and to find new forms of reading, of teaching, of writing.

    But what is caesura's history? It has a murky beginning, even an apocryphal one. Philologists looking for a clear etymology will not find one. But one thing that remains in these murky foundations is a relation, through Latin, to *caedere*, which implies a cutting action, a cutting apart, a cutting down, a cutting to pieces, even a slaughtering by so doing. This is a very particular sort of cutting, it is fatal, a sort of dismemberment, sparagmos. Caesura, death by a thousand cuts, the "breath in the line"—this is how Elizabethan courtier and soldier Sir Philip Sidney redefines caesura in his *The Defence of Poesy* (1595)—is a muffling of caesura that infects and inflects poetics even to the present; the "breath" in the line, however practicable, might be read as a masking of violence, an historical overwriting of "breaching" with "breathing," an oversimplification, the ultimate refusal of a speaking break, of the body or bodies sundered by the cut. This form of imperial masking, then, is one thing caesura carries with it. The normalization of this overwriting, the acceptance of the original violence of the caesura, can be seen in a wide range of poetry handbooks. Fussell, in the seminal *Poetic Meter and Poetic Form* (1979), indicates that to notice where caesura is placed is essential to technical understanding, and allows a reader to attend to poetic history, and to "the art of texture" in poetry (23, note that here history means the learning of a clearly canonical progression of forms); or as Philip Hobsbaum's *Meter, Rhythm, and Verse Form* (1996) glosses, "a slight pause occurring midline, not necessarily requiring especial marking" (185); Lennard's *Poetry Handbook* as "the medial pause/s in a line" (363); or in the first sentence of the (very short) entry for "caesura" in Edward Hirsch's *A Poet's Glossary* (2014): "From the Latin *Caedere*, meaning 'to cut'; a pause in the poetic line" (85). In Hirsch's description we see overwriting in action at the point of the semicolon: what is it here that allows for the move from "cut" to "pause"? Surely the poem which cuts and the poem which pauses are very different in their actions?

But interpretations of caesura, and caesural overwritings, are linked more closely to an imperialism, a masculinism. There is a neat substitution between *caesural* and *caesaral* which links the pause with the imperial form (beware being party to this parapraxis!). And there is also a second remainder in caesura's murky foundations that connects imperium, nation-building, and revolution with an exposed "second body" in the figure of caesura: the figure of the mother. Caesura's apocryphal foundations lie not only in a thousand, but also a single, significant, cut: the cut of the caesarean section, and the birth of Caesar in this way, a birth that is apocryphal not historical, but that nonetheless persistently haunts the figure of caesura. The first haunting: through the celebration in caesural diagnoses of the founding and forward movement of an imperial—caesaral—regime. The second: through the forgetting of the mother figure in the establishment of the logic of the caesaral over the caesural. Third, through the violence done to the female body subjected surgically to nonvaginal birth, and the forgetting of this body. If we remember this body, an alternative history of caesura begins to emerge that links a praxis of caesura in both reading and writing poetry to birth, to not one but two living bodies, to the mother (tongue). With this knowledge, what does it mean to claim when we read poetry, after Sidney, that caesura is a "breath" in the line?

Sure, caesura's cut is a breath-space, but one which is more complex than the early breathy (and often masculinist) commentators might lead us to believe. It is a breath of life (of more than one life)—a beginning-point. And it is a breath of pain—a death rattle. Its pause-making mechanism is quite literally vital. Caesura's pause is also anticipatory, marking the possibility of the continuation of the line; it is quite literally, perhaps, "pregnant." But pregnant with difficult implications. If mobilized in the wrong way, caesura's gap is a space of forgetting. And caesura's mask is the naturalization of its implications into dominant forms of poetic discourse, in particular those that are naturalized (or forgotten) in two caesural modes that are inherently political: when caesura is considered singular, the forgetting-art of the two bodies of caesura, as well as the cut itself, in the privileging of the (male) child over the mother-figure (a body and gender politics), and the becoming-tyrannical of caesura in the act of the cut and the privileging of the imperial male emergent from the caesarian cut over the colonized female body in which the cut has occurred.

Apocryphal and murky caesura's beginnings may be, and its radical, intimate violence cannot be denied. This ought not to be so effectively overwritten or eclipsed by supposedly softer or more clinically technical definitions that often hail from a critical mode which has, in more recent centuries, absorbed a lot from the messy legacy of close reading's faulty claim of neutrality (see the various definitions above, which are typical of the applications in critical reading and creative writing). These overwritings are a part of a mode in which caesura, even as it is perhaps one of the most ubiquitous immaterial effects in poetry, is naturalized within a critical discourse whose violent difficulties are exposed by its origin points.

To center our reading around caesura's forms and its burdens means finding a way to notice how certain forms of colonialism operate within the poetic line, recentering historical readings, shifting pedagogies, and tracing an old-new inheritance of caesura. To turn back to caesura in its difficulties means—with this break, this space in and of the line, this rupture—we may pose then a different aftermath to caesura than imperial colonization. To echo the first epigraph to this essay, yes: it matters where the line breaks, and it also matters how, and it matters how we recognize the breaks, and name them. To echo the second epigraph, it is the stories which emerge from the breaks which can tell us something about life, about living *on*. Attending to caesura's violent burden allows us to call it out, to make something else of the poetic line, to allow caesura, too, to tell the other sides of its story. Ankita Saxena's "Mother | Line (3)" (2023) makes caesura visible by formal means—creating a poem centralized around the mother line that is the caesural break. The central point of Shehzar Doja's "Let Us" (2023) shows us one way of marking caesura, of beginning to recognize the voices lost to the cut in the line:

Can you let us . . . ↓   *here? . . . ↓*
remember the line(s)
what for?

The arrow, the cut, is the gulping omission (15). Doja continues by transmuting the mark of the cut into the breath

                  There
         is always the next breath

   to look forward to

                            here the poet allows for the relationship between cut and breath to signal the possibilities of telling the other side of the caesura's story, to allow this, even, to infuse more widely the poetic form we take up (15).

    Teachers, writers, here is a preliminary exercise: find a notorious work of, for instance, the Renaissance poets. Make the caesura in the line visible by marking it, erasing what comes after. Write into the break, find in it a series of voices, alternative becomings, alternative aftermaths. Or, blow warm air into the lines, distribute them across the space of the page. How, in the act of writing into the break, does the reading of the poem, your reading of caesura, shift? Below are a series of preliminary lines with which such an exercise may begin. After the square brackets are the points at which speculative overwriting might occur, where new stories may be built. A first challenge may be simply to expand new writing from the caesura of the first line, to linger, as Fred Moten writes, "in the break" (6), working out the resistances to and the possibilities of finding a different voice in a poem. A second challenge may be to build from each caesura new lines, using the first part—the yet unbroken lines—as starting points or possibilities for conversations, for a call and response across the break between the poem and the present.

> 1. Take your line from Philip Sidney's sequence *Astrophil and Stella* (1598). What possibilities are there to write into the breaks of this quite conventional love poem? What new voices, what new actions, might occur if the breaks are considered differently?
> *It is most true, [that eyes are formed to serve*
> *The inward light [and that the heavenly part*
> *Ought to be king, [from whose rules who do swerve*
> *Rebels to Nature . . .*
>
> 2. Take your line from the opening of John Milton's *Paradise Lost* (1667). This presents a challenge to render from caesura here a new or unspoken story. You might invite students to take up here the counterpoint of Eve's voice, or of alternative possibilities of worlding that are not based on an Edenic break. What new epic tradition might rise from these breaks?
> *Of Man's first disobedience, [and the fruit*
> *Of that forbidden tree, [whose mortal taste*
> *Brought death into the world, [and all our woe*
>
> 3. Take your line from John Keats's "On First Looking into Chapman's Homer" (1816). There are possibilities here of commenting on the narrative of Empire that Keats outlines in his reading protocol here (towards the appearance of 'stout Cortez'). There are also possibilities of extending the practice here into a critique or explosion of the sonnet form by marking its caesuras, its erasures.
> *Much I have travelled [in the realms of gold*
> *And many goodly states [and kingdoms seen*

A different version of this exercise might be to take the lines given here and extend them further, letting new rhythms develop through the extension, transgressing the end-point of the line.

The bodies of caesura, the bodies forgotten by caesura's over-writing, are up for question. The very space of caesura, the cut, and its metapoetics (as multiplicity, as metamorphosis, as new birth) means that there is also inscribed a clear possibility for change, a possibility that has been too long taken only in one direction. I'm always reminded here of Saussure's famous analogy on language as interlinked thought and sound: "one cannot cut the front [of a piece of paper] without cutting the back at the same time" (113). Caesura cuts both ways at once.

To make clear the difficult burden of caesura, too long papered over or seen only from one side, is to finally be able to look forward to a future of caesura: to articulate both sides of caesura's story; to hear out of the other side of the divide of this divisive but very present part of poetry's being.

    To bridge the gap.
    To linger.
To read the breaks.
        To speak from, to hear the breaks speak back.

Further Reading

In the works cited list below, the poets Doja, Kunial, and Saxena all work with the difficult textures of caesura on both formal and metapoetic (thematic) registers; the theories of Singh, of Moten, address the implications and possibilities of the metapoetics of caesura. The works in the exercises above by Sidney, Milton, and Keats are all available freely online at sites such as poetryfoundation.org. For a longer essay on both caesura and enjambment which ends at the point this essay begins (asking what the "qualitatively different sense [of caesura and enjambment in a poem] might be [. . .] for the colonized rather than the colonial body [oeuvre, language]") see my own essay "On Toeing and Breaking the Line: On Enjambment and Caesura" (*An Introduction to Poetic Forms*, edited by Patrick A. Gill, Routledge, 2022, pp. 39–50).

Works Cited

Doja, Shehzar. *Let Us (or the Invocation of Smoke)*. Broken Sleep Books, 2023.
Fussel, Paul. *Poetic Meter and Poetic Form*. Revised edition, McGraw-Hill, 1979.

Hirsch, Edward. *A Poet's Glossary*. Houghton Mifflin Harcourt, 2014.
Hobsbaum, Philip. *Meter, Rhythm, and Verse Form*. Routledge, 1996.
Kunial, Zaffar. *England's Green*. Faber and Faber, 2022.
Lennard, John. *The Poetry Handbook*. Oxford UP, 1996.
Moten, Fred. *In The Break: The Aesthetics of the Black Radical Tradition*. U of Minnesota P, 2003.
Saxena, Ankita. *Mother | Line*. Verve, 2023.
de Saussure, Ferdinand. *Course in General Linguistics*. Translated by Wade Baskin, edited by Perry Meisel and Haun Saussy, Columbia UP, 2011.
Sidney, Sir Philip. "The Defence of Poesy." www.poetryfoundation.org/articles/69375/the-defence-of-poesy. Accessed 22 June 2023.
Singh, Julietta. *The Breaks*. Daunt Books, 2021.

5

Unpacking the Interpretive Toolbox
Historical Poetics in Introductory Courses

Caroline Gelmi

This essay makes the case for incorporating approaches from historical poetics into introductory-level classes tasked with teaching students the basics of poetry study. Historical poetics scholarship examines ideas about poetry and how those ideas change over time. As the historical poetics reading group explains on their website, they historicize the "terms through which we recognize, describe, and evaluate poems" and "encourage skepticism about the normative concepts that have been used to study and teach poetry." This skepticism is often missing from classes that teach foundational concepts and methods as ideas without a history, unchanging and uncontested. In what follows, I argue for why we need to begin to historicize these concepts in foundation courses and trouble the norms that govern our teaching of poetry to novice learners. I then outline a team-teaching assignment I use in my own intro to literary studies course at UMass Dartmouth to bring some of the methods of historical poetics to the classroom.

While you might recognize the kinds of courses I have in mind here by many different names ("Intro to Poetry," "Studies in Poetry," "Intro to English Studies," "Critical Reading"), I like to think of them as toolbox courses. At my university, the course is called "Literary Studies," a requirement for all English majors that also fulfills a general education requirement for nonmajors. It's designed to teach students how to close read texts while deploying discipline-specific terminology. It's usually taught using the most recent edition of the *Norton Introduction to Literature* and is organized into three units: poetry, drama, and fiction. Over the course of the semester, students develop their interpretive toolbox, as well as the ability to use it effectively. For example, a successful student would be able to both recognize that a given poem is a ballad and use their understanding of a ballad's formal characteristics to build a compelling, convincing analysis of the poem. This kind of course aims to give students knowledge and skills to build upon and build with, teaching them what is considered most essential to the discipline itself.

But as numerous scholars have argued, there are pressing political stakes involved in the question of what is essential to the discipline, and the toolboxes of poetry studies (like those of any field) are deeply ideologically inflected, are, in fact, cultural formations bound up with white supremacy, colonialism, classism, and nationalism. After years of teaching my institution's introductory course by the book, using the *Norton* and following my department's structure and objectives, I began to feel troubled by my sense that I was helping students to achieve the aim of building an interpretive toolbox at the cost of examining the tools themselves. In this way, intro-level courses can serve as sites where we unwittingly reproduce and shore up the white supremacist foundations of our discipline. At the same time, however, these kinds of courses present opportunities for powerful disruption, for the kind of work that Erin Kappeler points to when she urges us to "think seriously about how our fields remain racial formations, and about how we can dismantle and replace their compromised foundations" (2). Through toolbox courses, we can help our students (majors and nonmajors alike) cultivate skepticism about educational norms and empower them to thoughtfully and productively question what they're taught, to imagine other possibilities.

I chose to create a team-teaching assignment in which students collaborate in groups to teach a class session entirely on their own. I use this team-teaching format because it can be especially empowering for students when you ask them to take responsibility for helping one another to learn; however, if you have less class time to dedicate to an assignment like this, you might adapt what follows into a shorter in-class group exercise. Whether asking a class to work on this project for two weeks or one meeting, the key is to keep the approach active and student centered. My goals for the assignment are for students to consider the historical dimensions of a few of the terms from the poetry unit of the course and to articulate their understanding of some of the political, social, or cultural aspects of these terms. With groups of four to five students, each team was responsible for teaching the class about the use of a poetic term from a late nineteenth- or early twentieth-century American poetry handbook, textbook, or scholarly study. I provided the students with the appropriate excerpt from each reading, usually between twenty to thirty pages (you can, of course, shorten the reading if needed). The options included:

- "poetry" from Francis Barton Gummere's *A Handbook of Poetics: For Students of English Verse* (1885)
- "meter" and "vers libre" from John Livingston Lowe's *Convention and Revolt in Poetry* (1919)
- "ballad" from Bliss Perry's *A Study of Poetry* (1920)
- "rhythm" from Mary Austin's *The American Rhythm* (1923)
- "poetry" from Cleanth Brooks and Robert Penn Warren's *Understanding Poetry* (1938)

I use these terms because we worked with them in our class and students had read about them in our textbook. You might substitute whatever other poetic terms you'd like or even have groups discuss the same term in different books from different periods. As for the choice of texts, I use material I know mostly from my own research and cover a period that strikes me as especially formative for the development of literary studies in the United States, but this would be an equally rich and fascinating exercise with much earlier materials as well. If you're looking for texts to use, Google Books remains helpful and the stacks of libraries contain a wealth of older poetry handbooks. In my case, I also want texts that are old enough for students to perceive what is different, weird, or surprising in them, as well as what seems familiar or unchanged. This positioning means that students can often pick up on the social and political ideologies of the texts while still recognizing those ideologies as similar to the ones that structure their own lives.

As we go over the assignment in class, I explain why we're doing this team-teaching project, but I'm also sure to include an explanation on the assignment sheet:

> For these team-teaching class sessions, we'll be taking some time to learn a little bit about the deeper histories behind some of the interpretive tools and literary terms we're covering in our course. These are crucial tools and terms, but we sometimes tend to look at them in a vacuum and to think of them as neutral concepts that come from nowhere and don't have any histories or ideas attached to them. This is not at all the case. Ideas about poetry, and about all of literature, change over time and are often entangled with their own social, cultural, and political contexts. You will be more effective and aware as literary critics if you begin to develop some sense of these histories and contexts.

This kind of transparency is crucial when asking students to do an assignment or activity that may be different from what they're used to because it helps to get students into the mindset of thinking about their own learning. This early emphasis on metacognition aids students in the final stage of the project, which asks them to write a reflection paper addressing their experience and how this assignment affected their thinking about our course material.

The assignment begins with all students reading and annotating the excerpts from each text using a digital social annotation platform. Pre-class annotation helps to guarantee a certain level of comprehension and engagement with the material. Each team-teaching group is divided into two presenters and two discussion leaders. Presenters begin their class session with a ten- to fifteen-minute talk that responds to the following guidelines:

1. What do you think we should know about the author of the reading and the period in which it was published (stick to the information that is most relevant to the reading)? Are there any references in the reading that you think it would be helpful to explain to your classmates (again stick to the most relevant)?

2. In your own words, how does the author of the reading define the term you're going to be discussing. If the reading, for example, is about the ballad, then how does the

author define the ballad? If the reading is about the general definition of poetry, then how does the author define poetry?

3. What are some of the key passages from the reading that help to illustrate the authors ideas and how do they illustrate those ideas?

4. How do you think the author goes about supporting and developing their argument?

5. What parts of the reading do you not understand or do you have questions about? You aren't expected to be experts here, and it's ok if there are areas of the reading you're still confused about. Please tell us about them so we can work together to clarify.

Following this presentation, the two discussion leaders take over and lead the class in a conversation of the questions that they have created. I give them the following guidelines for creating their questions:

- You can ask your classmates to help with areas of the reading that were particularly difficult or confusing. You could use the areas of confusion brought up by the presenters and see what you classmates make of them.

- You can ask classmates to look closely at a particular passage from the reading and ask them questions about it.

- You can ask your classmates to consider how the reading relates to its social, political, and cultural context.

- You can ask your classmates to compare the way the reading discusses the literary term with the way our *Norton Introduction to Literature* discusses it.

This presentation/discussion structure produces a nicely balanced team-teaching session. The presenters provide context and background knowledge that enriches the subsequent discussion. For example, presenters on an excerpt from Mary Austin's *The American Rhythm* explained her work with Native people and how it influenced her writing. This gave students in the class the information they needed to have a lively conversation in response to the following prompt crafted by the discussion leaders: "Austin talks a lot about the importance of referencing back to Native American and African tribes to accredit rhythm. In this, she talks about how poetry and rhythm are the ways in which tribes communicate. In turn, she claims that it is the ONLY way they communicate. Do you agree with her opinion on the way race relates to rhythm? Given modern day standards, do you think that it has a negative connotation?" These questions got all the students talking, even those who had been silent for most of the semester (always a win!). And in their discussion, they were talking not only about racism and forms of white supremacy but about what racism and forms of white supremacy have to do with ideas about poetry. More than that, they wondered about whether their culture's own ideas about poetry, which they all agreed seemed pretty progressive, might be unwittingly racist.

For the final component of this project, I ask students to each turn in a short informal paper reflecting on the reading and on their experience teaching the class. This gives them an opportunity to close the metacognitive loop. For many of my students, it isn't surprising to see that academic work can be racist or classist. Some have experienced this racism and classism in very personal ways. But what they seem surprised by, and interested in, is how these ideologies inform discourses on poetry. They also often note how helpful it is to talk through these readings with one another. While there isn't time in a course like this one to give students the kind of history, context, and scope they might encounter in an upper-level course, there is great value in giving them a chance to have realizations about the longer histories of the course's primary concepts and to prompt those realizations from one another.

However you choose to experiment with this team-teaching assignment, I hope it inspires you to complicate your own toolbox course and to share your ideas with other instructors. For non-majors—those students who may never take another poetry (or even literature) course in their college careers—this experience with the methods of historical poetics provides a model for examining the core principles of their own disciplines. And early work with historical poetics prepares our majors to continue interrogating foundational concepts in their upper-level classes and empowers them to contribute to the larger, ongoing work of reshaping literary study.

Further Reading

For more on historical poetics, see Yopie Prins, "What is Historical Poetics" (*MLQ*, 2016), part of a larger special issue on the topic; the special issue of *Literature Compass* on historical poetics (July 2020); and the Historical Poetics group website (www.historicalpoetics.com). The publication section of the website provides a useful (though by no means comprehensive) list of historical poetics scholarship and the broader social and cultural turn in the field.

There is a wealth of scholarship out there on the science of learning and the role of student-centered classrooms and metacognition in teaching learning. Some resources I have found helpful include James Lang's *Small Teaching: Everyday Lessons from the Science of Learning* (Jossey-Bass, 2016) and *Make It Stick: The Science of Successful Learning* by Peter C. Brown, Henry L. Roediger III, and Mark A. McDaniel (Belknap Press, 2014).

Works Cited

Historical Poetics Group. "About." *Historical Poetics,* 2023, www.historicalpoetics.com/about.

Kappeler, Erin. "Free Verse, Historical Poetics, and Settler Time." *Literature Compass*, vol. 17, no. 7, 2020.

6

"I hear it now"; or, Teaching Students to Read Poems in Novels

ANNELISE CHICK AND GABRIELLE STECHER WOODWARD

How do we read poems embedded in novels, and how do we convince students that this generic navigation is a labor worth undertaking? Unprompted, students are likely to (at best) skim or (at worst) skip a poem entirely when it interrupts the prose of their assigned novel.

This reading malpractice is not without consequences. What is immediately at stake are students' awareness of how and why poems in novels, or versiprose, constitute verse as a form of shared knowledge between reader and author. Students miss out on the nuances of cultural knowledge afforded by intertextuality and embedded in the history and politics of editorial practice. Even more critical are the implications of the inclusion of poetry along the lines of identity politics with its canonical and national resonances, among others.

Not enough attention has been paid to the generic hybridity of versiprose, despite how frequently verse is embedded in novels. From Ann Radcliffe's Gothic novels of the 1790s to Margaret Atwood's *Odyssey* retelling *The Penelopiad* (2005), there is no shortage of texts that allow us to productively consider questions of genre and hybridity with our students. Despite how enthusiastic we literature teachers become when we are quick to recognize verse's added value to any narrative, our students are often less sure of how to navigate and make sense of these perceived obstacles. Students' tendencies to disregard the moments in verse that, to the untrained eye or ear, interrupt the momentum of the prose narrative result in a need to consider how we support and position students to actively engage with what these hybrid genres reveal about perspective and identity. Through the introduction of external voices, poetry affords the narrative an additional means of articulating affect or experience initiated by the narrator and through character dialogue. These fragmented or excerpted moments give readers associative knowledge, which promotes narrative empathy for characters and the identification of resonances across a vast expanse of literary texts.

As a brief case study, we consider *Bianca, or, the Spanish Maiden*, the posthumous novel of Bengali poet and novelist Toru Dutt that was serialized in the *Bengal Magazine* in 1878. *Bianca* concerns a young Spanish girl's coming of age in England as she navigates the complex terrain of courtship, grief and racial identity. This example provides a model for thinking critically about the rhetorical framing of poetry in novels. Dutt excerpts a variety of poetic forms and authors into *Bianca*, ranging from the opening epigraph of lines from a French song by Jean Bertaut (1552–1611) to American poet Henry Wadsworth Longfellow's *The Song of Hiawatha* (1855). *Bianca*'s layered voices represent the vast geographical and temporal expanse of its influence. Excerpts from Alfred, Lord Tennyson's *In Memoriam A. H. H.* (1850), an elegy written upon the death of Tennyson's beloved friend and poet Arthur Henry Hallam, and *The Princess* (1847) appear three times, making Tennyson the most quoted poet in the text. *Bianca*'s use of Tennyson, then, is reflective of the moves novelists make to associate their plots with other recognizable or meaningful texts and the overpowering emotions and experiences they convey.

Tennyson first appears in Dutt's narrative as Bianca grieves the recent death of her sister Inez. From a narratological approach, the discourse of *Bianca*—the ways in which the story is told—is intimately intertwined with the presence of poetic excerpts. The depth of Bianca's and her father's grief is articulated through their reading and recitation of Tennyson's work. Dutt explicitly frames the first use of Tennyson, an excerpt from canto LVII of *In Memoriam*, as necessary for the pursuit of narrating her characters' experience. We present this passage in full as a means of preserving its rhythm and editorial formation:

> She sat by the window; a book lay open on the table; her eye fell upon it; Inez was very fond of it; it was Tennyson's *In Memoriam*. The first lines Bianca came upon were

> Come, let us go, your cheeks are pale,
>> But half my life I leave behind:
>> Methinks my friend is richly shrined,
> But I shall pass; my work will fail.
> Yet in these ears till hearing dies,
>> One set slow bell will seem to toll
>> The passing of the sweetest soul
> That ever looked with human eyes.
>> I hear it now and o'er and o'er,
>
> How often had she heard Inez repeat these lines in her soft silvery voice!
>> I hear it now, and o'er and o'er,
>> Eternal greetings to the dead;
>> And 'Ave, Ave, Ave,' said,
> 'Adieu, adieu' for evermore!
>
> She closed the book and looked out of the window. Where was Inez now? Beneath the cold earth . . . (266)

Dutt excerpts Tennyson but maintains her control over his poem by interrupting him to tell the reader what it was like to hear Inez's silvery voice reciting those words. In doing so, Dutt disrupts the momentum of Tennyson's original canto and reasserts her control over the poem's meaning in its new narrative context. As poetry is used in service of Dutt's narrative vision, characters' actions and emotions determine the function and presence of poetry. At the time of the book's closure, the poem has served its purpose in sustaining Bianca's grief and allowing her a moment of closeness to Inez in spirit. While Dutt and Bianca turn to Tennyson to articulate grief, neither allows the poet's voice, his speaker, nor its subject Hallam to overtake the narrative. Tennyson is employed in service to Bianca's memory of her sister, and to Dutt who is calling on this shared literary knowledge between herself, her characters, and her reader.

The second use of *In Memoriam* is by M. Garcia, Bianca's and Inez's father, as a means of articulating his own experience of loss. Like the way *In Memoriam* was written as a sustained meditation on the loss of one individual, the Garcias reframe Tennyson's grief over Hallam's passing as a reflection of their own familial mourning. In this scene, we hear Tennyson through Garcia's murmuring—this is not Tennyson's booming voice but rather quiet whispers that Bianca overhears. Garcia's performance of the poem, then, translates one form into another, as Tennyson's elegy becomes for the Garcias a moment of lyrical effusion for Bianca to overhear. By having students ponder this whispered interruption of the poem, they can further investigate how Dutt reframes Tennyson's poetry for her own narrative purpose.

We can then prompt students to move beyond memorial poetry as a genre and think more explicitly about matters of recitation, appropriation and translation. Instead of reading Tennyson, as Bianca does, he recites lines from memory:

> After another pause, he murmured half to himself "Ah ! dear,
>   but come thou back to me
> Whatever change the years have wrought
> I find not yet one single thought,
> That cries against my wish for thee!" (273–74)

What does it mean for a poem to be performed by a character within the plot and appropriated for a personal context, rather than invoked or read in solitude? In order for students to appreciate and understand this mechanism, have students choose a nineteenth-century poem to memorize, recite, and recontextualize within their own lives. Writing reflectively about this recitation exercise can reveal the ways in which context can change or inspire new meanings for the source material. Recitation in the literature classroom is nothing novel; however, when it is used to reverse engineer something as distinctive as versiprose, its value emerges in the ways that it familiarizes the unfamiliar and personalizes the content students so frequently skip over.

Beyond recitation, Dutt's technique of infusing verse with affect has resonances with nineteenth-century editorial and excerpting practices, and this can serve as a launch point for discussing anthologizing practices. Anthologies prompt us to consider *whose* verses are chosen and cemented as relevant and *who* is doing the choosing or exercising cultural authority. It is important, here, to draw students' attention to the familiar anthologies that they have used previously: have them interact with the paratextual materials that reveal editorial influence, including critical introductions, thematic sequencing, and headnotes, for example, before pointing to the ways novels can act as poetic containers reflecting subjectivity.

In the case of versiprose, novels as containers of poetry are not unlike anthologies. Yet, instead of picking the most beautiful poetic "gems" or "flowers" in the mode of Palgrave, his *Golden Treasury*, and his predecessors, Dutt is highly selective in excerpting poems that best suit her imaginative purpose, allowing her to create familiar emotional experiences that our students can quickly access through these controlled effusions. Rather than explicitly describing her characters as distraught or grief-stricken, Dutt invites us to consider how grief and similarly powerful emotions are performed in an intertextual way, modeling how people use literature to navigate their own emotional experiences. In this way, Dutt demonstrates the ways in which canonical poetry can become embedded in our own mourning practices—we reach back and recall the literature that we have previously read or embodied as a means of articulating our own experience. *Bianca*, then, teaches us how literature can be employed to illustrate the depth of feeling or emotion in ways that those outside of ourselves can better understand.

Beginning discussions with *In Memoriam* provides students with a template for thinking about poetry's rhetorical function in the novel; however, as we have previously stated, *Bianca* is filled with a variety of other poetic excerpts. Once students have a handle on how to read poems in novels, they have the tools they need to begin thinking about broader thematic and cultural implications. In the case of *Bianca*, students might consider what the collaging of all its excerpts means for national identity, including not only the author's biography but how the text itself reflects a tension between France, England, and Bengal. For instance, (how) do we read with an author's biography—especially one so greatly impacted by and educated through British colonialism—in mind? An additional opportunity for further inquiry includes matters of recitation and performance, the value of which is connected to nineteenth-century educational and literacy practices and provides another means of visualizing the multiple voices that utter poetry. This, then, provides an opportunity to historically contextualize not just *why* Garcia chooses these lines to relate to his own grief but *how* he is able to do so, as these poems become embodied through the period's emphasis on memorization and recitation. These revelations show students the sheer volume of what gets missed when they skip over lines of poetry embedded in prose; we cannot fully understand such narratives without acknowledging and investigating its intertextuality.

Further Reading

For more information on the history of poems embedded in Anglophone novels, readers might consult G. Gabrielle Starr's book *Lyric Generations:*

Poetry and the Novel in the Long Eighteenth Century (Johns Hopkins UP, 2004), a text that examines the shared investment in emotion and individual experience between Romantic lyric poetry and the rise of the novel. Where versiprose embeds bits of poetry in prose, prosimetrum privileges verse. Stefanie Markovits's *The Victorian Verse-Novel: Aspiring to Life* (Oxford UP, 2017) surveys the generic hybridity of verse novels, a variation wherein the everyday lives common to novelistic plots are narrated in book-length verse.

It is also useful to consider the ways in which poetry has been historically reproduced—in full and in excerpts—across a variety of print matter, including anthologies. We recommend consulting Natalie Houston's essay "Anthologies and the Making of the Poetic Canon" from *A Companion to Victorian Poetry* (Wiley, 2008) as a means of surveying the relationship between poetry anthologies and nineteenth-century canonization practices that persist today. Houston points out that the anthology is not a genre with transferable conventions, as each collection has its own organizational, stylistic and hierarchical schema. Yet, the amalgamations produced perpetuate inequities in the canon as marginal writers still do not receive adequate recognition.

To learn more about the relationship between memorized poetry and nineteenth-century literature, we recommend consulting the scholarship of Catherine Robson. Her essay "Reciting Alice: What is the Use of a Book Without Poems?" (*The Feeling of Reading: Affective Experience and Victorian Literature*, edited by Rachel Ablow, U of Michigan P, 2010) considers Lewis Carroll's *Alice's Adventures in Wonderland* (1865) as a case study for examining generic hybrids that depict the impact of literacy instruction on characters' minds. While *The Feeling of Reading* does focus explicitly on Victorian reading practices, it provides a useful model for introducing students to the ways in which scholars have considered the relationship between feeling, individual and shared experience, and the texts we encounter. Additionally, Robson's book *Heart Beats: Everyday Life and the Memorized Poem* (Princeton UP, 2012) considers the long-lasting impacts of memorized and recited poetry as an Anglo-American curricular practice.

Works Cited

Dutt, Toru. *Bianca, or, the Spanish Maiden*. The Bengal Magazine 6, 1878, pp. 264–75, 279–94, 325–31.

Houston, Natalie. "Anthologies and the Making of the Poetic Canon." *A Companion to Victorian Poetry*, edited by Richard Cronin, Alison Chapman, and Antony Harrison, Wiley, 2007, pp. 361–77.

Markovitz, Stefanie. *The Victorian Verse-Novel: Aspiring to Life*. Oxford UP, 2017.

Palgrave, Francis Turner. *The Golden Treasury: The Best Songs and Lyrical Poems in the English Language*. Edited by Christopher Ricks, Penguin, 1992.

Robson, Catherine. *Heart Beats: Everyday Life and the Memorized Poem*. Princeton UP, 2012.

———. "Reciting Alice: What is the Use of a Book Without Poems?" *The Feeling of Reading: Affective Experience and Victorian Literature*, edited by Rachel Ablow, U of Michigan P, 2010, pp. 93–113.

Starr, G. Gabrielle. *Lyric Generations: Poetry and the Novel in the Long Eighteenth Century*. Johns Hopkins UP, 2004.

Tennyson, Alfred. *In Memoriam*. Edited by Erik Gray, Norton Critical Edition, 3rd ed., W. W. Norton, 2020.

7

Moving "Rooms" Across Borders

Putting Pressure on the Stanza

REEM ABBAS AND HEATHER H. YEUNG

We'll build in sonnets pretty rooms . . .

—John Donne, "The Canonization"

A couple of things about that room. They don't want you in it. It's true. But it's also true that it's a pretty whack ass room. Its outdated décor is garish and overstuffed.

—Barbara Jane Reyes, "Dear Brown Girl"

What is it to write from a between-place, a space where movement and travel meet borders and walls? This place—the ostensibly stable space of a house, a room—is to be desired as fostering and providing a safe space for generating the will to write, from which at least a temporary independence from imperial or cultural dictates might be allowed. This radical emancipatory tradition, even ontology, is now almost fully incorporated within a writer's toolkit. Its main modern touchstone, developed out of so many sociopolitical and literary mythemes, is Virginia Woolf's *A Room of One's Own* (1929). Yet the room is also to be feared as a space of immurement: the locked door, the forbidden space, the terrible secret, a hiding-space, the room become prison, the permanent threat of the foreclosure of the world. This, too, is part of the self-same tradition's foundation myths: the difficulty of choice and freedom, the locked room in Bluebeard's castle, Anne Frank's space between walls, Shahrazad's bedchamber, where we are trapped into the continuation of so many stories.

What is it to write from a place, then, from which the house, the room, might bear the possibility of emancipation and at the same time its opposite—at once desired and feared? While these spaces are always culturally inflected, moving the metaphorical as well as the real dimensions of the question of what a room is or does across borders means that the room itself becomes radically destabilized, if not entirely left behind.

Kojin Karatani writes that the architectural metaphor as explanatory of literary and philosophical thought exists only in—indeed is paradigmatic for—"the will to thought" and to form, in Western culture (xxxiii). But in such a definition of culture it is ubiquitous. All the more need, then, for us to put pressure on this question of the room. We already know the room represents power, ownership, imprisonment, and emancipation, and can be both a symbol and a reality of western imperial or bourgeois forms of life that all too often is taken for granted, its force even made invisible. The reality and idea of the room must both be contested. While the Western idea of the room can seem dominant, the room exists in different ways across cultures.

But what of poetry? Poetry, too, has its difficulty in and with rooms. The above outlined tradition of the room—the room whose foundations are coincident with the dominance of Western culture—we see too in poetry's building blocks. We are taught, often laboriously, to think about poetry as made up of stanzas (or, rooms), and indeed to teach stanza as an important term that students must learn to wield with accuracy. To forget what it is to have easy access to rooms is to become un-noticing of how thresholds to spaces can operate as guardians of or border controls to various forms of knowledge. All of us have left behind rooms, have left behind stanzas, and moved on to other forms of enclosure. To consider again the space of the poem and the stanza-as-room is to become attuned to a particular, difficult form of looking at poetry that demands attention and responsibility.

But to teach anyone to wield this term as a critical tool we must think about the cultural and imperial forms of the room, and think about where and when the use of the stanza is, and is not, useful or appropriate as a poetic term. To call something a room that is not a room is to exert a certain sort of Western imperial poetic domination, to become numb to the alternative mythemes and metapoetics that are bound, invisibly, powerfully, to the question of literary form, and that, along with words, make meaning.

We are wrong if we assume, even as it is ubiquitous, that the stanza is used as much outside of Anglophone poetics as it is within. *Stanza* is a borrowed word from Italian (*stanza* translates to "room") that came into use in Anglophone poetics to mean a section of poetic verse or strophic unit around the same time as the sonnet, too, was borrowed. This means that the stanza as much as the sonnet carries with it a beginning-point in a European, gendered, racialized, courtly tradition. The stanza carried over into poetry in English is a room of the highly privileged, to which many would not have access. Thus can John Donne's speaker-lover make the hyperbolic gesture quoted in the first epigraph to this essay. Such a gesture is not, not even in poetry, open to all, or interpreted—look to Barbara Jane Reyes's speaker in the second epigraph to this essay—in the same way. This is a tradition that the stanza collects and bears. This is a tradition, too, that allows the stanza to become part of an emancipatory poetics, as we can change what a room is and does, we can experiment with this in poetic form and fiction.

Move the poetic stanza over borders, even back into Europe, and one will be met with consternation. We must instead translate! Because there, stanza is not poetic, it is *only* a room. What we consider a stanza becomes, almost invariably, a strophe. With this move what is an imperial poetic architecture (stanza) transmuted into poetic form becomes a turn (strophe) or argument. This is not from early modern Italian but from ancient Greek, borrowed not from an architectural unit but from the movement of the bodies of a chorus in a play as they speak out judgments aimed to make civil society reflect. We lose space and enter rhetoric, but in so doing, our room falls apart and becomes quite something else. The poetry resonates differently with different terms applied. We learn to write differently, to consider different access points, to realize that what a poem is and can do changes when you travel. And we learn that to carry the stanza across borders means that—if it can get through poetic immigration points—we bring difficult expectations with us that are not necessarily naturalized within the place we arrive at.

So, first, consider the stanza as against the strophe, in German, French, and Italian. This immediately decenters the stanza's dominance, and makes it work harder to maintain this domination over how we think about poetic form—the room of the stanza, its modes of enclosure, become the movements of the masked, anonymous members of the Greek chorus within an amphitheatre, speaking out from the stage to a select audience. So where a series of stanzas might build a house, or hold us prisoner, a series of strophes form an argument and present it in a dramatic form.

Now let's go further and consider the stanza as against the bait, or bayt, of, for instance, Arabic, Persian, and Urdu poetries. We might think here that we have found our moveable form, as *bait* is taken from the Arabic for a house, or home, that has its origins in the tent of ancient nomadic Arabs. Here, the tent's structure governs the visual layout of the Arabic poetic line: the visual break—the caesura—that divides the line matches the flow of a tent's flaps. The first bait of a poem, then, is a point of entry, a threshold, into a space constructed to quite literally *house* poetic thought that, in keeping with its material form, can just as easily be left (aside) or deconstructed only to be reconstructed elsewhere. And so we have an idea of a metapoetics suitable for the nomad, the border-crosser: the idea of home rather than the static structure of a house. We can't fold a room into a bag but to create a home? Perhaps! But wait. However seemingly impermanent, this portable architecture of poetic belonging carries with it also legacies of difficult structures of domination—the ubiquity of this metapoetics in various cultural geographies gives pause. We must also be vigilant, then, of seemingly easy border crossings.

Such poetry collected in its imperial form converses architecturally: the divan—a council space or smoking room, a collection of short poems of a great poet—fosters at a glance the exclusive nature of poetry, where *exclusive* means at once "chosen, special," and "preventing access, barring." In both cases it is private, privative, excluding privation, exuding privilege, protective. Watch out, then, for rooms of poets, and what cultural forms these collections operate within! Hover by the doorway and notice the rules of engagement: who and what does not enter, and how. Each doorway is different in form and function, and so is each space, and thus is poetry conditioned.

For sure, the strophe is no less a difficult, elite, imperial, cultural inheritance than the stanza, nor the bait or the divan, but staging these things together, collectivizing around them with the consciousness of their inheritance, means that we begin to think about poetry differently. More particularly, we begin to think differently about how much we take for granted in the formal work poetry does. What happens if our base structure of poetry is a tent, rather than a room or a theater? What happens if we are reading a poem which stems from a completely different terminological tradition—numerological or descriptive of the poetic function (as in some Chinese and Japanese poetics), for instance? How do we occupy, or colonize, the stanza, or does the stanza occupy, or colonize, us (in the ways we read, write)? How do we give (or take away, or overwrite) the names of poetic form?

A poet writing now carries these spatial challenges. In their poetry they will make decisions about form in which engagement with form's difficult histories is essential: to choose to write in chunks of verse, or to choose to explode such verse is all writing with and against "verse forms" (stanza, strophe, bait, pailu, jueju, etc.). To teach and to write, and to teach the writing and reading of poetry demands attunement to the nuances of these inheritances. Poetics requires a reflection on the reader or writer's responsibility in their act of reading and writing. We ask, from our position, dwelling on the threshold of the room, always moving in and out of this space, what this mobility means and how best to articulate it. Here, in this exploration, you—all—are welcome, and welcome to settle space on your terms.

Teaching practice gives us a material, practical zone in which the difficulty with the stanza-room or strophe-theatre or bait-tent sometimes quite dramatically exposes itself: we teach poetry lessons in rooms (a physical room, a Zoom room), each space requiring a particular form of navigation. Each teacher must be conscious of the idea of the room and their use of it, in order to try to create as well as possible a free, exploratory space to foster what Marina Warner calls "the whirr and hum of thought . . . woven of reciprocity, willing, ambition, the impulse to translate fugitive thoughts into communication with others," or, the hospitality that should be the foundation for any emancipatory teaching practice.

We believe that teaching poetry, poetry's 101, ought to begin with a consideration of the room, to open the room, to un-settle the room from the threshold to the chair to the window-view by opening access to all; that to approach the study of poetry on equal terms we must first encounter the inequalities that may predetermine any reader's approach to poetry—to the stanza—what causes so many people to halt at poetry's threshold and turn away.

"We'll build in sonnets . . . rooms": Classroom Exercise

In each stage of this exercise you are asked to work with your imagination, and then to write a series of guided lines. It does not matter what, or indeed how many, languages you write these lines in nor if they are grammatically "proper," or even complete as thoughts.

> 1: *writing from the threshold*
> Imagine: standing on the threshold of a space that you have to enter. (This classroom, a museum, your bedroom at home, a completely unknown room in your rich fantasy life.) Hold this close and write:

One line about what it feels like to stand on the threshold. (Does your breathing change? How does your body react to being on the threshold?)

One line about what you see as you stand on the threshold. (Does the light change as you look inside the room? Is the room large or small?)

One line about a thing in the room that arrests your vision or distracts you.

The final line about what it is behind you as you face into this room. (This could be what is literally behind you, or what you have left behind to get here—literal or figurative.)

2: *navigating the space*

Imagine: slowly moving into this space. Write:

One line about how you feel walking into the space.

One line about how the ground feels under your feet.

One line about what the room *sounds* like. (Are your footsteps loud or quiet? Can you hear the outside of the room or is the room noisy?)

One line about the thing you saw (line 3 above) that has drawn you in. (Does it change as you get closer?)

3: *remarking on the objects*

Imagine: pausing and looking around you. Write:

One line where you reach out and touch the thing you saw (line 4 above). (In your imagination, close your eyes: what changes about the thing when you no longer see how it looks?)

One line where you turn away from the thing that you saw, slowly opening your eyes again, turning your back on the thing. (How does it feel to do this?)

One line about the next thing you see.

One line about another thing you see.

4: *looking out*

Imagine: the space you are in has windows. Write:

One line about what you see when you look out. (Open the windows!)

One line reflecting on how it feels to be in the space looking out.

You now have in front of you a poem whose framework is a so-called English Sonnet. How does this make you look back on the poem? What would you change? How does this affect the way that you think about how a stanza works? What walls or lines do you think we need to break down, bolster up, or put windows or doors in, or even walk away from? Who would you want to welcome into the space you have built, what ghosts would you banish? Or, would you like to escape this space and take the poem into the wild? Breathe or break these thoughts into a second edit of your lines.

This exercise is a practical groundwork for an understanding of the ways that poetic form can work. Teachers—you may want to modify this exercise to be explicitly about the classroom space in order to find creative feedback on barriers to access and to practice. You might want to set pertinent restrictions in order to teach a historical lesson. You might want to use the exercise to encourage reflection on imagined, utopic, speculative spaces. However conceived, the exercise provides us with a structure to make within and break out of in our own writing practice. To travel across threshold-zones. It also provides a way into reading certain sorts of poems—both those which are constructed in stanzaic forms, and those which break with these forms. In this way we can see the real meaning of these breaks with/in the stanza: whether they are to destroy or to emancipate, to free or to shackle, and how to call out these functions.

We might all think—and sometimes are forced to think or be—in stanzas, but these stanzas are all different. Such an approach allows us to begin to address these differences, to learn the wild and variable conditions of poetry. Using this exercise to begin to think independently about what the control and poetics of the stanza are to us allows us also to bring the stanza into conversation with the classroom space, and other spaces, and address difficulties and hierarchies of access and expectation through poetic means, opening the threshold, then, to a shared articulation of what poetry does and means, and how it travels.

Further Reading

Our talisman-poems for this essay and exercise are: Basil Bunting's "Ode 36" (*Complete Poems*, Oxford UP, 1994), Elizabeth Bishop's "Sonnet" of 1972 (*The Complete Poems 1927–1979*, Farrar, Straus, and Giroux, 1984), Evie Shockley's "in a no win zone" (*semiautomatic*, Wesleyan UP, 2017),

Victoria Adukwei Bulley's "[ ] noise" (*Quiet*, Faber and Faber, 2022), Solmaz Sharif's "Look" (*Look*, Graywolf Press, 2016), Zeina Hashem Beck's "Ghazal: With Prayer" (*O*, Penguin, 2002), and Raymond Antrobus's "I Move Through London Like a Hotep" (*The First Time I Wore Hearing Aids*, prod. Ian Brennan, Bandcamp, 2022). By *talisman* we mean poems which carry condensed within them in diverse ways the practice, the theories, and the ethics that we elaborate in this essay, poems that we carry with us in order to help focus and refocus thought, poetic talismans that are, as Olivia Sudjic describes, "to be held against annihilation" and that galvanize continued practice from the threshold-space (7). These are also poems that (from both of our experience) are excellent examples to use in classroom teaching about the stanza in particular and poetic form more generally.

Works Cited

Donne, John. *Selected Poems*. Penguin, 2006.

Karatani, Kojin. *Architecture as Metaphor: Language, Number, Money*. Translated by Sabu Konso, edited by Michael Speaks with Cynthia Davidson, MIT Press, 1995.

Reyes, Barbara Jane. *Letters to a Young Brown Girl*. BOA Editions, 2020.

Sudjic, Olivia. *Exposure*. Peninsula Press, 2018.

Warner, Marina. "Learning My Lesson." *The London Review of Books*, vol. 37, no. 19, 19 Mar. 2015. *The London Review of Books*, www.lrb.co.uk/the-paper/v37/n06/marina-warner/learning-my-lesson.

8

Under the Sonnet's Menace

Helping Students Navigate Race, Constraint, and Rage in the Post-Romantic Sonnet

ANTON VANDER ZEE

In *Forms of Contention*, her 2020 study of the African American sonnet tradition, Hollis Robbins recalls a poetry reading she had recently attended in which the former poet laureate Natasha Trethewey discussed her engagement with the sonnet: "She touched on her use of the sonnet as a 'received European form,'" Robbins writes, "and spoke of using the master's tools to dismantle the master's house. "The audience," she continues, "was transfixed" (2).

After the reading, Robbins offers a question as applause dissipates: "Why," she asks Trethewey, "do you still characterize the sonnet as a form received from white poets?" The question is motivated by a strong desire to see the form not just occupied but owned by Black poets. After listing a series of prominent Black sonnet writers, her question continues: "How many poems will have to be written before someone will say she received the form from a black poet?" Robbins notes that, before responding, Trethewey is silent for a while: "You're right, I can't say that anymore," the poet concedes. "I received the form from Gwendolyn Brooks" (2).

The critic seems satisfied that her counter-narrative of influence has prevailed, though she notes a tension between them after the reading. For Robbins, this tension suggests a difficult truth in African American poetry, one that also drives her book's argument that a distinct African American sonnet tradition has been overlooked. "Why not say," she asks, "that Dunbar, McKay, Brooks, Hayden, Baraka, and Hayes stole the sonnet form and made it different and better?" (5). One might, however, read Trethewey's silence—and that noted tension—differently.

While Robbins's argument informs how critics view the sonnet tradition, she risks conflating the critical act of recovering the African American sonnet tradition with the poetic act of composing within that tradition. For Trethewey, what the sonnet form would seem to make available over its many reincarnations, it also, historically, withholds: the invitation to self-fashion, the freedom to express love and desire, the permission to express inviolate inwardness, the right to protest and proclaim. The sonnet becomes, then, a potent synecdoche for a white tradition, white institutions, white supremacy. Black poets often turn to the sonnet not simply as an expressive vehicle that they might finally call their own, but to stage an encounter with both self and world. And that encounter persists in the form and the idea of the sonnet. When Trethewey frames the form as a distinctly "European inheritance," she indicates that while it cannot be simply stolen, as Hollis suggests, it can certainly be *possessed*.

At a pedagogical moment in the US when conservative school boards and state school trustees ignore how deeply our institutions inscribe white supremacy, the sonnet becomes a cultural space in which white poetic tradition can be unsettled, and in which intensive engagements with white institutions are suggestively staged. To students, the sonnet can seem to be a small poetic machine made of too many parts. But when they come to understand how poets engage the tradition, they come to see the sonnet as a space in which one might explore the very idea of rules and the deeper relationship between constraint and freedom.

This essay focuses the pedagogical effort to center Black voices in the sonnet tradition, framing this effort through the work of the Jamaican-born Harlem Renaissance poet Claude McKay. McKay's work stands out for its post-Romantic figural transformations, repurposing the standard tropes and obsessions of the sonnet tradition in ways that deliver incisive critique. And these transformations are, uniquely, *post*-Romantic. Key Romantic poets developed the canonical sonnet to a point where it had reached a sort of maximal tropic capacity. In centuries prior, Petrarch, Sidney, Shakespeare, Milton, and Donne variously imbue the form with tortured selfhood, lyric longing, spiritual pining, and political assertion. The Romantics add a heightened melancholic interiority and an attention to self in relation to urban and pastoral environments. Beyond this expanded topical terrain, the Romantic sonnet also amplifies a long-standing metapoetic engagement with the sonnet's fundamental tropes of space, constraint, and enclosure. Pushing against these constraints, the Romantics also bring to the sonnet an occasional penchant for finely calibrated rage—though it would take a distinctly post-Romantic poet like McKay to give these tropes of constraint and rage truly extraordinary power.

At the start of such a discussion, I find it helpful to divide the class into groups, asking each to lead a conversation about a poem I assign them from the handful of sonnets discussed below. Attending to the poem's broader themes, I ask them to create a list of all the ways a given poem offers figures for boundedness, constraint, and enclosure. How, I ask, do these various figures work alongside one another? Then, attending to what their assigned poem achieves formally, I ask them to discuss where the sonnet seems to abide by its own rules. Introducing the key formal attributes of the sonnet, I ask them where the iambic rhythm holds and where it breaks, and whether their sonnet neatly fits a traditional rhyme scheme and argumentative structure. And, if not, how are these formal deviations meaningfully related to their thematic meditations on constraint?

From the very beginning of McKay's sonnet-crafting, the form functioned as an alien space. In his "Invocation" (1917), he calls upon his ancestral spirit to help "bring ancient music into my modern heart" (7) as he seeks to make a dead form sing. Speaking as much to his literal environment in a hostile and racist country as to the bindings of the sonnet itself, he calls out: "Lift me to thee out of this alien place / so I might be, thine exiled counterpart, / the worthy singer of my world and race" (12–14). This early urge to transcend the sonnet's—and the white world's—constraints initiates a core tension in McKay's work between the illusion of the unbound and the fetters that remain to be tested and broken.

In "Samson" (1920), McKay provides another spatial metaphor for the sonnet when he calls out to "Sable Samsons in white prisons bound / wounded and blinded, in your hidden strength" (9–10) as he relishes the walls coming down. In "Negro Spiritual" (1922), the sonnet's space is figured as a "garish marble hall" (9) as McKay meditates self-reflexively on how his own authentic voice of blackness, like those spirituals, must be deformed in the formal walls of the sonnet, performing what he calls an "alien vandal mind" (12). His sonnet "The White House" (1922) is more direct in its performance of righteous anger pushing against these constraints. The sonnet begins: "Your door is shut against my tightened face / And I am sharp as steel with discontent" (1–2). Facing the sonnet's exclusive white space, the poet seeks to repossess the "grace / to bear my anger proudly and unbent" (3–4). The iambs here feel tense—more like a clenched fist than a mere poetic exercise. While John Keats, in his famous metasonnet beginning "If by Dull Rhymes Our Sonnet Must be Chained" (1819) blithely sought what he called those "sandals more interwoven and complete / to fit the naked foot of poesy," McKay must go unshod: "The pavement slabs burn loose beneath my feet," he writes (5). The very poetic ground is unstable in this white house. As the poem continues, we see McKay's rage emerge in response to white space that depends upon the shuttering and othering of the poet: "passion rends my vitals as I pass / A chafing savage down the decent street / Where boldly shines your shuttered door of glass" (6–8). McKay's perfect execution of the sonnet here masks the power it takes to stand strong and achieve a voice when the white world, looking through those closed glass doors, gives back to the poet only a dehumanizing reflection.

To enter the sonnet form is to be doubly bound for McKay. In the sonnet "In Bondage" (1920), he speaks less to the constraints noted above, and more to his attachment to his brothers in struggle. The poem begins with a pastoral scene in a subjunctive mood that resembles many pastoral sonnets of the Romantic era: "I would be wandering in distant fields / Where man, and bird, and beast, lives leisurely / And the old earth is kind" (1–3). "But," McKay concludes, revoking this image, "I am bound with you in your mean graves / O black men, simple slaves of ruthless slaves" (13–14). The initial sense of boundedness suggests a combination of solidarity and entrapment that forms the backdrop for how all human actors here are more nefariously bound to the complex and ruthless ideology of white supremacy. The sonnet, throughout McKay's work, is the space where these double bindings can be fretted and strained to create a distinctly intensive music.

McKay's engagements with the sonnet's constraints transform, most famously, into a quiet rage in his sonnet "America" (1921). Here, McKay performs a seething anger pressing against the walls of constraint. "Although she feeds me bread of bitterness" (1), he writes in lines that refer to both America and the sonnet itself, "her vigor flows like tides into my blood, / Giving me strength erect against her hate" (5–6). The often noted echo of Percy Bysshe Shelley's "Ozymandias" (1818) is clear in the sonnet's final lines:

Darkly I gaze into the days ahead,
And see her might and granite wonders there,
Beneath the touch of Time's unerring hand,
Like priceless treasures sinking in the sand. (11–14)

Obstructing the sonnet's neat iambic rhythm, McKay's vision breaks "darkly" into the sonnet tradition. In "America," the poet arrives "as a rebel fronts the king in state" (8), standing within the walls of the sonnet, quietly confronting its power. McKay, here, executes a brilliant mastery of form and a simultaneous deformation from within, combining constraint and rage in a way that later Black poets would continue to explore.

The contemporary American poet Terrance Hayes's recent book *American Sonnets for My Past and Future Assassin* (Penguin, 2018) includes a sonnet that deftly voices and then reverses McKay's trope of intensely claustrophobic poems. To prepare my students for Hayes's amped-up density and complexity, I ask them to think about the poem's rhetorical situation: who or what is the speaker? Who or what is being addressed? Although the addressee in Hayes's sonnets is often shifting, the addressee in this specific sonnet can be read as a mirror self, a narrating poet and a narrated poet: "I lock you in an American sonnet that is part prison, / Part panic closet," the sonnet begins, "a little room in a house set aflame. / I lock you in in a form that is part music box, part meat / grinder to separate the song of the bird from the bone" (1–4). Here, the sonnet transforms into a torture chamber. In a surreal turn, the poem's speaker proclaims: "I make you both gym and crow here" (7). Students will often note the clear Jim Crow reference here, but this reference also disguises something more subtle. "Gym" here is a space of enclosure—a space of performance amidst constraint. To "crow," however, takes on a verbal sense—an ambiguous cry of torment or triumph emanating from blackness—the sonnet's little song, just off-key.

Under this intense pressure, however, something gives: "You undergo a beautiful catharsis trapped one night," Hayes writes (8). In the final three lines, the repetition of "I lock" that initiates the poem transforms into an act of intentional poesis: "I make." "I make you a box of darkness," Hayes writes, "with a bird in its heart. Voltas of acoustics, instinct, and metaphor" (12–13). The poem forms an insinuating shadow-version of Keats's sonnet of chained rhymes mentioned above. In both poems, the prison-like enclosure and the fetters invite the construction of a *made place*. There's a concession to the sonnet's constraints in both poems, but then a repossession of them. Keats, in his sonnet, calls on poets to be misers of sound, and Hayes impeccably crafts his voltas of acoustics, instinct and metaphor. Hayes's poem ends with an ambivalent reflection on poetic tradition as the addressee shifts to include the self, but perhaps also the sonnet itself and the white world it represents as the poet speaks out from and into that box of darkness: "It is not enough / to love you," the poem concludes. "It is not enough to want you destroyed" (14). Poets come to the sonnet to confront this ambivalence and this brokenness, this rage against constraint. It can't be stolen, only possessed.

This engagement with how teachers can center Black voices in the sonnet tradition could be accomplished at a smaller pedagogical scale: a weeklong unit in a survey course, for example. On a larger scale, one might develop a course such as "Sonnet Bound: Claude McKay and the Sonnet Tradition," which would center the broader sonnet tradition—in both its European inheritance and its later possessions—in the figure of McKay. In addition to his remarkable sonnets of bounded rage, McKay refigures just about every trope in the sonnet handbook: Petrarch's wayward ship courses through his sonnets, as does Milton's trumpeted politics, Baudelaire's spleen, Donne's agitated devotional orientation, Wordsworth's meditations on space and place (both urban and rural), and Keats's reflective melancholy. Such an approach would help loosen the relentlessly diachronic approach that we see so often in handbooks and histories of the sonnet. McKay, in such a story, would center a network of connections, and perhaps the sonnet might be less bound to the traditional ways we talk about it, frame it editorially, and present it to our students.

Further Reading

In addition to Robbins's work, Timo Müller offers a complete literary history in *The African American Sonnet* (UP of Mississippi, 2018). Both works trace the African American sonnet tradition into the twenty-first century. *Complete Poems: Claude McKay* (U of Illinois Press, 2008) is the essential resource for study of McKay's poetry. Terrance Hayes's most recent book-length engagement with the sonnet form continues his long-standing investment in the sonnet form. Jericho Brown takes the sonnet form to new places with the invention of his "duplex" form in his 2019 Pulitzer Prize-winning collection *The Tradition* (Copper Canyon Press). One could also turn to John Murillo's powerful sonnet series, "A Refusal to Mourn the Deaths by Gunfire, of Three Men in Brooklyn," which appears in his recent *Kontemporary Amerikan Poetry* (Four Way Books, 2020) and represents ongoing engagement with the sonnet that begin in his debut *Up Jump the Boogie* (Cypher Books, 2010). Sonnets also recur in the recent work of Evie Shockley, Shane McRae, Roger Reeves, Amaud Jamal Johnson, Tyehimba Jess, A. Van Jordan, Patricia Smith, and Erica Dawson, among others. There has also been renewed attention to the sonnets of post-WWII poets, including the recent publication of *Heart First into This Ruin: The Complete American Sonnets* (Black Sparrow Press, 2022), which collects Wanda Coleman's sonnets. Another key resource is the broadly representative collection *The American Sonnet: An Anthology of Poems and Essays* (U of Iowa P, 2022) edited by Dora Malech and Laura T. Smith, which situates Black voices at the heart of the tradition.

Works Cited

Hayes, Terrance. *American Sonnets for My Past and Future Assassin*. Penguin, 2018.
McKay, Claude. *Complete Poems: Claude McKay*. Edited by William J. Maxwell, U of Illinois P, 2008.
Robbins, Hollis. *Forms of Contention: Influence and the African American Sonnet Tradition*. U of Georgia P, 2020.

9

Rawest Radical Material
Teaching Poetry's Diction

WILLIAM FOGARTY

Twentieth-century and twenty-first-century English-language poetry has been especially pointed in demonstrating that diction is not just word choice but a multidimensional formal element with the capacity to unite aesthetic and social spheres. Words, after all, construct the forms of poetry and manifold forms of social life. Teaching diction in all its diverse manifestations can, I suggest, answer some of the imperatives outlined by Dorothy Wang in "The Future of Poetry Studies" (2021) for "taking seriously the work that poems themselves do" by poets from marginalized social positions (230n6). For diction presents a way to apprehend how BIPOC and LGBTQIA+ poets are not, to borrow Wang's terms, "just . . . examples of difference" who provide "ethnographic reportage" but are "creators of core concepts of poetics" (229–30; 230n6). In what follows, I offer strategies for teaching diction and for illuminating the ways in which words themselves can be radical formal features with the capacity to advance trenchant social critiques.

My poetry classes begin with discussions about diction with the following broad questions:

- *What is diction?* Diction refers to "word choice." However, I emphasize not just authorial choice but diction's constitutive structural function. Diction comprises words and phrases, the building blocks of poems that coordinate as they assemble: as Helen Vendler explains, "the meaning of a word in a poem is determined less by its dictionary definition . . . than by the words around it. Every word in a poem enters into relation with the other words in that poem" (147).

- *What are the denotations and connotations of the phrase "word choice"?* "Word" denotes utterance, unit of language, written and spoken expression, but it suggests consensus, too, a sound formation whose signification we generally agree upon, suggesting as well, divergence—what different connotations do we each detect? "Choice" means preferential determination, selection, agency, option. But it also implies power, the presence of options—who gets to choose, and from among what?

- *What assumptions do we have about "poetic diction"?* Answers tend to include words like flowery, exaggerated, emotional, elevated, elaborate, descriptive, long-winded, difficult, abstract, confusing. It is easy to find poems that undo these presumptions. Terry Eagleton has observed that at least since the twentieth century there has been no such thing as "poetic diction": "Diction means the kind of vocabulary conventionally considered suitable for poetry; and the point about modern poetry is that there isn't one" (144).

To identify different kinds of diction and to illuminate the variances of denotation and connotation, I provide a pair of poems that use the same or similar words while drawing out different resonances from those words. For example, I compare a poem about trees by Louise Glück and one by Lucille Clifton. Glück's poetic study of "Elms" (1985) employs a generalized lexicon—"I," "need," "dark," "sadness," "wood," "tree"—as it imparts a valuable aesthetic lesson: private torment is productive for art because it "twists" the forms art makes (189). Glück often chooses from a simple lexicon of the natural world, making tableaus with pond, moon, lake, "wild iris," "hawthorne tree." She has described her aim as creating paradigms, avoiding the troubled designation of the term *universal*. But we might still ask: paradigms of what and for whom? Lucille Clifton's untitled poem that begins "surely i am able to write poems" (2004) considers "trees" in similarly elemental diction, but her lesson extends to history and society: the "knotted branches" in her tree poem give way to what she calls "an other poem," one whose trees and branches and the twisted forms they make connote lynching and the ongoing catastrophes of American racism (581).

To examine a specific poem's diction in relation to its social and historical context, I often turn to the first section of Gwendolyn Brooks's three-part sequence "Riot" (1969) because of the way it orchestrates different registers of diction in response to racism and social upheaval. I explain first that the poem is set during an uprising after Martin Luther King's 1968 assassination and that it depicts a white man's fatal attempt to escape it. We talk about the title and the poem's famous epigraph taken from King: "A riot is the language of the unheard" (470). I bring our attention to diction by posing questions about our expectations of this particular poem's diction based on its title and epigraph:

- *What does the title and epigraph prefigure about the poem?* That it's going to be concerned in some way with civil rights; perhaps that it's going to protest racism and King's murder; that it will have a political edge.

- *What kind of diction might we expect in a poem that begins with that epigraph?* That the poem will make a connection between rioting and language. What we will find is that the poem presents a language that does not explicitly make such a connection.

We then listen to Brooks reciting the poem. I ask students to complete several activities in groups:

- In two or three sentences, write out the plot of the poem.

- Annotate the poem with a brief glossary that defines its unusual words and proper nouns: John Cabot, Wilma, Wycliffe, Jaguar, Lake Bluff, Grandtully, Richard Gray and Distelheim, Maxim's, Maison Henri, Winnetka.

- In two or three sentences, describe John Cabot.

- Identify different formal aspects such as line length, stresses, rhyme, alliteration, and repetition.

Finally, I ask student groups to designate the various types of diction the poem employs in categories such as proper nouns, product names, colloquialisms, pejoratives, polysyllabic words, languages other than English (the list can go on). I want them to use their groupings to answer these specific questions: does the poem portray John Cabot and the riot realistically, or does the poem's diction suggest something less realistic, something representational?

Their findings suggest that although the events the poem refers to are historical, the poem presents embellished language that is representative rather than realistic. This is, after all, a poem that combines historical characters in a composite (John Cabot and John Wycliffe), fuses multiple words ("whitebluerose"), imagines angels in the sky, and presents "doubt" as a speaking entity. Its words generate an aesthetic response in their inventiveness that it then deploys for political purposes in its context. For the poem's fusions of French, satirically preposterous exclamations, altered biblical allusions, and exaggeratedly refined standard English shuttle in blank verse toward an imagined execution of its racist white character that comes to symbolize at once the absurdity, hopelessness, and death of racism. The poem is an innovation of language that mixes ordinary and extraordinary speech: a white character symbolically and satirically named "John Cabot . . . once a Wycliffe," conjuring early European so-called discoverers of North America, expresses racist repugnance in French ("Que tu es grossier!"), in absurd exclamations ("Don't let It touch me! the blackness! Lord!"), and finally in a racist biblical allusion ("Lord! / Forgive these nigguhs that know not what they do"). In contrast, the language representative of the Black rioters is composed and refined, direct and crystalline: "You are a desperate man, / and the desperate die expensively today" (*Blacks* 470–71). Likewise, the litany of stereotypical referents related to the wealth of the poem's representative white character sets the Black rioters in high relief: a sportscar, a rarefied liquor, an art gallery in New York and at a Chicago college, restaurants in Paris are all blunt superficialities contrasted to the riot of "Poor" Black people figured in more traditionally lyrical language: they approach in "rough ranks," in "seas" and a "windsweep," "not detainable. And not discreet" (470). The poem is a motley containment of diction held together by the forms it produces—iambic pentameter, alliteration, blank space between stanzas—creating an ironic steadiness as it renders verbal outbursts of racism, outrage, and violence.

Twenty-first-century poets have in a sense made it inevitable to study diction because they have foregrounded their experimentations with it.

In fact, innovation of diction is the central formal property of two of the most lexically complex books of poetry released in the twenty-first century, Cathy Park Hong's *Dance Dance Revolution* (2007) and Jos Charles's *feeld* (2018). Both texts are made from explicit originations in diction, each creating a new version of English from an array of linguistic sources and wielding those creations of diction to examine distinctly political conditions.

Hong's *Dance Dance Revolution* demonstrates that words in a poem can be at once alienating in their initial peculiarity and unifying in their ultimate intelligibility. The book is a narrative of interrelated poems set in a dystopian world in which a Korean tour guide speaks "Desert Creole," a lingua franca based on many languages but rooted in both standard and dialectic versions of English. The effect seems at first to be deterritorialization. Yet for all its uprooting effects, the outcome is orientation. The tour guide invents a poetic language whose communicative capacities are far-ranging and effective: "I train mine talk box to talk yep-puh, as you / 'Merikkens say 'purdy,'" the guide says about her linguistic services that are and are not like a typical consumer product: "no goods only phrases, betta de phrase, 'purdier' de experience" (25). The book portrays the tour guide's life in this "purdy" global tongue as it shuttles toward climactic poems that depict the real-world Kwangju uprising, a mass protest against the South Korean military government that took place in 1980. The tour guide describes essential political instruction she learns from her father about language, his speech distinguished from hers with italics: "*You can be the best talker but no point if you can't / speak the other man's tongue*," the father explains to his daughter. He then enumerates the strategies that not knowing a language can preclude: "*You can't chisel, con, plead, / seduce, beg for your life*" from another person if you don't know their language, "*So learn them all*" (46). While the tour guide has learned "all" the languages, Hong teaches us her book's translingualism, and the local is rendered translocal. I ask students to translate the book's invented lingua franca into other versions of English, any version as long as they stay as close as possible to the essence of the original. The guiding questions of this exercise are, what is lost in the translation and what is gained from executing the translation? How are our creations at once estranging and engaging like Hong's word choices? How are they not?

Charles's *feeld* operates similarly in that it is also a text with its own invented lingua franca that simultaneously familiarizes and defamiliarizes. The book is a sequence of sixty brief poems expressed by a transgender consciousness moving through various settings in the contemporary world: a garden, a bathroom, a supermarket, an inn. The settings are commonplace and public, but the compressed lines transform the ordinarily social into private extraordinariness as they respell words using, as Charles explains, a combination of "Middle English," "internet speak," and the poet's "own . . . idiosyncrasies" (YouTube). The result is a lyrical, almost hermetic language of the mind embedded with historical and social valences with their medieval spellings and text-message-style misspellings. I ask students to identify different possible meanings in the words that Charles remakes and to rewrite the poems with the spellings "corrected": for example, a "tran" is a trans person, a train, a prefix meaning across; "hiv" is a receptacle for bees, the hive mind of the web, the diagnosis HIV; "hole" is an opening, a hollow place, an orifice, also unity, completeness. How do standard spellings change the meanings of the original poems? We learn from Charles's word choices that everything fits and doesn't fit, that nothing is singular but expands into multiplicities, that experience is not definitive but overdetermined: nothing is noting, to be alone is to be allowed, the world is a whorl and a whirl, the space the book asks us to traverse is a field of language and a field of feeling. Like Hong's book, Charles's has done us the service of teaching us its language—again, of simultaneously familiarizing and defamiliarizing—so that by the end of the collection we have become if not fluent at least practiced.

What I hope to have communicated with all these poems is that diction is not just word choice but a complex, relational, formal tool that not only makes and undergirds a poem's overall structure but communicates its methods, dispositions, claims, and sociopolitical critiques. It is a fruitful, rigorous, and enlivening teaching tool for poetry.

Further Reading

Some introductory texts on poetry that have helpful discussions of diction include Terry Eagleton's *How to Read a Poem* (Blackwell, 2007), Helen Vendler's *Poems, Poets, Poetry* (Bedford, 1997), and the entry on "Diction" in the *Princeton Encyclopedia of Poetry and Poetics* (Princeton UP, 2012). Essays for contextualization of Brooks's "Riot" include James Sullivan's "Killing John Cabot and Publishing Black: Gwendolyn Brook's Riot: Document View" (*African American Review*, vol. 36, no. 4, 2002, pp. 557–69) about how the poem coincides with Brooks's shift from a corporate to an independent Black-owned publisher and Annette Debo's close reading of the poem's linguistic violence, "Reflecting Violence in the Warpland:

Gwendolyn Brooks's *Riot*" (*African American Review*, vol. 39, no. 1, 2005, pp. 143–52). As for Hong's and Charles's books, numerous reviews, articles, interviews, and talks are available on the internet. I find especially helpful Justin Parks's open-access essay, "Reading and Teaching Cathy Park Hong's *Dance Dance Revolution* Beyond National Borders" (*American Studies in Scandinavia*, vol. 49, no. 2, 2017, pp. 93–108); Ruth Williams's analysis of Hong's language as a globalized English, "A Poet's 'Canny Acts of Sabotage': Diasporic Language in Cathy Park Hong's *Dance Dance Revolution*" (*College Literature*, vol. 43, no. 4, 2016, pp. 645–67); "Synthetic Economies," a review of *feeld* by BK Fischer on the *Kenyon Review* website (kenyonreview.org/reviews/feeld-by-jos-charles-738439); and a filmed reading available on YouTube that Jos Charles gave from *feeld* at the Chicago Humanities Festival (www.youtube.com/watch?v=Z3pMcmnc16M).

Works Cited

Brooks, Gwendolyn. "Riot." *Blacks*, Third World, 1987, pp. 470–71.
Charles, Jos. *feeld*. Milkweed, 2018.
———. "Jos Charles: *feeld*." YouTube, uploaded by Chicago Humanities Festival, 3 November 2018, www.youtube.com/watch?v=Z3pMcmnc16M.
Clifton, Lucille. "[surely i am able to write poems]." *The Collected Poems of Lucille Clifton: 1965–2010*, edited by Kevin Young and Michael S. Glaser, BOA, 2012, p. 581.
Debo, Annette. "Reflecting Violence in the Warpland: Gwendolyn Brooks's *Riot*." *African American Review*, vol. 39, no. 1, 2005, pp. 143–52.
"Diction." *The Princeton Encyclopedia of Poetry and Poetics*. Edited by Stephen Cushman and Roland Greene, 4th ed., Princeton UP, 2012, p. 358.
Eagleton, Terry. *How to Read a Poem*. Blackwell, 2007.
Fischer, BK. "Synthetic Economies." Review of *feeld* by Jos Charles. *Kenyon Review*, 7 Sept. 2018, kenyonreview.org/reviews/feeld-by-jos-charles-738439.
Glück, Louise. "Elms." *Poems: 1962–2012*, Farrar, Straus, and Giroux, 2012, p. 189.
Hayes, Terrance. "George Floyd." *The New Yorker*, 6 June 2020, www.newyorker.com/magazine/2020/06/22/george-floyd.
Hong, Cathy Park. *Dance Dance Revolution*. Norton, 2007.
Parks, Justin. "Reading and Teaching Cathy Park Hong's *Dance Dance Revolution* Beyond National Borders." *American Studies in Scandinavia*, vol. 49, no. 2, 2017, pp. 93–108.
Rankine, Claudia. "Weather." *New York Times*, 15 June 2020, www.nytimes.com/2020/06/15/books/review/claudia-rankine-weather-poemcoronavirus.html.

Sullivan, James D. "Killing John Cabot and Publishing Black: Gwendolyn Brook's Riot: Document View." *African American Review*, vol. 36, no. 4, 2002, pp. 557–69.

Vender, Helen. *Poems, Poets, Poetry: An Introduction and Anthology*. Bedford, 1997.

Wang, Dorothy. "The Future of Poetry Studies." *The Cambridge Companion to Twenty-First-Century American Poetry*, edited by Timothy Yu, Cambridge UP, 2021, pp. 220–33.

Williams, Ruth. "A Poet's 'Canny Acts of Sabotage': Diasporic Language in Cathy Park Hong's *Dance Dance Revolution*." *College Literature*, vol. 43, no. 4, 2016, pp. 645–67.

10

Reading, Misreading, and Rereading "We Real Cool"

MIKE CHASAR

First published in the September 1959 issue of *Poetry* magazine, and then included as the fifth poem in her third collection *The Bean Eaters* in 1960, Gwendolyn Brooks's "We Real Cool" is standard if not compulsory reading in high school and college classrooms. "We Real Cool" may well be, as Christopher Spaide has argued, "the most anthologized postwar American poem (a delicious irony for a poem about seven adolescents skipping school), and certainly the most conspicuous pronouncement of 'we' in American poetry" (249). Because the poem is so widely encountered in educational contexts, because its effect in those contexts is one of students representing themselves to other students, and because the homogeneity of that "we" has implications for how students are encouraged to imagine Black youth as a group, the stakes of reading "We Real Cool" are especially high.

In this essay, I want to argue that prevailing literary interpretations of "We Real Cool" reflect and replicate the social system of racial profiling that disadvantages and harms Black youth by criminalizing minor infractions—a system often represented by the "school-to-prison pipeline" but that, as with George Zimmerman and others, extends to the behavior of individuals outside of those institutions as well. It is a sad fact that the history of interpreting "We Real Cool" has frequently reinforced and legitimized this system's logics, and it is sadder still that, by virtue of its use as an educational tool, the poem is used to conscript and train students in racial profiling while at the same time even encouraging students to practice policing on their peers. The poem does not have to be read or used in this way, however. That its speakers can be easily acquitted of wrongdoing by revisiting the statements they make from another perspective offers further proof of the long, prejudicial ways of reading it and, by extension, similar ways of reading social behavior in real life.

Spaide is not the only one to characterize the poem's speakers as truants—or worse. Nor is he alone in focusing on that "we" in order to make the subject of group mentality an organizing principle of the speakers' behavior. For Spaide, the poet's "scolding reservations" are evident to an audience for whom literary and social "reading" skills are mutually reinforcing. "Socially astute readers," he explains, "can infer the necessary knowledge about these seven from [Brooks's] epithet (these are truant POOL PLAYERS, not developing STUDENTS)" (249–50). Spaide's presumption about the nature of the author's disapproval echoes Helen Vendler, who similarly imagined, a quarter century earlier, that "Brooks's judgmental monologue . . . barely conceals its adult reproach of their behavior" (384). Given permission by what they imagine to be the author's disapproval of her protagonists, the critics have piled on. Craig Hansen Werner goes a step further than truancy and calls the students "a group of dropouts" (155). Betsy Erkkila sees them not just as dropouts but as gangbangers "defined and entrapped by the nihilistic and ultimately deadly mythology of the black gang" (207). They are, for Wynn Yarbrough, "violent and self-serving" (192). Explaining that "they don't need school, they stay out late, they fight, they drink, and engage in sexual mischievous behavior," Harold Bloom deems their behavior "monstrous" (43, 42). They are, Hortense Spillers has argued, "dudes hastening toward their death" who "make no excuse for themselves and apparently invite no one else to do so" (120). Elizabeth Alexander says that, having been "seduced by the finger-popping siren song of the street," the speakers "have frittered their lives away" (xxi–xxii). Their deaths, writes James D. Sullivan, are the "consequences of coolness" (33).

Brooks's poem is tricky because it plays to poetry readers' desire to see in words and phrases "something more"—symbols, metaphors, irony, unreliable narrators, etc.—and layers that commonly taught reading practice on top of a system of racial profiling that calls on people and institutions to interpret Black behaviors as an indication of "something more." This should, in part, make us think for a moment about the objection that poetry-resistant students commonly raise: *Why do you have to read so much into it!?* But if we detach our close reading practices from practices of racial profiling and reconsider from an anti-racist lens what the speakers say they do and the fate they meet, another poem begins to emerge—one not about the consequences of coolness, gang life, or dropping out of school, but about the consequences of racial profiling that criminalizes relatively innocuous behaviors as "monstrous."

Critics jump to the conclusion that the speakers in "We Real Cool" are truants, but the speakers actually say that they "left school." Given the poem's heavy alliterative patterning—one that Gary Smith for some reason believes "belies any possibility for mental growth" on the speakers' part—it would be entirely reasonable for the protagonists to have said "skipped school," but they don't hew to that pattern because they aren't in fact truants and they haven't dropped out (49). If they really were the violent, nihilistic, aggressive, monstrous gang of dropouts that critics have made them out to be, they wouldn't have hesitated to alliterate in order to: a) brag about skipping school, and b) emphasize the force of that action via the alliteration they use later in the poem; even "cut school" would have worked more toward that purpose. Students might have many reasons to leave school early, especially if they are graduating (according to Chicago Public Schools Archives, graduation dates in 1958 and 1959 were June 27 and June 26). Because the speakers are Black, however, readers like those I've cited above assume via the logics of racial profiling that the most likely reason for a Black student to leave school is to in fact play the truant. Brooks herself avoided passing judgment on the subject at least twice. One time she commented, "they are *supposedly* dropouts, or at least they're in the poolroom when they should *possibly* be in school" (Brooks and Stavros 9; emphasis added). Another time, recounting the poem's origin, she explained, "I was passing by a pool hall in my community one afternoon during school time, and I saw, therein, a little bunch of boys . . . but instead of asking myself, 'Why aren't they in school?,' I asked myself, 'I wonder how they feel about themselves'" (Brooks, "We Real Cool," audio recording). That so many readers in educational contexts involving and emphasizing "close reading" have gone on to twist the phrase "We left school" to mean "We skipped school" is one of the great misreadings in the history of American literature, and it's a misreading that not only has at its roots the history of racial profiling that I've cited but that activates and extends that practice in the present every time the misreading is repeated.

Hopefully, you can see for yourself where the misreading of "We Real Cool" has gone from here. Seven Black adolescents hanging out and having a good time playing pool get called a gang. "Strike straight" gets interpreted as violent behavior rather than a manner of playing pool or a mode of communicating, or in relation to any of the positive connotations of "straight" (such as going straight, being straight-laced, or being on the straight and narrow). Clint Eastwood can be admired for being a "straight shooter," but seven young Black men are called violent for saying they "strike straight." They may "sing sin"—who hasn't sung along to song lyrics that have sinful content?—but they don't appear to commit much of it, even though a subset of readers insists on reading the "Seven at the Golden Shovel" in relation to the seven deadly sins. Even though the act of thinning gin is to water down and therefore dilute the alcohol, the poem's speakers are faulted for drinking, and critics are quick to seize on the sexual connotations of the word "jazz," because it feeds the tropes of the aggressive, hypermasculine, sexually predatory Black male that profiling insists on identifying; Bloom even argues that "Jazz June" might plausibly imply "a horrific gang rape scenario" (43). We can put this another way: if your average white kid and his six friends spent the last month of school playing pool, staying up late, drinking a little bit of watered down gin, singing music lyrics, and generally jazzing June, would you call them, as Bloom has called the poem's speakers, "monstrous"? Would you, as Erkkila has, describe them as "defined and entrapped by the nihilistic and ultimately deadly mythology of the . . . gang"? As "hastening toward their death"? As "frittering their lives away"? As having been—despite having stayed in the pool hall for the entirety of the poem—"seduced by the finger-popping siren song of the street"? No, you wouldn't. Instead, you'd be watching something like the scenario for a John Hughes film.

Read from an anti-racist perspective, the poem's turn to "We / Die Soon" doesn't lose any of the literary effect for which it's been celebrated. Rather, in the interpretive approach I take here, the poem leaves its reader wondering about how and why Black youth would die from relatively innocuous behavior. Their activities—to hang out in a group, to not be in school, to talk a big game, to water down alcohol, to perhaps sing raunchy song lyrics, and so on—don't even rise to the level of minor infractions. But teachers, police, judges, peers, fellow citizens, and, it turns out, poetry scholars will misinterpret their behavior as criminal gang activity and shift the blame for dying young onto the Black youth themselves and away from the system of profiling set up to misread them. The fact that the speakers know that this is the consequence of being a Black teenager—it's made to feel like their fault when it's not—makes them not just self-aware but socially aware, too, of the suspicion, judgment, and discrimination they will face. This, then, is why they speak as a group. The "we" of the poem is not an assertion of group mentality, but an assertion of group *identity*—not people thinking alike, but people facing and thereby bound together by a shared set of living conditions. (It is no accident that in *The Bean Eaters*, "The Last Quatrain of the Ballad of Emmett Till" follows on the heels of "We Real Cool" three poems later.) The speakers' realization at the end of the poem lines up with how Brooks herself encouraged us to read and hear that "we" as well. Those pronouns, she explained, "are meant to be said softly, as though the protagonists in the poem are questioning the validity of their existence" (Eady).

Further Reading

To better understand "We Real Cool" not just as a literary text but as a *pedagogical* text whose various meanings are affected by its situation in the classroom, I turn for background reading to two books about the longer history of teaching poetry: Angela Sorby's *Schoolroom Poets: Childhood, Performance, and the Place of American Poetry, 1865-1917* (U of New Hampshire P, 2005) and Catherine Robson's *Heart Beats: Everyday Life and the Memorized Poem* (Princeton UP, 2012).

Works Cited

Alexander, Elizabeth. Introduction. *The Essential Gwendolyn Brooks*, edited by Elizabeth Alexander, Library of America, 2005, xiii–xxvi.
Bloom, Harold. *Gwendolyn Brooks: Comprehensive Research and Study Guide.* Edited and introduction by Harold Bloom, Chelsea House Publishers, 2003.
Brooks, Gwendolyn. *The Bean Eaters*. Harper and Brothers, 1960.
Brooks, Gwendolyn. "We Real Cool." Audio recording, www.youtube.com/watch?v=oaVfLwZ6jes.
Brooks, Gwendolyn. "We Real Cool." Poetry Foundation, www.poetryfoundation.org/poetrymagazine/poems/28112/we-real-cool.
Brooks, Gwendolyn and George Stavros. "An Interview with Gwendolyn Brooks." *Contemporary Literature*, vol. 11, no. 1, winter 1970, pp. 1–20.

Eady, Cornelius. "Gwendolyn was Here." *Lincoln Center Theater Review*, no. 69, summer 2017, p. 69.

Erkkila, Betsy. The *Wicked Sisters: Women Poets, Literary History, and Discord*. Oxford UP, 1992.

Smith, Gary. "Brooks's 'We Real Cool.'" *The Explicator*, vol. 43, no. 2, winter 1985, pp. 49–50.

Spaide, Christopher. "Multiple Choice: Terrance Hayes's Response-Poems and the African American Lyric 'We.'" *The Cambridge Quarterly*, vol. 48, no. 3, Sept. 2019, pp. 231–57.

Spillers, Hortense. *Black, White, and in Color: Essays on American Literature and Culture*. U of Chicago P, 2003.

Sullivan, James D. *On the Walls and in the Streets: American Poetry Broadsides from the 1960s*. U of Illinois P, 1997.

Vendler, Helen. "Rita Dove: Identity Markers." *Callaloo*, vol. 17, no. 2, spring 1994, pp. 381–98.

Werner, Craig Hansen. *Playing the Changes: From Afro-Modernism to the Jazz Impulse*. U of Illinois P, 1994.

Yarbrough, Wynn. "Playing It Real: Nonsense Poetics, Identity, and African American Poetry for Children and Young Adults." *Children's Literature Association Quarterly*, vol. 46, no. 2, summer 2021, pp. 178–200.

Part 1 Cluster

Ideas on Teaching Lyric

11

Retheorizing Lyric via the Pedagogy of Eighteenth-Century Antislavery Poetry

CHRIS CHAN

Since the late twentieth century, literary scholars of poetry and poetics have vigorously contested the nature and interpretation of *lyric*. Across various contexts, the term has been used to name an entire poetic genre, to describe artworks that evoke particularly "poetic" responses, and to characterize a mode of reading which abstracts a poem's intrinsically literary elements (its rhythm, voice, structure, and so on) from its extrinsic, contextual features. Yet perhaps lyric's most consequential feature is what I call its quasi-imperialistic grip over the interpretation of poetry and, by extension, its pedagogy in the classroom. This is to argue that the skills we teach our students—to read poems as self-contained texts, and to identify the relationships between their form and content—resonate with the logic of Anglo-American imperialism: namely, its elision of cultural and material specificities into presumptively universal modes of feeling, knowledge, and judgment. Indeed, as Suvir Kaul has claimed of eighteenth-century British poetry, the diachronic "functions" of poetic form remain embedded in the English and European exploitation of indigenous peoples across the globe, and in the tensions between the worlds they imagined and those they overpowered (132).

This essay argues that the mutually constitutive legacies of empire and lyric also lead to a pedagogical imperative: that presuming lyric's immanence (if not innocence) from imperialism risks reproducing the latter term's exploitative logic in the study of poetry in the classroom. To teach poetry through the voices of its canonized masters; to presume that a poem's "speaker" projects a universally accessible feeling or perspective onto a common readership; to present poems independently of their historical environments—these are just a few ways in which a putatively "lyrical" pedagogy of poetry perpetuates the erasures occasioned by empire in exchange for literary mastery.

How, then, can we resist these tendencies in the classroom and encourage students to read English poetry with a more nuanced awareness of its contexts and consequences? Here I propose that teaching eighteenth-century antislavery poetry offers us an invaluable opportunity to unpack the relationship between poetic production and lyric interpretation. More specifically, I present such poetry to my students as a case study in what I call the *representational stakes* of lyric expression: the poet's ability to present anew difficult subject matter, and the power relations—between speaker and listener; between enslaved African subjects and free British observers—that undergird familiar tools like metrics and address. As such, students learn to interrogate the deep entanglement between slavery's hegemonic practices and lyric's universal ambitions, and to comprehend poetry as a vital (if imperfect) tool for navigating their shared legacy.

Teaching the Representational Stakes of Lyric in Antislavery Verse

I have taught eighteenth-century antislavery poetry in two different undergraduate courses at two institutions: an introductory survey of "British Poetry, 1660–1918" at the University of Pennsylvania, and an upper-level seminar on "Slavery and Enlightenment in Eighteenth-Century British Literature" at Ghent University in Belgium. In both courses, antislavery poetry plays a central role in helping students understand how poets articulated their political demands through specific literary choices. What challenges did eighteenth-century poets face in denouncing the crimes of British slavery? What do their engagements reveal about the limits of poetic form and lyric expression?

In the British poetry survey course, my students and I engage these questions across three ninety-minute class sessions. I find it especially effective to begin with the poems of Phillis Wheatley, paying careful attention to how she positioned herself as an enslaved woman writer to her readers. The stakes of this positioning become clear when students are tasked with reading her poems alongside the prefatory materials to her 1773 volume *Poems on Various Subjects*: the famous frontispiece illustration featuring a pensive Wheatley with a quill in her hand; the title page and dedication to her patroness Selina Hastings, Countess of Huntingdon; her master John Wheatley's letter to the publisher; and the list of public signatories testifying to Wheatley's poetic qualifications. Discussing the differences that these various materials pose to our understanding of her poetry, in turn, can lead to deeper considerations about what precisely constitutes her lyrical "voice."

Such considerations come to the fore in her famous eight-line poem "On Being Brought from Africa to America," which conspicuously reframes the circumstances of her captivity in the language of Christian gratitude. In my experience, students who read this poem for the first time are most struck by Wheatley's rhetorical composure, her characterization of the Middle Passage as an act of redemptive "mercy," and her seeming apology for the conversion of other enslaved Africans to Christianity. Their initial surprise, in turn, leads us to discuss how much creative license Wheatley may have had in writing her poetry, and to what extent her voice emerges from her literary choices (such as her use of heroic couplets) and the ideological expectations of her Anglo-American readership. From there, I encourage students to decide whether Wheatley's poem marks a tactful compromise between her authorial freedom and her audience, or whether it radically challenges contemporary sensibilities on Christianity, race, and enslavement.

Another productive way to explore this tension between poetic self-presentation and personal testimony is to examine how contemporary white English poets described the injustices of slavery to their readers. Three model poems in this regard include William Cowper's "The Negro's Complaint" (1785) and sonnets II and IV of Robert Southey's *Poems on the Slave Trade* (1787), all of which condemn slavery by claiming intimate knowledge of enslaved Africans' experiences. Two passages demonstrate how this works in practice:

> Still in thought as free as ever,
> What are England's rights, I ask,
> Me from my delights to sever,
> Me to torture, me to task?

Fleecy locks and black complexion
Cannot forfeit nature's claim;
Skins may differ, but affection
Dwells in white and black the same. ("The Negro's Complaint,"
   lines 9–16)

Why dost thou beat thy breast and rend thine hair
And to the deaf sea pour thy frantic cries?
Before the gale the laden vessel flies;
The Heavens all-favoring smile, the breeze is fair;
Hark to the clamors of the exulting crew!
Hark how their thunders mock the patient skies!
Why dost thou shriek and strain thy red-swoln eyes
As the white sail dim lessens from thy view? (Sonnet II, lines
   1–8)

After identifying the poetic structures—composite ballad stanza and Petrarchan sonnet, respectively—that shape these subjects' complaints, students are usually quick to note how Cowper's enslaved speaker and Southey's persona lend greater rhetorical force to their antislavery arguments. But I also encourage them to consider whether such lyric figures metonymize the ideology and practice of imperialism: whether these speakers, in other words, testify as much to the poets' *possession of,* if not *mastery over,* their own subjects as they do to the experience of enslavement. This last prompt has helped students generate fruitful responses: as one of them eloquently observes of "The Negro's Complaint," Cowper's ventriloquism "force[s] his audience to recognize the voice of this slave as the voice of a 'real' person . . . thereby legitimizing the topics they discuss," yet the poet's own status as a free white man "also work[s] against him, bringing a sense of illegitimacy, perhaps even appropriation, to his work."[1] Still, teaching Cowper's poem in a survey course like "British Poetry, 1660–1918" can also pose more immediate (but no less teachable!) challenges. Another student, for example, once mistakenly reasoned that Cowper himself was the enslaved sufferer in question, a misreading which underscores the poet's presumed authority to speak for his own subject.

In teaching antislavery poetry through the lens of lyric representation, then, I show students not just how familiar poetic devices were marshaled to present unsettling subjects to readers, but also how attention to context can help us "unsettle" those same devices. I develop these considerations at greater length in my upper-level "Slavery and Enlightenment" seminar, where we read three longer works: John Bicknell and Thomas Day's *The Dying Negro, A Poetical Epistle* (1773), Hannah More's *Slavery* (1788), and John Jamieson's *The Sorrows of Slavery* (1789). As in the British poetry survey course, students are tasked with evaluating these poems' lyrical efficacy: their capacity to present British slavery as both a pressing crime against humanity and a suitably "poetic" subject for their readers. I stimulate these discussions by assigning several excerpts from contemporary periodical essays on lyric poetry, so that students can assess whether these antislavery poems achieved the period's lyrical standards of harmonious expression and sustained imagination. This approach often produces useful insights: one of my students, for example, interprets *The Dying Negro*'s use of the heroic couplet "as a way of mocking the English elite," given that it demands recognition of the enslaved speaker within a legible poetic medium. Another student, meanwhile, argues of the same poem that "the highly sentimental and immersive [rhetoric of] love tragedy . . . diverts attention away from the actual matter, that is, the slave's loss of freedom."[2]

Both readings thus raise important ethical questions over white writers' authority to appropriate enslaved African subjects in condemning transatlantic slavery, reminding us that these features remain inseparable from an imperialist poetics: one characterized by possessive practices, universalizing ambitions, and celebrations of technical mastery. In turn, reevaluating familiar lyric terms like *voice*, *address*, *form*, and *representation* against the longer, unresolved legacies of transatlantic slavery and British imperialism helps us become closer readers of poetry as well as more resistant interpreters of literary language. Our heightened sensitivity to the long arc of imperialism therefore encourages more nuanced modes of identification than the patronizing pity that antislavery poets all too often evoked for their suffering subjects.

Further Reading

Thanks to the painstaking efforts of literary critics and historians, there is now a wealth of scholarship on eighteenth-century antislavery poetry and its role in contemporary and modern debates over race, labor, empire, and poetics. A few studies to which I am especially indebted include Tim Burke, "'Humanity is Now the Pop'lar Cry': Laboring-Class Writers and the Liverpool Slave Trade, 1787–1789" (*The Eighteenth Century*, vol. 42, no. 3, fall 2001, pp. 245-63); Brycchan Carey, *British Abolitionism and the Rhetoric of Sensibility* (Palgrave Macmillan, 2005); and Robert Mitchell, *Sympathy and the State in the Romantic Era: Systems, State Finance, and the Shadows of Futurity* (Routledge, 2007). For more recent and revelatory examinations of poetic voice in antislavery verse, see Deanna P. Koretsky, "Habeas Corpus and the Politics of Freedom: Slavery and Romantic Suicide" (*Essays in Romanticism*, vol. 22, no. 1, 2015, pp. 21-33); Ivan Ortiz, "Lyric Possession in the Abolition Ballad" (*Eighteenth-Century Studies*, vol. 51, no. 2, winter 2018, pp. 197-218); and Andrea Haslanger, "The Speaking and the Dead: Antislavery Poetry's Fictions of the Person" (*The Eighteenth Century*, vol. 60, no. 4, winter 2019, pp. 419-40).

For notable works which situate antislavery poetry at the heart of modern lyric theory, see Debbie Lee, *Slavery and the Romantic Imagination* (U of Pennsylvania P, 2002); Max Cavitch, "Slavery and Its Metrics" (*The Cambridge Companion to Nineteenth-Century American Poetry*, edited by Kerry Larson, Cambridge UP, 2011, pp. 94-110); Meredith L. McGill, "Frances Ellen Watkins Harper and the Circuits of Abolitionist Poetry" (*Early African American Print Culture*, edited by Lara Langer Cohen and Jordan Alexander Stein, U of Pennsylvania P, 2012, pp. 53-74); and John Michael, "Lyric History: Temporality, Rhetoric, and the Ethics of Poetry" (*New Literary History*, vol. 48, spring 2017, pp. 265-84).

Such renewed interest in antislavery verse has likewise spurred its increasing availability in modern poetry anthologies. Two collections published in the early 2000s—Marcus Wood's *The Poetry of Slavery: An Anglo-American Anthology* (Oxford UP, 2003) and James Basker's *Amazing Grace: An Anthology of Poems about Slavery, 1660-1810* (Yale UP, 2005)—remain the most comprehensive and contain all of the poems discussed in this chapter. Also notable are Carolyn Forché and Duncan Wu's *Poetry of Witness: The Tradition in English, 1500-2001* (W. W. Norton, 2014), which includes excerpts of More's *Slavery*, James Field Stanfield's *The Guinea Voyage* (1789), and other contemporary antislavery poems; and Vincent Carretta's *Unchained Voices: An Anthology of Black Authors in the English-Speaking World of the Eighteenth Century* (U of Kentucky P, 2004), which situates Wheatley's poetry both in its eighteenth-century context and in the longer Black Anglo-American tradition of abolitionist literature.

On Wheatley's poetry in particular, see Carretta, *Phillis Wheatley: Biography of a Genius in Bondage* (U of Georgia P, 2011), which provides a definitive account of her writings built upon archival readings and extensive historical context; and Betsy Erkkila, "Phillis Wheatley on the Streets of Revolutionary Boston in the Atlantic World" (*Early American Literature* vol. 56, no. 2, 2021, pp. 351–72), a recent provocation for us to memorialize Wheatley as both an accomplished poet and an active colonial insurrectionist.

Notes

1. My thanks to Alan Ismaiel, who took my British poetry survey course at Penn in the fall 2020 semester, for graciously granting permission to share his comments from his poetry reading worksheet on "The Negro's Complaint."

2. My thanks to Lara De Geest and Beau Serrus respectively, both of whom took the course in the spring 2022 semester, for their insights into this poem.

Works Cited

Cowper, William. "The Negro's Complaint." London, 1788.

Kaul, Suvir. *Poems of Nation, Anthems of Empire: English Verse in the Long Eighteenth Century.* U of Virginia P, 2000.

Southey, Robert. "Sonnet II." *Poems*, London, 1797, p. 34.

12

Lyric Borders

Reading and Writing with Gloria Anzaldúa's New Mestiza

Leah Huizar

The lyric poem has the potential to be a radical mode of creativity and inclusivity in the poetry classroom. Yet too often it serves as a limitation. Though much discussed among critics, in many creative writing classrooms, the lyric often diffuses along its narrowest parameters. The *Oxford Dictionary of Literary Terms* (4th ed., 2015) offers a basic account of the lyric as "any fairly short poem expressing the personal mood, feeling, or meditation of a single speaker." The American critic Helen Vendler in *Poems, Poets, Poetry* (3rd ed., 2009), a textbook aimed at undergraduate writers, further defines the lyric as that which "represents a moment of inner meditation, it is relatively short, and always exists in a particular place—'here'—and a particular time—'now'" (xl). We can conclude from these that a lyric is typically meant to be personal and grounded in the poet's direct experience and perception. These lyric parameters invoke a single speaker reflecting on a singular moment in time. The lyric poem, as such, is singular, immediate, and local.

In my own writing, however, I often struggled with this form of lyric. It did not come naturally. I found myself uncertain when or where to begin: how to situate myself—a Mexican-American, working-class woman—to be best understood. I wanted to write about my experience in the world but would fumble in the entanglements of my own sense of self that seemed to bleed into other voices, other places. As I wrote, I often felt weighted by all the unspoken layers of identity. I could not conceive of how to capture the present moment unfreighted by context. Instead, I felt as if any statement needed a supporting cluster of explanatory notes, and each landscape felt like contested territory.

Of course, how could it not? Wasn't my own identity and situation in the non-poem world often contested? I wondered, how could I make my own experience coherent in this mode? What was my responsibility to explain or consolidate for the reader? Further, as a poetry professor, I wondered what happens when a student feels this way also? Can the lyric make room for another approach that is no less lyrical but avoids norming dominant expectations for identity and cultural situation? Finally, for those already cutting their own lyric paths, can we read and see them more fully for all that their poems accomplish?

In this essay, I aim to describe an approach to the reading and writing of lyric poetry which overcomes the lyric boundedness of its typical parameters around identity, time, and place. Though no less personal and potent, this approach to lyricism is meant to be an inclusive, capacious poetics. I draw directly from Gloria Anzaldúa's new mestiza in which subjectivity may be multiple and liminal. I suggest that we can teach the reading and writing of lyric poetry as not only "I" but "we." Not only "here and now" but "there and then." Not only local but historic, global, and the vast between. By approaching the lyric with a borderlands sensibility, we gain multiplicity and connection.

Approached in this way, the lyric comes alive with possibility. I quote from *The Gloria Anzaldúa Reader* to suggest that this sensibility goes far beyond the material or literal borders of the original *Borderlands* text. In these essays, Anzaldúa writes, "Multicultural texts show the writer's or artist's struggle to decolonize subjectivity. . . . Perspectives based on representation problematize these binaries, asking how people negotiate multiple worlds every day. My identity is always in flux; it changes as I step into and cross over many worlds each day" (Anzaldúa and Keating 209). The poem's subjectivity exists within a state of ambiguity, liminality; it is interstitial, between, multiple. Conceived in this way, I suggest the lyric subject is enlarged. Not only does it better serve those that see themselves as between but it allows for new and invigorated possibilities of perspective in crafting the lyric.

Additional lyric features begin to take on a different scale as well. Consider the familiar spatial phrase invoked among Latinos/as/xs to describe their cultural betweenness as that of *ni de aqui, ni de alla*. Neither of here, nor of there. So much for the "here and now" of the lyric. It is as Anzaldúa wrote, "the new mestiza is a liminal subject who lives in borderlands between culture, races, languages, and genders. In this state of in-betweenness the mestiza can mediate, translate, negotiate, and navigate these different locations" (Anzaldúa and Keating 209). Thus, the poem's lyric subject is also informed by seemingly disparate geographic, historic, and cultural realities. In poems like these, the scope or scale of the locale may be expansive. Likewise, the lyric can come to accommodate different experiences of time and place: of the "here and now" *and* the "then and there" all at once.

Turning back to the classroom, this approach impacts poetry pedagogy in both the reading and the writing of poems. Student-poets in my classes are prompted to write a new lyric poem each week. These assignment prompts invite them into this lyric approach and offer new options for conceiving of their voice and place in poetry.

As we prepare to write, we'll often explore a dynamic poem together, such as Ray Gonzalez's "Axis," from the collection *Beautiful Wall* (2015). We'll note how its initiating memory spins, like an axis, to reveal its subject through first and third person lenses. We'll consider the poem's "here" which at turns is a village, a volcano, the globe. We'll note how the "now" tethers its present to geologic and historic pasts. Distinctly lyric, the poem's revolving perspectives, its shifting local to global scales, its annular vision of time all lead to a complex and rich lyric of connection and identity. One in which students can take up for themselves as they begin to write their own lyrics. Below is an excerpt of one of the writing prompts I often assign my student-poets:

> *Exploring the Lyric I:* Write a lyric poem where the poetic *I* is given the space to be liminal, multiple, or absent. Allow the constitutive components of one's identity and subjectivity to roam, layer, intersect. Not all parts of one's identity need to be foregrounded (nor must they be suppressed or simplified for potential readers). For multilingual speakers, one is welcome to invite multiple languages into the poem.

Traditional lyric approaches (perhaps, an imagistic meditation set in the solitude of one's dorm room) do not always allow student-poets to get at that which was most vibrant in them. Too often young writers then struggle to conceive of a lyric *I* that they feel has something interesting to say. I am convinced it is not that they do not have something interesting to say—they very often do—but they are coming up against barriers to the form. With this in mind, I have endeavored to create lyric prompts, such as the one above, to center that which students care most about, that which is central to who they are and how they see themselves in this world. For many students the sense of betweenness, the messy edges of the lyric *I*, the liminal space of where to situate oneself in and through various times and places, provides an entrance into poetry.

Using the prompt above, an introductory poetry student once wrote movingly about visiting her hometown of Cuernavaca in Mexico after many years away. As the young poet worked to depict the place, the poem blurred the past and the present. It wove together her English- and Spanish-speaking selves, her memories and those inherited from a parent. The poem itself inhabited the personal, the cultural, and the political to express a sense of what it means to belong and not belong to a place. The poem crossed borders real and imagined. Had the student attempted a standard lyric, the poem would have lost not only half of its language but would have been unable to leap easily between these perspectives, positions, and times.

In another weekly poem prompt, I asked students to write from an unexpected central consciousness. In doing so, students wrote lyrics which moved beyond reflecting on an artifact to identify with it. When I assign this prompt, I teach Brenda Cárdenas's "Zacuanpapalotls" (2009) as part of our preparations for writing. In the poem, which tracks the migration of butterflies, students are always struck by the opening word: "We." It suggests an expansive identity and invites engagement with the human and nonhuman, the environment, the migrant and local. When I have taught this prompt students often surprise me in their explorations. There is a kind of freedom in choosing to write on that thing which is both beyond and within. In fact, in embracing the lyric as described on these pages, my sense is that your students, like mine, may find the roominess of its parameters liberating.

As the final part of our lyric writing work, students share their poems with each other. Of course, it would be a shame to spend so much time enlarging the lyric poem to increase its inclusivity only to then reproduce workshop habits which have not always served all students well. Traditionally, much of the burden for understanding fell on a silent writer sharing a contextless poem. Instead, we prepare for peer workshops by acknowledging that in writing these poems, it may involve work for the reader that they are not accustomed to performing, and that's okay. As a class, we expect that at a minimum a good reader will follow up on any areas beyond their knowledge to avoid privileging dominant perspectives. Especially in the age of automatic translation and information access, this is not especially burdensome. There may remain gaps in some readers' comprehension, but that's okay too. A writer may choose who their poems are written for and how much they expect the reader to rise to meet them. For many new writers, the idea that they might have expectations for the kind of reader they want is revelatory.

I believe that the ideas outlined above offer important creative possibilities for the writing and reading of writers of color, women and queer writers, and historically underrecognized writers. This approach advocates for an inclusive poetics capacious enough to serve diverse subjectivities across time and place. Student-poets have license to share more of their complex selves. Here, the lyric *I* may exceed the singular. It may invoke a multiplicity of languages and ways of knowing. It may depart from the immediacy of "now" or even allow the "here and now" and "there and then" to operate in the same lyric space. In scope and scale, the lyric may move beyond the private life to encompass multiple perspectives, voices, vantage points. The poem arises from one's many possible selves to build and/or collapse time, place, and history.

Poem prompts for the classroom:

1. Write a lyric poem where the poetic *I* is given the space to be liminal, multiple, or absent. Allow the constitutive components of one's identity and subjectivity to roam, layer, intersect. Not all parts of one's identity need to be foregrounded (nor must they be suppressed or simplified for potential readers). For multilingual speakers, one is welcome to invite multiple languages into the poem.

2. Write a poem inhabiting an unexpected central consciousness: Be the butterfly, be the drone.

3. Write a poem that moves on a different geological and geographic scale. Consider your own connections to time and place. Write from inside the fossil record as it's covered over at the close of an era. Take out your microscope or telescope. Write from below the earth. Write from space.

4. Write poems from the archive and from primary and secondary sources. Explore and haunt the "there and then" of it. Ask questions of it; seek out its knowledge.

5. Write a poem that moves through connected linguistic layers and logical leaps. Allow your poem to unfold as you give language to an experience, even if the subject of the poem must shift. Follow it outward however far from your immediate perspective.

Further Reading

Central to this approach to lyric has been my reading of the work of Gloria Anzaldúa. My advanced creative writing students often read excerpts of Anzladúa's *Borderlands/La Frontera: The New Mestiza* (Aunt Lute Books, 2012) as part of their critical and creative reading homework. I would also recommend *The Gloria Anzaldúa Reader* by Anzaldúa and AnaLouise Keating (Duke UP, 2009), which I cite from "The New Mestiza Nation" chapter in the above essay.

Many of the foundational pedagogical assumptions of this essay originate in my reading of bell hook's *Teaching to Transgress* (Routledge, 1994) and Paulo Freire's *Pedagogy of the Oppressed* (Bloomsbury Academic, 2018). I approach the teaching of poetry with a desire to encourage self-actualization and foster an environment where students' own knowledge is celebrated and integral to our learning. In lyric poetry, these concepts are especially important as the personal rests at the heart of the poem-making.

Given the focus of this essay, there is not enough space for a complete discussion on inclusive workshop practices. I note that there are several kinds of inclusivity-minded interventions one can make in the creative writing classroom to foster an inclusive writing space—workshop format, peer expectations of feedback, and centering the writer in discussions all come to mind. For more on this topic, I recommend *The Antiracist Writing Workshop: How to Decolonize the Creative Writing Classroom*, by Felicia Rose Chavez (Haymarket Books, 2021). Particularly helpful in organizing workshop methods is chapter 6, which discusses Liz Lerman's critical response process. I use my own modified workshop model which, while not identical to this recommendation, joins in the aim of centering the poet-writer during feedback discussions and thus avoiding privileging dominant perspectives.

Works Cited

Anzaldúa, Gloria, and AnaLouise Keating. *The Gloria Anzaldúa Reader*. Duke UP, 2009.
Oxford Dictionary of Literary Terms. "Lyric." 4th ed., Oxford UP, 2015, www.oxfordreference.com/display/10.1093/acref/9780198715443.001.0001/acref-9780198715443-e-678.
Vendler, Helen. *Poems, Poets, Poetry: An Introduction and Anthology*. 3rd ed., Bedford/St. Martin's, 2009.

13

Lorenzo Thomas's Griot Lyric

Reading Persona and Race in the Digital Age

Lukas Moe

What do we learn, as teachers of poetry, by making the poem a scene of instruction? The New Critical idea of the "little drama" of lyric naturalized the dynamics of the poetic speaker in the page-bound poem (Brooks and Warren 20). During and since the Jim Crow era, this style of lyric pedagogy elided the racial dimensions of the poem as a social utterance—what it does, for whom, and why—not to mention the poet. As an alternative, this essay explores the poetics of the griot, the African storyteller figure that I draw from the work of Panamanian American poet Lorenzo Thomas. Less bound by nation than the bard, the griot is a mobile yet durable agent of Black diaspora, knitting together its linguistic community across space and time. Thomas's griot poetics suggests a framework for students to approach poetry in terms of their own language communities and practices, in particular those of social media, and to consider how the lyric may function as a vehicle for telling stories without losing sight of its formal specificity. The poet as storyteller—like the online personality or the blues musician—encourages students to reflect on the historical, racial, and media conditions in which they encounter poems.

I'll begin with a teachable moment from my own classroom. Jim Crow racism caused Black poets such as Paul Laurence Dunbar to reflect on the pain and pleasure of lyric performance, for example in Dunbar's "We

Wear the Mask." I've paired Dunbar's poem with Emily Dickinson's "I'm Nobody! Who Are You?," signaling to my students these poems' shared concern with authorship and audience. I find that the parallel between platforms such as Instagram and TikTok, and the sense of persona from the Latin verb *personare*, "to speak through a mask," is intuitive to my students. But I didn't foresee how this affinity would overshadow the historical difference of Dickinson's lyric persona from Dunbar's. In an online discussion thread, several students posted thoughts about anxiety and hidden pain. A few students took enthusiastically to Dickinson's sense of "How dreary–to be–Somebody." Wrote Daniel Redondo-Macias, "There are so many people that seek out and crave the spotlight, but with this line, Dickinson expresses her disdain for it."

A lively discussion ensued. But as we speculated on the poem's myriad meanings, we also threatened to collapse the specific meanings we might take from Dunbar into those we teased out of Dickinson. My students attributed a generic speaker to "We Wear the Mask," and while registering the pathos of the poem's imagery ("With torn hearts and bleeding hearts we smile"), they struggled to account for how Dunbar's figure of performance becomes reflexive in the next line: "And mouth with myriad subtleties." Who is mouthing, Dunbar or his persona? Social media blurs the distinction between self and selfie, the person and the post, and this makes the distance between a poet and a poem's speaker all the more relevant to our students today, as they navigate misinformation, trolling, and bots. Poems throw light on the dangers of collapsing person and utterance, but also on the ways that online life licenses irresponsible and hateful speech by distancing the speaker from both platform and audience.

I see now that "We Wear the Mask," removed from the context of Jim Crow minstrelsy, risks becoming a screen for the projection of white, or at least nonracialized, subjectivity. Indeed, the dynamics of my classroom reflected the problematic race blindness of *lyricization*, the term we've learned from historical poetics scholarship for the myriad ways we've come to treat poems as monoliths rather than contingent products of genre and occasion. As Virginia Jackson shows of Dunbar, the lyricization of verse culture circa 1900 overlapped with the rise of post-Reconstruction white supremacy. The topical meaning of a ballad about lynching, for example, was muted by a style of reading that emphasized the dramatic premise of a poem's form rather than the literal identity of a poem's speaker. Mid-century lyric reading took "every poem" as "a little drama" in which the poem's speaker reacts "to a situation, a scene, or an idea," as stipulated in

Cleanth Brooks's and Robert Penn Warren's 1938 textbook, *Understanding Poetry* (20). Brooks and Warren imagined that the encounter of speaker and audience encompassed poetry's generic situation writ large and thus equated lyric with soliloquy. Erecting a fourth wall between the fictitious lyric speaker and the poem's actual reader, *Understanding Poetry* gave broad dispensation to the formalist principles that shaped the college learning experience of many who teach poetry now. These principles may lead to quite dubious conclusions. "It does not matter who wrote the lyric," Helen Vendler argued in 1997, by way of correcting "those who believe that only [African Americans] can speak of the black experience" (187).

Poems certainly bridge gaps of race, class, and gender—a possibility I don't wish to foreclose when I teach a poem by Gwendolyn Brooks or Phillis Wheatley. But to subordinate the perspectives of Black poets to the supposed universality of lyric, as Vendler does, is to downplay the historic struggles needed to win recognition of Black lyric speakers on their own terms. In this regard, the pairing of Dickinson's "I'm Nobody!" and Dunbar's "We Wear the Mask" obscured interpretations that my students would have been excited to make: for instance, that the animating concerns of publicity and exposure for Dickinson's speaker rely on the relative absence of bigotry and violence endured by Dunbar's "We," for whom civic personhood ("to be—Somebody") might well have been unavailable. Offering a scene of instruction rather than a little drama, Dunbar's poem breaks the fourth wall between performer and audience by naming it as today's climate of resurgent white nationalism. Black lyric texts such as Dunbar's push students to see how the particular mediates the universal in self-expression, and help to complicate what has become a common refrain among Gen Z readers: "Can I relate to this?" Insofar as relatability is a powerful if distorting lens, I try to focus it on my students' experience. "Can I relate?"—the very question close readers supposedly should not ask about a poem—can be turned on its head through follow-up questions: Who are we as readers? What is the magnetic pull that some texts exert on us, and what makes us respond? What is it like to read poems in a world of endless feeds and magic screens? Questions of relatability becomes more interesting as sites of self-reflection.

In the survey course I taught at a large public university, I found that it softened my students' resistance to poetry to measure a poem's capacity to communicate and to tell stories against narrative genres—not only those on my syllabus but the soliloquys of TikTok and Instagram, which tell us how to dance, how to be happy, how to hustle. This wasn't to divert attention from a poem's unique tone, diction, or rhythm, but to acknowledge, and learn from, the modes of scrutiny Gen Z already exercises. Asking students to read poetry through the lens of their own scrolling habits has pitfalls, but that lens trains their focus on devices of rhetorical and literary distancing, such as Dunbar's "mask." Certain senses of "we" exclude, perhaps antagonize, others.

Let me offer another example by way of Black poetry's blues tradition. Here again, my hope is to leverage rather than avoid the apparent anachronism of reading poems in an age of social media. For this the poetry of Lorenzo Thomas is "fit music," the title of Thomas's 1972 chapbook. Drawing inspiration from movies, television, and radio, shuttling between first-person and collective pronouns, modernist and vernacular idioms, Thomas modeled the poet's role on "the African griots—the oral historians and traditional bards" (*Extraordinary Measures* 111). Like the blues, the art of the griot is to lighten tales of hardship with humor and wit: "Traveling light or heavy burdened," the griot is on the road from gig to gig, "In passage—/ Chasing the tortoise and the hare / In endless round" (Thomas, *The Collected Poems* 493). From Thomas's 2001 poem "An Arc Still Open," these lines cut a haunting middle passage between history and myth, the unfinished arc of the poem's title echoing Martin Luther King Jr. The blues; the fable of the tortoise and the hare; the Atlantic slave trade; Civil Rights: dropping breadcrumbs for students to follow, the poem moves in a circular but open-ended way. Dwelling in "this world of entropy and haste" yet positing the "neverending journey" of "we" and "us," the poem stakes a claim on "humane understanding" and "the sanity of spirit known as grace" in the way that a grandparent or a trusted counselor might. This is Thomas speaking as "Griot, storyteller / soft-spoken but loquacious sage" (*Collected Poems* 493).

What story does this poem tell? A good starting point for classroom discussion, this question cues up others: What is the poem's emotional register? What about its insistent use of "We"? What sort of storyteller could claim to speak for all of us? The poem invokes big abstractions such as "Memory" and "Art" while placing them in tension. It defines the poet in orphic terms—a singer responding to loss—as well as through the West African trickster figure of "Anancy, spinner of magic phrase." Circling back to the question of author and persona, does the "griot" change how students think about lyric? Must there be a formal distance between poet and speaker? The poem begins provocatively by doubting its own semantic medium: "Words . . . tarnish over time," and part of the griot's labor is "burnishing" them back into splendor (*Collected* 492). Raised in a bilingual family, Thomas returned continually to the question of "American English." For L2 students, the stylistic range of his writing exemplifies that of a first-generation immigrant who wrote in activist and avant-garde settings, national and diasporic traditions, folkways as well as mass culture.

At this point, students may enjoy listening to a recording of Thomas's own voice, included in the episode of Al Filreis's *Poem Talk* podcast about "An Arc Still Open." Filreis's discussion with Tyrone Williams and William J. Harris offers a rich close reading of "An Arc" and covers the poem's ekphrastic inspiration, John T. Biggers's 1997 mural, *Salt Marsh*. Listening to the podcast and looking at an image of *Salt Marsh*, students gain context for Thomas's life and career. They hear the poet performing the role of griot, whose art is rooted in local community and simultaneously, as Thomas says of Biggers's mural, "the whole universe." Unlike the false universality of whiteness, however, griot poetics tells stories through history, not to avoid it.

All of this can be brought back to the question of social media through a final example. Nicely apposite to the poems by Dunbar and Thomas is "If We Must Die" by Claude McKay, originally published by *The Liberator* in 1919. McKay's poem was read by Winston Churchill over the BBC airwaves during World War II, found in the debris of the Attica prison riot, and reprinted in magazines like *Time* as a beacon of resistance—a provenance and afterlife that Thomas traced in a 1989 lecture at Naropa. The transit of "If We Must Die" fascinated Thomas: an English sonnet occasioned by distant historical events, in this case the brutal police violence against Black Chicagoans in summer 1919, that would go on to circulate across media, history, and racial identity. "If We Must Die" offers our born-digital students a lively example of Black poetic experiment in genre and diction as well as poetry's capacity for mythmaking and political resilience—a style of agency many of our students yearn to think about and practice themselves. McKay is timely for weaving new political histories out of old literary-historical threads.

Endeavoring to make poems relevant to the social problems and media forms of today, I've found it helpful to meet my students on their terms, inviting them to read lyric as they might listen to music or scroll a feed, to think of poets as analogous to storytellers of all stripes—an influencer, a grandparent, a "legend" of pop culture. This is not only a way of adapting lyric reading practices to a digital age but of discovering a strong justification for including lyric poems on the syllabus as resilient, mobile, and indeed, relatable texts. Such is a tradition in which anyone may belong.

Further Reading

On race and lyric in nineteenth- and twentieth-century contexts, particularly in the African American tradition, see Virginia Jackson, "The Cadence of Consent: Francis Barton Gummere, Lyric Rhythm, and White Poetics" (*Critical Rhythm: The Poetics of a Literary Life Form*, Fordham UP, 2019); Sonya Posmentier, "Lyric Reading in the Black Ethnographic Archive" (*American Literary History*, vol. 30, no. 1, 2018, pp. 55–78); Anthony Reed, "Sing It in My Voice: Blues, Irony, and a Politics of Affirmative Difference," in *Freedom Time: The Poetics and Politics of Black Experimental Writing* (Johns Hopkins UP, 2014); on race and the lyric speaker in contemporary poetry, see, for example, Kamran Javadizadeh, "The Atlantic Ocean Breaking on Our Heads: Claudia Rankine, Robert Lowell and the Whiteness of the Lyric Subject" (*PMLA*, vol. 134, no. 3, 2019, pp. 475–90).

Works Cited

Brooks, Cleanth and Robert Penn Warren. *Understanding Poetry*. 3rd ed., Holt, 1960.
Jackson, Virginia. "Specters of the Ballad." *Nineteenth-Century Literature*, vol. 71, no. 2, 2016, pp. 176–96.
Thomas, Lorenzo. *The Collected Poems of Lorenzo Thomas*. Edited by Aldon Lynn Nielsen and Laura Vrana, Wesleyan UP, 2019.
———. *Extraordinary Measures: Afrocentric Modernism and Twentieth-Century American Poetry*. U of Alabama P, 2000.
———. "The Poetics of the Blues." Jack Kerouac School of Disembodied Poetics, 24 July 1989, archive.org/details/naropa_lorenzo_thomas_lecture_the.
Vendler, Helen. *Poems, Poets, Poetry: An Introduction and Anthology*. Bedford/St. Martin's, 1997.

14

Lyric After Lyricization

Learning and Unlearning the Lyric *I* in the Activist Classroom

Anastasia Nikolis

Teaching the lyric *I* is tough in the wake of arguments about lyricization. Scholars like Virginia Jackson and Yopie Prins have argued that the category of *lyric* is problematically capacious and anachronistically ascribed by twentieth-century critics to poems that belong to more nuanced poetic genres and traditions (2–3). Other critics, such as Jonathan Culler and Eric Hayot, defend the category of lyric as an opportunity for theorizing about poetic construction and comparing across traditions (Culler 6, 9–10; Hayot 1419–20). In light of the complexity of this scholarly debate, teachers might wonder if it's worth teaching the lyric *I* at all, especially in classes that are not explicitly dedicated to poetry. For example, should I teach it in my first-year college writing classes, where students only encounter a couple of poems throughout the semester? Or in my continuing education courses at a local literary center, which only meet for three sessions?

I teach the lyric *I* in even my most abbreviated courses because I believe the lyric *I* presents an opportunity for students to rethink the assumptions, blindness, supremacy, and grasping after false universality that is caught up in both their own sense of (white) subjectivity and the history of lyric subjectivity. This feels especially urgent since I teach in

Rochester, New York, which has been in the news multiple times in recent years due to rampant police brutality, the murder of Daniel Prude, and subsequent protests. Moreover, although Rochester's population is more than 50% people of color according to 2022 census data (census.gov), my classes at both the college and literary center are majority white.

While my case study for this paper is drawn from my continuing education class at the Writers & Books literary center, I have also used this lesson in my first-year college writing classes with similar results. These might seem like completely different classroom dynamics, and they are. But they are similar in their shared interest in self-exploration and subjectivity. The typical eighteen-year-old just starting college is, rightfully and earnestly, obsessed with trying to find their place in the world outside their family of origin. The typical continuing education students who stumble into a Poetry 101 class are similarly preoccupied with trying to find themselves after their kids have left the nest, divorce, retirement, or the death of a partner. Whether they are eighteen, fifty-five, or seventy, these students are similarly reeling in their new worlds and seeking new ways to understand themselves. Lyric poetry, with its emphasis on subjectivity, is an access point for these students who are trying to understand their own. This interest in subjectivity maps on to what we might call the lyric *I* in poetics discourses.

To give a little more context about Writers & Books, it is a local nonprofit located in the middle of the city. It has an independent bookstore, runs reading groups and reading series, holds a summer camp for school-age kids, and conducts adult education creative writing classes. For a couple of years, I taught a recurring Poetry 101 class every quarter that was accessible for brand new poetry writers but had enough variety in the course material that students could take it repeatedly. It introduced students to fundamentals of poetics and gave prompts so they could write independently. The typical continuing education student at Writers & Books is white and relatively affluent. They identify as liberal, live in suburbs that are upwards of 70% white, and engage minimally with the social and political dynamics of the city (NYSED.gov). For all of these reasons, I don't feel comfortable leaving the conversation about subjectivity for more extended poetry classes.

At its best, I believe that teaching is activism. I also believe the best opportunities for classroom activism are where students already have personal investment. This means that even in a condensed format poetry class, or in a few sessions over the course of a first-year writing class, I want to meet my students at their interest in subjectivity. I want to seize that interest and use it as an opportunity to dismantle their assumptions about how to read the *I* in a poem—as a signifier of "universal" experience that is whitewashed, ableist, and sexist—and their corresponding assumptions about their own subjectivities.

But how much should students learn about the lyric *I*? Enough so they can unlearn their corresponding assumptions. The historical context for what I do in my classes starts with the tension between New Critical and confessional approaches to the lyric subject. In the New Critical model, the *I* indicates the poem's "speaker," rather than the poet. It is read purely as an impersonal rhetorical construction that can be universalized to stand in for all of human experience. But, of course, a rhetorical construction theorized by a predominantly white male hegemony isn't universal at all. The emergence of confessional poetry in 1959 is often explained by scholars as a direct rejection of the universalizing, impersonal, and overcooked New Critical framework. Poets like Robert Lowell, Sylvia Plath, and Anne Sexton start writing poems that explicitly draw on their personal experiences, mostly describing personal, "taboo" subject matter such as mental illness, addiction, adultery, or sex. The confessional poetic project suggests that autobiographical readings of the lyric subject, in which the poem's *I* and the poet's *I* are the same, is the best method for particularizing and frustrating the New Critical universal subject.

While a confessional, autobiographical reading of the lyric *I* solves the problem of New Critical universalizing, it presents others. There is a fairly consistent rejection of autobiographical reading among the confessional poets themselves, but it's even stronger among the post-confessional poets who follow. Poets like Louise Glück don't want to be thought of as writing "merely" women's poetry, so they complicate the *I* in their lyrics. Glück famously speaks through the personas of the wild iris and other plants in order to distance her own lived experience as a white woman and foreground the rhetorical construction of feminine subjectivity in her work. Meanwhile her student, Claudia Rankine, famously eliminates the *I* in *Citizen* (2014), using a *you* throughout the first, third, and fourth sections, in order to distance her own lived experience as a Black woman in the United States and foreground the poetic construction of racialized subjectivity.

This post-confessional tradition demands that we attend to the rhetorical construction of the lyric *I* while simultaneously confronting its positionality within systems of power. The rhetorical constructions employed by both Rankine and Glück invite readers to position themselves as the speaker in the poems, but with contextual details that remind readers there are limits to how universalizable the lyric *I* (or *you*) can be. These lyric subjects *are and are not* the poet (Culler 107–09). They *can and cannot* speak for universal experience. This is-and-is-not framing of the lyric subject destabilizes the false universality of the New Critical *I* without overcorrecting to read poems "merely" in terms of the poet's autobiography.

This concept of "is and is not" and "can and cannot" is a difficult one to drop on a first-year writing student who enjoys reading a poem because they can identify with the emotional experience described. It is equally difficult to drop it onto continuing education students who say they prefer and relate more to Mary Oliver than overtly political poets. So, while this is-and-is-not framing of lyric subjectivity does not capture the full historical complexity of the lyric *I*, it does convey that the lyric subject is not as simple as inexperienced poetry readings might suggest. Moreover, it begins to destabilize the assumptions that often inform those inexperienced readings.

To these ends, my lesson uses two poems by the same poet to teach students about these two extreme ends of the lyric subjectivity spectrum. Then, it asks students to reconcile these two poems with one another in order to account for a more complex lyric subject. For example, in one class I shared two poems by the contemporary American poet, Aimee Nezhukumatathil, who draws on her Filipina and South Indian background in her work. First, we read her persona poem, "Self Portrait as Scallop," to understand how the lyric subject can be used as a rhetorical device, which approximates how the New Critics described the lyric subject. Then, we read "On Listening to Your Teacher Take Attendance," which encourages an autobiographical, or confessional, reading of the poem's lyric subject. Both poems appear in her collection, *Oceanic* (2014).

When we read the persona poem, "Self Portrait as Scallop," the students are drawn to the lines they identify with. Lines like, "by then I will have opened up to you," speak to their own experiences of being vulnerable and gesture at some kind of universal human experience (Nezhukumatathil 3). But they are equally drawn to lines that are clearly not relatable and wonderfully unfamiliar in their descriptions of the scallop's "hundred blue eyes" or "the small hinge of its umbo" (3). These lines provide an opportunity to discuss how certain lines invite identification while others do not. With the framework of invitation, the students are quickly able to explain how the scallop-as-lyric-subject is available as a mask for anyone to identify with because it isn't a person. But, with the framework of invitation, students also start questioning their impulses to identify with the *I* of the poem, since none of them are scallops.

At this point, they are primed to evaluate if they want to accept the invitation to identify with the lyric subject when we turn to "On Listening to Your Teacher Take Attendance,"

> Your teacher means well,
> even if he butchers your name like
> he has a bloody sausage casing stuck
> between his teeth, handprints
> on his white, sloppy apron. And when
> everyone turns around to check out
> your face, no need to flush red and warm.
> Just picture all the eyes as if your classroom
> is one big scallop with its dozens of icy blues (5)

My students' first impulse is to identify with the *you*. They share their own stories of having their names mispronounced by a teacher—Smythes became Smiths, Peetones became Pythons. After they get that out of their systems, we talk about Nezhukumatathil's uncanny return to the scallop's haunting blue eyes. I ask them to consider if the *you* in this poem is an invitation to identify or an address. Then, I ask if they've ever been in the position of listening to someone *else's* name get butchered and to reposition themselves as the scallop. What happens when the name of a student of color is mispronounced in a classroom that is majority white? How does the situation change when colonial dynamics are considered—when the student comes from a historically colonized group and the teacher represents the colonizer? Nezhukumatathil uses the *you* to invite identification with the speaker in her poem, much as Rankine does in *Citizen*. But, like Rankine, she also wants readers to question that identification, which is why she doesn't use a more standard *I* and brings back the scallop.

By starting with a persona poem, students are more primed to decouple the pronoun from the poet and see it as a rhetorical feature, as any New Critical reader would. But, when we turn to the more overtly autobiographical poem, they have to account for positionality, too. I have found the trick is getting the students to see both things happening at once, in both poems. By pairing the two poems that each use the scallop as a foil for the *I* of the poem, the students start to see how the lyric subject isn't a static device, but one that can be manipulated for a variety of effects. Once they see this, it destabilizes their impulses to always read the lyric subject the same way—as a universalizable subject. In turn, they start to destabilize universalized readings of subjectivity that play into the American history of systemic racism and white supremacy, without falling prey to overly marginalized autobiographical readings as a simplified corrective.

There is room for improvement in this approach, but it achieves four main goals:

1. Encourages student interest in poetry by allowing them to enjoy the access point they are attracted to. In this case, personal content that examines subjectivity.

2. Introduces the lyric subject as a complicated poetic device that can be manipulated for a range of effects.

3. Encourages students to question when they are invited to identify with rhetorical constructions of lyric subjectivity.

4. Destabilizes the assumption that expressions of personal emotional experience are always universalizable.

Given that the history of the lyric is so complicated, should lessons on lyric subjectivity be cut from shortened introductory poetry classes? I don't think so. While this approach essentializes the New Critical and confessional approaches, it does so in order to teach that there are complexities to lyric subjectivity that early poetry students have a tendency to overlook. The more I reflect on the demographics of my students and teaching in Rochester at this particular historical moment, the more urgent it seems to at least introduce them to the past mistakes of hegemonic lyric subjectivity and use it as an opportunity for them to reflect on their own. This kind of reflection is one small step toward changing the patterns of racialized marginalization that pervade small cities like Rochester across the United States. Reflection is quiet activism. Recognizing student access points to poetry—whether it's their own sense of subjectivity or something else—should provide our points of entry for activism as poetry teachers.

Further Reading:

For more about confessional and post-confessional poetry see M. L. Rosenthal's review "Poetry as Confession" in *The Nation* (1959); Robert Lowell's 1960 National Book Award acceptance speech, "The Raw and the Cooked" (www.nationalbook.org/robert-lowells-accepts-the-1960-national-book-awards-in-poetry-for-life-studies); Deborah Nelson's "Confessional Poetry" chapter in *The Cambridge Companion to American Poetry since 1945* (Cambridge UP, 2013); and Christopher Grobe's *The Art of Confession* (NYU P, 2017).

For more about lyricization and universalizing the lyric subject see Kyoo Lee's "YOU Affect: U, a new-I?" in *Evening Will Come* (no. 55, 2015); Dorothy Wang's *Thinking Its Presence* (Stanford UP, 2013); Anthony Reed's *Freedom Time* (Johns Hopkins UP, 2014); Kamran Javadizadeh's "The Atlantic Ocean Breaking on Our Heads: Claudia Rankine, Robert Lowell, and the Whiteness of the Lyric Subject" in *PMLA* (vol. 134, issue 3, May 2019, pp. 475–90, 2019). For more about the poets referenced, see Robert Lowell's *Life Studies and For the Union Dead* (Farrar, Straus, and Giroux, 2007); Sylvia Plath's *The Collected Poems* (HarperPerennial, 1992); Anne Sexton's *The Complete Poems* (Mariner Books, 1999).

Works Cited

Census. "Quick Facts Rochester city, New York." *American Community Survey*, United States Census Bureau, 2022, www.census.gov/quickfacts/fact/table/rochestercitynewyork/RHI125222#RHI125222. Accessed 6 July 2023.

Culler, Jonathan. *Theory of the Lyric*. Harvard UP, 2015.

Glück, Louise. *The Wild Iris*. Ecco Press, 1993.

Hayot, Eric. Against Historicist Fundamentalism." *PMLA*, vol. 131, no. 5, Oct. 2016, pp. 1414–22, doi.org/10.1632/pmla.2016.131.5.1414.

Jackson, Virginia, and Yopie Prins. Introduction. *The Lyric Theory Reader: A Critical Anthology*. Johns Hopkins UP, 2014, pp. 1–8.

Nezhukumatathil, Aimee. *Oceanic*. Copper Canyon Press, 2018.

NYSED. "Monroe County Data." *Student Information Repository* System, New York State Education Department, 2021–2022, data.nysed.gov/profile.php?county=26. Accessed 6 July 2023.

Rankine, Claudia. *Citizen: An American Lyric*. Graywolf Press, 2014.

Part 2

What We Do With Poems

15

Poetry as Empathetic Praxis
Black Poetics and the Creative Writing Classroom

Monique-Adelle Callahan D.

Plato affirmed poetry's ability to create a well-integrated community and, as Carolina Arujo notes, he believed strongly that the empathetic understanding of others was an essential ingredient for "political and personal flourishing" (83). Teachers of poetry recognize the vigorous and intentional teaching of reading and writing as an essential contribution to the fabric of society. We promote the ability to effectively read our world and write about it, most importantly the world of people, all of whom are at once the same and different from one another. For the poet Kwame Dawes, the "instinct to empathize" is in fact a "human and morally critical act," a lived experience that is "an act of the imagination." He concluded that he must "master empathy, and to do so, [he] must imagine, imagine fully and imagine with discipline and commitment" ("Back to Empathy"). Poetry as empathetic praxis can prepare us for positive, authentic, transformative encounters with other human beings.

Empathetically attuned poetry praxis is aggressive training for a kind of penetrating travel. In her powerful essay collection *Empathy Exams*, Leslie Jamison reminds us that empathy is "a penetration, a kind of travel. It suggests you enter another person's pain as you'd enter another country, through immigration and customs, border crossing by way of query" (6). In the classroom that embraces these concepts, poetry becomes a space that is both, to use Janina Levin's terms, personally therapeutic and socially productive (189). This classroom is therapeutic in that it has the potential to trouble the lines of the oppressive inscriptions on each of us imposed by legacies of systemic *isms*, and to aide in the healing process. This classroom is socially productive in its ability to build positively fruitful habits in the inevitable intermingling of familiarity and strangeness in human social encounters. The classroom dedicated to empathetic praxis involves an intentional effort to inform and educate students about how these practices reconfigure their orientation to their classmates and the world outside of the classroom.

When we challenge our students to reflect on and be aware of themselves as subjective readers of poems and of people and to perceive matrices of meaning, simultaneities, and irreconcilable tensions, our students learn to wrestle with—but not eviscerate—a poem, to acknowledge, respect, and pursue its fractal and multiple meanings that are refracted through multiple lenses. To accomplish this reflection, we can employ practices in our classrooms that slow down our students and fix their attention on that essential component of effective art—and, I maintain here, effective social life—*process*. For instance, in my poetry writing workshops, I assign and assess my students on substantive, sequential revised drafts of their poems. I ask them to highlight revisions that reflect the observations of their classmates that have provided new possibilities for craft choices and meaning. As a part of their final portfolio, I ask them to submit a written reflection about how they have incorporated this important feedback into their drafting process. Each time we incentivize students' willingness to allow the influence of others to impact their creative process, we further detach them from valuing fixed *knowledge* produced in analytic isolation and to valuing *understanding* cultivated through a collaborative process involving openness to others, vulnerability, and a willingness to change prior conceptions of meaning or form. These exercises and others like them build a bridge that conjoins habits of empathy and poetic praxis.

As we attune our students to empathetic praxis we actively reward the poetic process that requires the poet-as-writer to divorce themselves from the power of their own will—that is, the willful intention for meaning of the poem. The poet-as-reader divorces themselves from the impulse to know—that is, to translate into the language of the familiar. At times in my classes I ask students to deconstruct their poem drafts by physically cutting them into pieces of words and lines that they can reconfigure in various ways on a fresh page. Other times I ask them to recompose the poem by writing backwards—beginning from the poem draft's final line and working upwards. These and similar activities not uncommon to the poetry classroom challenge students to defamiliarize themselves with their immediate orientation to the poem and to allow for a process of inquiry, discovery, and reconfiguration that opens them to new possibilities for the poem's form and meaning. While these specific activities are not new to the poetry workshop experience, the kind of empathetic praxis I suggest here gives students an opportunity to reflect on their writing process and, even more critically, to do so in productive community with other students. As I encourage my students to discuss their poems in small groups and pairs, I open up space for them to consider how the poems engage with the life experience and perspectives of their classmates.

Empathetic praxis embraces the unfamiliar in the poem as structure, the poem as idea, the poem as expressed experience, the poem as speculative act. The process of writing and reading poems then becomes an exploratory process, heavily conscious of a relationship between language and its representation of human experience, thought, and connection. This process is deeply introspective, reflective, and empathetic, and ultimately provides a model for ethical engagement with the world. The teaching of reading poems can model a kind of engagement with the world of people and ideas around us that does not *other* the other and that acknowledges the fragile fallibility of the self, while at the same time allowing space for that self to exist wholly and integrally. Poetry instruction that forges beyond the constraint of singular, translatable meaning, and encourages the brazen authenticity of reader and writer, paves the way for evolving modes of human connection across racial, social, and cultural boundaries. In this context, the ideal relationship between poet and poem is characterized by empathetic process and inquiry. Poet and trained reader write and read from a position of abstention from fixed knowledge.

We can foster this kind of community in our classrooms by creating a classroom culture and system of rewards that counters the fear of fallibility and risk. Instead of asking our students to write *about* a topic—a prompt with knowledge as a point of entry—we can ask them to describe, or to react, or to abandon traditional syntax and align words and phrases according to their sound, for one instance. Resisting assumption, first the poet and then the reader of the poem each pursue an experience with the poem through inquiry. Ultimately, meaning emerges as a composite of the fused and interdependent processes of inquiry and imagination. As we invite and positively reinforce multiple interpretations of lines, images, and formal choices when we discuss poems; as we provide group work that rewards the number of possible interpretations or perspectives on and in the poem; and as we explicitly affirm our students for risk-taking in reading and writing through our assessment and grading, we determine what success looks like in our classrooms and actively nurture the courage for empathetic praxis.

Effective teachers of poetry teach this process intentionally. They remind students that they do *not* already know what even their own poem is trying to do, have *not* already processed the experience they are engaging through the poem, and have *not* already accessed all they need to fully realize the poem. We begin this work by making the poetry workshop a democratic space where students develop their voices and apply empathetic praxis to the work of their classmates. As teachers we step back and ask each student to offer their questions and their perspectives on the poem so they can engage in the kind of perspective-taking required of empathetic praxis. Having each original poem read by multiple voices, including but not limited to the original composer also reinforces this multivocal space. Students can then write authentic poems that surprise them, poems that open them to self-estrangement and new understandings of themselves and the world around them. At times this new understanding is embodied in the "world" that is an *other* person. As poets and students of poetry are trained in this empathetic praxis, they are groomed to see the poems in the people around them. In the act of paying attention, the poet begins to start seeing in the way Leslie Jamison articulates empathy—a process in which one learns to start seeing (217). As the student-poet is well trained in abandoning preconceived knowledge and approaching the poem draft as an unknown entity, so then does this student grow in the ability to live this modus operandi in the social world. In other words, the student-poet learns to embrace the simultaneity of familiarity and strangeness as it manifests beautifully in human beings.

Black writing is especially entangled in this familiar strangeness. At the turn of the twentieth century W. E. B. DuBois identified this familiar strangeness as endemic to the Black experience in America when he coined the term "double consciousness," a state of being Black and American as an irreconcilable tension that ultimately split the Black consciousness. The violence of racism is, in part, in its forceful imposition of interpretation onto the body of another. It is in the unmitigated interpolation of the self into the other. It is in the unconscious and unchecked imagination—which we refer to as bias—and the absence of critical self-awareness of what Ibram

X. Kendi refers to as "racist policies and racist ideas" (17–18). When we incorporate Black poetry in particular, we invite our students to engage the complexities of being through a conscious evaluation of what constitutes identity and an empathetic process of engaging a community of others, both in contemporary practice and in our negotiation of national and global history.

When the poets we study can engage students around identity and empathy, the classroom becomes charged with transformative potential. In his collection *asked what has changed* (2021), poet Ed Roberson confronts this dynamic of seeing and its relationship to meaning and identity. His speaker laments the destructiveness of a mind that "fails to be the other persons" (8), essentially a mind that fails to empathize in that it is incapable to stepping out of its insular knowing and skillfully engage an *other*. Reading Roberson while students study and work on persona poems like "Skinhead" by poet Patricia Smith in which the poem becomes a portal into a wholly other identity, for example, empowers students to explore the dynamism of difference. In *Playlist for the Apocalypse* (2021), poet Rita Dove enters the lives of Holocaust survivors, Trayvon Martin, the segregated Deep South and contemporary Ferguson, Missouri, and more people and spaces with the surgical skill of an empathetic poetic discipline. Ultimately, she concludes the collection with a courageous disclosure of her own interiority as she wrestled with a debilitating physical disease, reminding us of the bidirectional relationship between empathetic praxis and self-exploration. It is this existential interconnectedness that Tracy K. Smith explores in her collection, *Life on Mars* (2011). Smith debunks the myth of a distinctly constructed, isolated "self" separate from other matter. Incorporating Dove and Smith while asking students to write about aspects of their life experiences, establishes the delicate balance between self-exploration and moving beyond the self to understand one's integral connection to a diverse community. As I ask students to look deeply into their own life experience, I do so with the intent to instigate a dialog between their voice and that of the poets they read and the classmates they sit next to.

Ultimately, the writing and teaching of Black poetry enacts a mode of imaginative meaning-making and identity formation that promotes empathetic and ethical interconnectedness across inscribed boundaries (be they geographic, social, or temporal), and can function in the classroom as a speculative mode that can be used to ethically engage a rapidly evolving global future. While poetry is not a social, political, or economic practice, the practice of poetry can transform the way we approach this tripartite. When we acknowledge the intimacy of the moment between reader and poem, writer and poem, and facilitate that process with perspicacity, we empower our students to allow the reading and writing of poems to prepare them for the practice of empathy in their daily lives. Writing poems and engaging poems with skill and vigor can be an invaluable exercise in empathy that provides a model for an ethical engagement with a diverse and interconnected world of people. The dynamic space both of the poem and of the poetry classroom represents a space of intimate encounter and rigorous reconfiguration of the self, other, and representations of the internal and external world through acts of imagination. In this space we can interrogate the intricacies of our interconnectedness, mediated through empathetic poetic praxis. As Claudia Rankine provokes us to see in the following lines from her eclectic, interrogative masterpiece *Just Us*: "I am here. Whatever is / being expressed, what if, I am here awaiting, waiting for you" (7).

Further Reading

Leslie Jamison's *The Empathy Exams* (Graywolf, 2014) is a thought-provoking collection of personal essays on empathy. For more on literature and empathy, Janina Levin's article "Productive Dialogues across Disciplines" (*Journal of Modern Literature*, vol. 39, no. 4, 2016, pp. 187–92) defines empathy as an interdisciplinary concept. For empathy as an aesthetic concept, consider Carolina Araujo's "Plato's Republic on Mimetic Poetry and Empathy" (*The Many Faces of Mimesis: Selected Essays*, Parnassos, 2018).

Eve. L. Ewing's article "The Quality of the Light: Evidence, Truths, and the Odd Practice of the Poet-Sociologist" (*Black Women's Liberatory Pedagogies*, edited by Olivia N. Perlow, Palgrave Macmillan, 2017, pp. 195–209) discusses the impact of poetry on the social world. Nicole Rangel's article "An Examination of Poetry for the People: A Decolonizing Holistic Approach to Arts Education" (*Educational Studies*, vol. 52, no. 6, 2016, pp. 536–51) explores poetry and alienation. For a modern and contemporary take on the cultural and sociological impacts of American racism, read Ibram X. Kendi's book *How to be an Antiracist* (Random House, 2019) and W. E. B. DuBois's *The Souls of Black Folk* (1903).

For contemporary black poets referenced: Ed Roberson's *asked what has changed* (Wesleyan UP, 2002) explores interconnectedness and alienation in a global ecosystem and Tracy K. Smith's collection *Life on Mars* (Graywolf, 2011) considers identity through the lens of the universe. Rita Dove's *Playlist for the Apocalypse* (W. W. Norton, 2011) examines national and global attempts at co-existence and democracy. Claudia Rankine's *Citizen* (Graywolf, 2014) explores race and citizenship in America through contemplations on popular culture and other forms of Americana.

Works Cited

Arujo, Carolina. "Plato's Republic on Mimetic Poetry and Empathy." *The Many Faces of Mimesis: Selected Essays*, Parnassos, 2018.

Dawes, Kwame. "Back to Empathy." *Poetry Foundation*, Apr. 2010, www.poetryfoundation.org/harriet-books/2010/04/back-to-empathy.

Jamison, Leslie. *The Empathy Exams*. Graywolf, 2014.

Kendi, Ibram X. *How to be an Antiracist*. Random House, 2019.

Levin, Janina. "Productive Dialogues across Disciplines." *Journal of Modern Literature*, vol. 39, no. 4, 2016, pp. 187–92.

Rankine, Claudia. *Just Us: An American Conversation*. Graywolf, 2020.

Roberson, Ed. *asked what has changed*. Wesleyan UP, 2002.

16

Performing Desire

Collaborating with Sex Worker Poets in the Composition Classroom

PHILIPPA CHUN

Introduction: Why Drag Sex Work into the Composition Classroom?

The composition class may not seem the obvious place to teach poetry about sex work (SWer poetry). Mastering academic norms and writing are necessary evils to most students, not skills that will empower them in their professional and personal lives. Few students plan to major in the humanities. This creates challenges for instructors who must "sell" composition courses to an overworked, often disinterested group of largely STEM students.

Most students have never met a sex worker. Their limited knowledge of sex work comes from mainstream media: dead sex workers in crime dramas; crying children on anti-trafficking billboards; exchanges of sex for drugs on ghoulish reality television. Teaching SWer poetry and inviting sex workers into the classroom as colleagues humanizes sex workers, undermines mainstream discourse about sex work, expands the literary canon, and promotes inclusive learning. Students think critically about how their own experiences of marginalization and activism might overlap with sex workers' demands for rights, labor protections, and freedom from violence. Finally, the criminalization of sex work disproportionately affects LGBTQIA+ workers, people of color, and immigrants. Teaching with sex workers foregrounds the necessity of applying intersectional approaches to literature and social justice issues: sex workers are *already* your students, friends, and colleagues.

Poetry and Sex Work

Most students are intimidated by poetry. They feel unequipped to read it and are frustrated by its opacity. Most students approach poems as math problems, eager to learn the formula for producing the "correct" reading. Traditional poetry pedagogy encourages students to mine a poem for literary devices and then locate it within a canon overrepresented by dead white men. When most students hear *poet*, they do not picture a sex worker.

Teaching SWer poetry serves several pedagogical functions. Poetry's playful subversion of language, its rejection of straightforward narrative arcs, its ability to make the ordinary unfamiliar and the extraordinary relatable, and its emotional honesty make it ideal for writing about sex work. Poetry invites students to remember the power of language free from academic jargon or the "five-paragraph essay." Poetry's negative capability troubles binary understandings of sex workers as victims/criminals or oppressed/empowered. Most academic writing stages an ethnographic encounter with the sex worker as an exoticized "other." Her[1] life is radically inaccessible to the "civilian" (non-sex worker) world unless through trite narrative clichés: the "happy hooker" or the mute victim. Teaching SWer poetry foregrounds the various identities of sex workers, amplifying the voices of those facing multiple, intersecting forms of identity-based discrimination. For example, it directs student attention towards the disproportionate risks faced by transgender workers and workers of color.

Finally, some of the most vibrant and exciting contemporary poetry is being written about sex work by those with either direct experience in the industry or decades of experience organizing alongside sex workers.[2]

Forms of Collaboration

My collaborations with sex workers have taken two forms, both using video conferencing software. I have invited published poets to visit the class, and

I have invited artists currently working as sex workers to co-teach with me.

The authors I have collaborated with have written publicly about doing sex work in the past (Jamie Hood) or have a long history of campaigning alongside sex workers (Cassandra Troyan). During the visit, authors read from their poetry, answer questions, and discuss their work. Students relish the opportunity to meet young, published authors, fostering close engagement with their poetry.

This is often the first time students have met a published author. Discussing the writing process demystifies poetry and makes writing in general seem less intimidating. Hearing how Hood integrates her life into her writing enabled students to relate to her work. Hearing Hood and Troyan read their work made students consider the value of outside perspectives to their academic education. As one student wrote, reading poetry and meeting poets was a reminder that "prose, especially in academia, does not have a monopoly on critical thought and wisdom!"[3] Writing emerges from these visits as exhilarating, accessible, and powerful, and students choose to write poetry in and outside of the classroom.

I have also co-taught poetry in collaboration with current sex workers. I collaborated with "Bella,"[4] a sex worker-artist, for several years. Introducing Bella as a sex worker *as well* as an artist, activist, and educator emphasizes her humanity and broad expertise, not simply her job. We regularly co-taught Rachel Rabbit White's *Porn Carnival* (2019); this collaboration enhances the teaching of poetry about sex work in ways that I could not achieve alone. As co-instructors, we model a nonhierarchical classroom space. Bella's instruction demonstrates to students what feminist standpoint theory posits: all knowledge is socially situated. Based on their lived experience, marginalized groups are better positioned to reveal certain information about power and oppression. Bella's privileged insight reveals the stakes of academic exclusion; it not only harms individuals and communities, but robs the world of the insights that marginalized folks can offer. Bella's presence unsettles the notion that literary scholars are the most (or only) qualified to teach poetry.

Safely Collaborating with Sex Workers

The biggest challenge to collaboration concerns the criminalization of full-service sex work (FSSW) in the US. Collaborating with academics involves significant risk to sex workers, even those engaged in legal sex work such as stripping or working in countries where FSSW is not criminalized. Sex workers face being outed, housing discrimination, loss of "civilian" jobs and income, incarceration, travel bans, and harm from law enforcement. Recognizing and minimizing such risks is important given the growth of sophisticated surveillance technologies.

Instructors should explain the scope of the project, discuss benefits of collaboration for students *and* for sex workers, enact safety measures, and listen to collaborators' input. If possible, offer collaborators stipends, assign their writing, and think creatively about how your professional skills and institutional affiliation can be used to provide nonfinancial compensation. Be prepared to justify these collaborations and these pedagogical benefits to your institution. Define clear parameters for students about what is acceptable to ask your collaborator. Avoid discussing specific sexual acts, prices, or providing information about sex worker-only spaces or safety strategies. If your collaborator is not publicly "out" as a current or former sex worker, these precautions are even more vital.

My call for collaboration is tempered by awareness of the ongoing harm the academy causes sex workers. Academics often use sex workers to further their own agenda, at the expense of sex workers' own needs or desires. Sex workers receive frequent requests for their unpaid time and expertise which can jeopardize their safety and privacy. When searching for a collaborator, contact an intermediary to approach sex workers on your behalf and vouch for your credibility and credentials.

Intermediaries may include academics already working with sex workers, sex worker collectives, and experienced nonprofit and campaigning organizations. If you contact someone directly, always use their professional email or contact form, not their private social media accounts. Be prepared to answer questions about your credentials and your project. Listen to feedback from your collaborator about the project's feasibility, benefits, and safety measures. Be willing to revise your original plan.

Sex workers will advise you of necessary safety measures. These may include: using a pseudonym; not uploading recordings to the internet or university course management systems; streaming recordings only from your personal computer so students cannot download files; and, using masks, filters, or audio only when recording or streaming to prevent the use of facial recognition software. If you cannot enact appropriate safety measures, *do not collaborate.*

Poetry in Practice:
Teaching Rachel Rabbit White's *Porn Carnival*

I led the following exercise individually and with Bella. By midsemester, students have already analyzed poetry and linked its formal qualities to meaning. Students are familiar with literary techniques and terms such as alliteration and metaphor. However, I encourage students to approach poetry intuitively. How students respond to an idea or poetic feature matters more than whether they can identify techniques like assonance by name. To introduce students to Rachel Rabbit White's poetry and poetry about sex work, I adapt Jennifer Minnen's excellent teaching exercise "Explode the Poem" (130–02). Minnen emphasizes poetry's orality, a quality frequently overlooked by students. Minnen asks instructors to read a poem aloud three times: students listen, annotate a single line, and say their annotation out loud immediately after the relevant line is read.

For this exercise, I use White's poem "Cabaret" from *Porn Carnival*, a collection written while White was working as a high-end escort in New York City. The poem adopts a first-person persona to describe the beauty and banality of escorting. It performs an anti-capitalist critique of labor, wealth inequality, and the commodification of women's bodies. "Cabaret" finds beauty in the abject—a dominatrix looks "like a goddess" as she defecates on a client—and rejects Christian notions of sexual purity, advising that "anyone who thinks sex / is inherently precious / is not your friend" (109).

I play a recording of White reading "Cabaret" rather than reading it myself. The first time, I turn off the lights. Students close their eyes as they listen without visual distractions. I play the recording again. Students annotate a line of the poem. Finally, Bella or I read the poem slowly, pausing at the end of each line so students can comment. The exercise's structured nature makes participation easier for shy students. Their voices mingle with those of the poet, the instructor, and each other. This exercise produces insightful comments from students who find themselves in direct dialogue with the poet, discovering new interpretations by hearing the poem performed.

When I last did this exercise, several students commented on White's voice. Its slow, feminine, "breath-y" quality is intimate and sensual, positioning the listener as a voyeur to White's performance. Like a client, White's listener is being seduced. Students are reminded that a poem's narrator is always a persona even when poets draw upon lived experience.

One student commented on the personification of "pussy" in the line "pussy pays the bills / pussy keeps the lights on" (109). This student rarely participated in class due to insecurities about speaking English as a second language. I gently pushed them to expand on their comment. What effect does personification have? How does it feel hearing the word *pussy* in a poem? They responded, quite reasonably, it was strange! This led to a discussion of assumptions about what is and isn't "poetic" language. We examined how the literary canon excludes marginalized voices, including those of queer and transgender poets and poets writing about criminalized activity. Another student observed that the personification of "pussy" pithily reveals how sex workers, like White, harness the financial power of female sexuality. They added that the lines normalize sex work as simply one job among many, albeit one that is criminalized and stigmatized.

Another student identified allusions to fairy tales and Disney films towards the end of the poem: "bunnies gather / birds land on my shoulder / the curtains close" (110). The woodland creatures invite ironic comparisons between escorts' explicitly sexual labor and the sanitized romance of Disney movies. However, a different student observed that the poem's reclamation of female sexuality contrasts starkly with fairytales such as "The Little Mermaid" and "Snow White" that punish female desire. In Disney's *The Little Mermaid* (1989), the mermaid must sacrifice her beautiful voice to walk on land and pursue love. In the 1836 Hans Christian Andersen story, the mermaid has her tongue cut out and is cursed with agonizing pain every time she uses her new legs. Sex workers' suffering becomes yet another example of the patriarchal suppression of female sexuality. White seems to suggest: at least sex workers get compensated for their objectification!

White's use of contemporary slang, references to group chats and social media, and her refusal to adhere to divisions between "high" and "low" culture (descriptions of getting a nose job nestle alongside references to Sappho and Nietzsche) make her work accessible to undergraduate students. Most students have not studied poetry since high school and are only familiar with a handful of established canonical poets. White's references to orgies, drug use, and sex work challenge preconceptions about what subjects poetry can address. Students have also expressed relief and gratitude at having an academic space to interrogate ideas around sex and sexuality.

Ultimately, sex work loses its shock factor. It is normalized through poetry that positions sex work as a labor issue, something Troyan's collection, *Freedom & Prostitution*, does particularly skillfully. Sex work can be exciting or dangerous but is mostly tedious and exploitative, like many jobs. White gives us glimpses of the reality of escorting: yeast infections, annoying clients, performative desire. SWer poetry challenges popular misconceptions—that it is inherently degrading and that sex workers are desperate victims. White's collection provides an intimate look into a stigmatized and misunderstood industry but her poetry eludes the confessional. It denies readers sordid, traumatic details about sex work and makes explicit the partial, subjective nature of its account. Students become aware that sex work is the work of fantasy, performance, and artistry, much like poetry itself.

Conclusion

The pedagogical success of this project can be measured by the excellent written work students produce, course evaluations, and the ongoing nature of these collaborations. Students make podcasts and write papers about the decriminalization of sex work. Many prefer to write about poetry rather than prose. They enroll in related courses, minor in the humanities, and win writing awards. Students' academic and creative writing improves and they are more comfortable reading, writing about, and producing poetry.

In course evaluations, students overwhelmingly state that learning about sex work challenges their misconceptions about it. It humanizes sex workers as "just normal people" and leaves students "feel[ing] a lot more knowledgeable" about sex work and the struggle for labor rights. Meeting current and former sex workers and activists put faces to an invisible community, provides novel insights, and makes learning about the realities of sex work important and urgent. One of my students summarized the impact of this work: "Learning about [sex work] for the first time was extremely interesting. But most of all, it was enlightening to learn how academic and artistic work can humanize people in ways I did not expect."

Acknowledgments

I owe an enormous debt to Bella and the UK-based Queer Whore Collective. I am equally grateful to Cassandra Troyan and Jamie Hood for collaborating with a stranger and sharing their beautiful writing and wisdom with students; your influence will be felt for years to come. Thanks to Kitty for practical advice on how to contact sex workers, to Eli Dunham and James Hundley who patiently read multiple drafts of this essay, and to my mentor, Professor Shirley Samuels. Thank you to all of the students who took my course: your curiosity, engagement, and feedback made this project possible. Finally, thanks to all the current and former sex workers whose poetry, strength, expertise, and generosity fuels my teaching and activism.

Further Reading

I highly recommend the two poetry collections I refer to in this essay: Jamie Hood's *How to Be a Good Girl: A Miscellany* (Grieveland, 2020) and Cassandra Troyan's *Freedom & Prostitution* (The Elephants, 2020).

In addition to the texts cited, *Hustling Verse: An Anthology of Sex Workers' Poetry* (Arsenal Pulp Press, 2019), edited by Amber Dawn and Justin Ducharme, offers a great introduction to SWer poetry. For student-friendly introductions to sex work, my collaborators and I recommend the books *Revolting Prostitutes: The Fight for Sex Workers' Rights* (Verso, 2018) by Juno Mac and Molly Smith, and *We Too: Essays on Sex Work and Survival* (Feminist Press, 2021), edited by Natalie West and Tina Horn. The Sex Worker Syllabus (twitter.com/SWSyllabus) provides an evolving list of literary, academic, and nonfiction texts written by sex workers, as well as resources for academics considering collaborating with sex workers.

Notes

1. The majority of sex workers in the US are women. Here I use *women* inclusively to refer to cisgender and transgender women.
2. See Works Cited and Further Reading for more information.
3. All student quotations are from anonymous course evaluations.
4. "Bella" is a pseudonym.

Works Cited

Dawn, Amber, and Justin Ducharme. *Hustling Verse: An Anthology of Sex Workers' Poetry*. Arsenal Pulp Press, 2019.

Hood, Jamie. *How to Be a Good Girl: A Miscellany.* Grieveland, 2020.
Mac, Juno and Molly Smith. *Revolting Prostitutes: The Fight for Sex Workers' Rights.* Verso, 2018.
Minnen, Jennifer. "Explode the Poem." *The Pocket Instructor: Literature: 101 Exercises for the College Classroom,* edited by Diana Fuss and William A. Gleason, Princeton UP, 2015, pp. 130–32.
Troyan, Cassandra. *Freedom and Prostitution.* The Elephants, 2020.
West, Natalie and Tina Horn, editors. *We Too: Essays on Sex Work and Survival.* Feminist Press, 2021.
White, Rachel Rabbit. *Porn Carnival.* Wonder, 2019.

17

Oral Poetries Are (Not) Lost to Us
Ethnopoetics in the Digital Age

Kenneth Sherwood

As a student of American poetries and spoken word, I always value a chance to hear poets giving a poetry reading, particularly if their practice is informed by oral or performance traditions. Delivery by voice can add emotional power to the poems and move an audience in ways that a printed text, read in silence or solitude, may not. We respond to the voice of mourning or the song of lament, the cry of jubilation and the whisper of awe, with a physical connection between speaker and listener. But attending a reading—or even listening to a recording of one—is only part of what it means to attend to poetry's oral cultures. Indeed, an urge to witness and document oral poetry can also inspire a sense of loss over what hasn't been documented. Teachers may be familiar with a similarly problematic dynamic as they develop a syllabus and note a pattern in anthologized poems that seems to invite students to focus on loss and absence. What happens when the ethos of loss becomes the dominant note in a classroom? As teachers, are there ways in which our multicultural classrooms unintentionally reproduce the century-old framing of oral traditions as products of the "vanishing other," anthologized before their culture was lost?

An anti-racist pedagogy cannot be satisfied with a song of mourning. Writing here as an Anglo-American male who teaches primarily non-indigenous students, I am convinced it is possible and desirable to work towards engaging with the cultures of others on their own terms and contribute to the work of reconstitution. Without diminishing the cultural violence and displacement of the last five hundred years or minimizing the ethical and intellectual challenges that occur when students, teachers or scholars from outside a culture choose to read, transcribe, interpret, and represent poetry from a culture to which they do not belong, we teachers ought to consider how we can better teach oral poetries in a digital age.

Imagine a night in the cold of winter where an audience has gathered on a college campus in Minnesota (*Mni Sota Makoce* [Dakota], "land where the waters reflect the clouds") in the country of the Anishinaabe, to hear a speaker. He begins the reading or performance with formal welcomes in Zuni (a language from 1300 miles to the southwest). We hear oral poems and stories in three languages, translated by an individual who was not born into the traditions but devoted a life to their teaching and study. For just under an hour, we are invited to become open listeners, and we begin to engage with poetic others. We were moved by the distance between us and the poems we heard but also by the prospect of cross-cultural connection and reconstitution.

The notion that the academy can and should study and teach oral and traditional poetries from global and indigenous cultures as literature is neither new nor uncontroversial. It dates back some fifty years to the advent of *ethnopoetics*, a term associated with the poet, translator, and editor Jerome Rothenberg—who coined the term in 1968—and poet, translator, and anthropologist Dennis Tedlock, who gave the performance described above. Prior to the 1970s, the American academy tended to see oral traditional poetry as primitive "seedlings" (in departments of literature) or valuable for mining linguistic and cultural information (anthropology and linguistics). Ethnopoetics aimed to center the full range of human poetry, encourage cooperative projects among artists and scholars, poets and communities, across cultures and disciplines; combat "cultural genocide" and "encourag[e] a knowledgeable, loving respect" for other cultures "past and present" (see the 1970 "Statement of Intention" [*Alcheringa/Ethnopoetics*, vol. 1, no. 1]). As a practice and a term, ethnopoetics has not been without its critics. In 1973, Helen Vendler's *New York Times* review of a Rothenberg anthology saw it as a threat to the traditional literary canon, proposing facetiously, "Perhaps we should have two concurrent courses in our schools—one with Samoan myths, Hopi chants, Eskimo drawings, Indian mantras and anything else the world-poetry advocates care to include; but let us keep, too, the intimacy, familiarity and love that our children can have only with the poetry, and the greatest poetry, of their mother-tongue."

Too often, the poems, songs, and stories collected by ethnographers were recorded or transcribed in ways that have come under criticism, or even come to be seen as cultural theft (see Jensen's *Travels with Francis Densmore* [2015] and Robinson's *Hungry Listening* [2020]). In the present moment, ethnopoetics needs to be responsive to concerns around appropriation, false claims of indigenous identity, and ethical recognition of cultural sovereignty that have led institutions such as museums to repatriate cultural objects.

In 2024, the need for ethnopoetics remains. In the preface to the anthology *The Serpent and the Fire: Poetries of the Americas from Origins to Present*, Rothenberg and Javier Taboada observed "an upsurge of new or ongoing nationalisms and racisms, directed most often against . . . diversity of mind and spirit" (xli) in contemporary culture. Continuing the ethnopoetic project in many ways, they propose the alternative framing of "[a]n omnipoetics of diversity against a false universality"(xliii), which would "attempt to create a horizontal corpus of works that can facilitate a mutual communication across borders, to bring the works of all into a continually expanding 'symposium of the whole' " (xli). In a tribute to Rothenberg, who passed away in April 2024, Jon Kalish recounts how Rothenberg himself enacted this omnipoetics, writing, "Rothenberg recalled seeing a photo of a thin and gaunt Native man who reminded him of Nazi death camp survivors . . . when the man was asked his name, he responded, 'Ishi,' the word for person or man in the language of an Indigenous group known as the Yana. The linguistic coincidence was not lost on Rothenberg: the Hebrew word for man is *ish*. He remarked . . . that the Yana Indians, like the Jews, had been exterminated" (quoted in Kalish, *The Forward*). For fifty years, it has been a creative and an ethical project: "To confront this implicit, sometimes rampant ethnic cleansing, even ethnocide, there is the need for a kind of omnipoetics that tests the range of our threatened humanities wherever found and looks toward an ever-greater assemblage of words and thoughts as a singular buttress against those forces that would divide and diminish us" (Rothenberg and Taboada, "An Omnipoetics Manifesto").

The challenge for teachers then is how to teach ethnopoetics appropriately, to unsettle rather than colonize poetry. One place to start is the *Alcheringa* digital archive, where the flagship publication of ethnopoetics is now freely available for students and teachers. Accessible for many years only in special collections, the digital archive gives access to over 1700 pages of oral materials as well as MP3s of the nearly twenty audio recordings initially issued with the journal as accompanying fold-in 45-rpm records. Students can encounter songs from the Quechua in Peru and Serbo-Croation legends, Coyote Songs from the Nez Perce of Idaho/US and stories by Son House (US blues musician), Somali Tales, Yaqui Deer Songs, and Christian sermons, in addition to written poems by contemporary poets from the US, the Caribbean, and elsewhere, publishing in print, whose poetry is in conversation with oral traditions.

In thinking about how to teach while reconstituting oral traditions for a digital age, we can perhaps be guided by parallel challenges in the field of music where artists and advocates have increasingly recognized the limits of inclusion models and multicultural enrichment. Dylan Robinson asks us to imagine that instead of inviting a native drummer or flute player on the concert hall stage with the dominant "concert protocols" in place so that music can be "an object of aesthetic contemplation," "the music [should be] presented using Indigenous logics . . . [serving] one of the many functions that Indigenous songs do: as law, medicine, or primary historical documentation." An unsettling requires allowing "indigenous songs and musicians . . . [to] disrupt [. . .] the norms of concert music performance" (8).

Most high school and undergraduate teachers of literature will recognize the possible parallel risks in the way we read and teach poetry. Catherine Quick emphasizes the importance of understanding the language and culture when she encourages "a critical distance from preconceived notions" without which "ethnopoetics faces the possibility of misrepresenting and even patronizing the 'primitive' culture" (100).

We are teaching "other" poetries through a western logic and not an ethnopoetics paradigm if we take as givens: the poem as individualistic expression (created by a singular author, product of romantic inspiration, prizing novelty); the poem as decontextualized (detached from history); the poem as compressed, purely verbal text, a polished aesthetic "object" (aesthetic norms of craft and compression, functions of print-textual normalization); the poem as an object for passive reception.

To teach oral poetries in an unsettled way is first to presume a plurality of forms, traditions, and imaginations, and suspend expectations that the poetry of an "other" will map immediately onto our own experience and expectations. We recognize the possibilities for: poems as communal expression, traditional; contextualized and part of tradition or history;

expansive, possibly loose or multiform; inviting participation. Expanding the range of poetries taught, by drawing on *Alcheringa*, is a start, but if we want to move beyond the concept of inclusion, ethnopoetics invites us to rethink numerous aspects of the dominant critical paradigms for teaching poetry. Over the years, I've had the chance to explore some of these activities in classrooms from high school to introductory literature, advanced undergraduate, and most recently at the graduate level. Some adaptation will be called for depending on the context. As initial steps, teachers at nearly any level might begin by exploring the ethnopoetic practices of open listening and deep contextualization.

Open Listening

Speaking of universals is dangerous, but all known cultures have poetic traditions. What counts as poetry for any of them is language use that is set apart from the "ordinary." If it is poetry, we can anticipate special words, spoken in a special way, and segmented somehow into formal patterns. Framed this way, poetry becomes something that students can listen for without forcing it into a culturally narrow frame.

Activity 1: Listen to poetry in a language unknown to you.

One of the most suggestive recordings in *Alcheringa* is a compilation of "performances in three different languages by a total of six different speakers." The recording of "Oratory in Three Languages" was frequently used by Tedlock in his teaching to demonstrate how open listening to performance in even unfamiliar languages reveals how we can learn to hear some of the contours of oral tradition. He wrote: "As an experiment, you may wish to guess at the general themes of the speeches or at the types of occasions on which they were delivered" by listening alone (*Alcheringa*, vol. 4, no. 1, back cover). Impressively, students are usually quite able to discern the oral genres—even without knowing the languages.

Audiences for oral poetry respond to its sound contours, the rhythm, intonation, and special features that complement and extend beyond the content of the words. Ask students to listen and describe what they hear. We may note formal features in teaching metrical verse (asking students to identify meter or rhyme scheme, alliteration and assonance), but each oral performance tradition has its own sounds (technically patterns of paralinguistic features) which—as when we learn a new language and have trouble hearing new sounds we cannot yet pronounce—are not immediately recognized by outside listeners. Open listening invites us to tune in to these new sound patterns and begin to appreciate them, whether we are listening to language from another part of the world for from a community close by that is not usually invited into the classroom as poetry.

Activity 2: Listen and then transcribe.

Provide students a short recording of an oral performance in a language they speak; this could be audited in class or as a homework assignment. Poems might be chosen from the *Alcheringa* archive or from sources of local relevance to the students. The next step might seem paradoxical, given that we are talking about oral poetry sometimes from traditions which may make no use of writing systems or whose poetic traditions developed through voice and ear with no textual mediation. But using an audio recording, I like to ask students to repeatedly listen and then to begin to transcribe what they hear. At first, they may be content to transcribe for content, capturing words accurately. In a group setting, even this may show some differences in what we hear and how we parse words and phrases. But we quickly turn to whether punctuation should be notated, whether there are lines, whether we hear phrases or grammatical sentences, what marks such a formal unit (is it a pause, a rhyme, a change in intonation?), and how we want to notate that. Are lines grouped into stanzas? How do we know? What other features seem important to the performer? If we can also hear an audience, what do they respond to the most?

Any method of aural transcription necessitates repeated and careful close-listening; it tunes the ear of the reader, brings awareness of voice characteristics, subtle sound patterns; depending on selected features, it may also render available some contextual and social dimensions of the poetry reading event such as audience response or the historical/social conventions of given reading contexts. While the practice of oral poetry transcription dates to nineteenth-century ethnography—prior to the technology of audio recording—traditional listening and transcription remains pedagogically useful. To return again to the analogy of music, students in traditions from classical to jazz also practice melodic and rhythmic transcription as a form of ear training.

In teaching ethnopoetic transcription, I have had students explore both very strict standardized transcription schemes and more free, expressive approaches. There are advantages to either. In a more advanced class, we might discuss issues of transcriber bias—from the way one's ear hears in terms of the phonology of one's first language to selection effects, when a researcher invites an informant to share certain materials, songs but not jokes. Students can be invited to explore how questions of authorship and cultural ownership might differ, asking who has the right to perform a song and who is allowed to hear it?

Option 1: Standardized transcription.

In one course, we developed a standardized practice beginning with the determination of a set of desired features and the selection of a coding or markup vocabulary. We adapted terms from music in order to tag **Loudness** (f: forte [loud]; ff: very loud; cresc: crescendo [getting louder]; p: piano [soft]; pp: very soft; dimin: diminuendo [getting softer]), **Tempo** (a: allegro [fast]; aa: very fast; acc: accelerando [getting faster]; l: lento [slow]; ll: very slow; rall: rallentando [getting slower]), **Pitch** (asc: [ascending]; desc: [descending]), **Voice** (qualitative descriptors such as harsh; whispering; melodic), and **Pauses** (notable passages of silence).

Using this somewhat strictly agreed system meant that we were all listening for similar things and using a shared vocabulary, notwithstanding the irony that we had imported terms associated with western classical music. We marked them in the same way with xml tags (for example, <pause type="brief"/>) and thus were able to share what we heard quite transparently. Of course, the rigidity of this approach can seem confining and a bit mechanical, so for some classes it might be preferable to take an expressive transcription approach.

Option 2: Expressive transcription.

Alternatively, learning to perceive previously unregistered dimensions of aesthetic language can be approached as a more creative and individualistic project. So, one student or small group may choose to focus on changes in intonation, another might notice that laughter and approval from the audience shapes the performance, deciding to foreground those features. Similarly, after being introduced to some exemplary transcription models, students are free to choose how they would like to represent certain aural features on the page. Does a larger font or ALL CAPITALS do a better job of signaling shouting? Should a pause be represented with _____ blank _____ space or a visual mark? Do we want to be very precise ("0.35 second pause") or more reader friendly ("short pause")?

Such activities allow students to come to appreciate the interaction of form and content, of sounds' pleasures and functions in another poetic tradition. Inevitably, some will feel that we have still not "captured" the performance on the page in a full sense—which is a lesson in itself. They may also recognize that what they hear and interpret is limited by their unfamiliarity with the tradition or context. Beyond what their beginner ears can hear, what do the poets, singers, or audiences themselves in this tradition value?

Deep Contextualization

In study of ethnopoetics, *listening* can be both a literal and metaphorical descriptor.[1] To appreciate, to enlarge our subjectivity, to cross cultural divides, to enter into reciprocal arrangement—we may ask students to be good listeners in the metaphorical sense as well—responsive, thoughtful, hesitant to provide our own answers too quickly. Unsettling poetry can lead to increased awareness of the constraints of experience and a crucial recentering of marginalized voices.

Self-conscious awareness, as well as discomfort with the positionality of the ethnographer doing fieldwork, does risk the scenario where students may feel they cannot approach experiences or texts with which they do not personally identify. As desirable as it is, the ethical awareness of their positionality or privilege backfires if it becomes a justification for disengagement. When we discuss this explicitly, I sometimes find it helpful to foreground the unique provisionality of the wiki platform. Each entry is created and each edit is made with an effort to be informed and ethical, but the format reminds them that, structurally, they are not writing the final, authoritative word. In fact, other readers will be invited to modify the work they have shared.

As one step towards a productive engagement with these tensions, I created an ethnopoetics wiki for the collaborative writing of my students (contexts, analysis, transcription, and commentary). Pursuit of collaborative research can be one way to help students deepen their appreciation of contexts and engage with what it means to begin to contribute to a body of knowledge. The wiki is always open to revision and correction. Even as one authors a page, it is open to the input and views of a larger community. It can be productive even as it is necessarily limited, provisional, always in process. With the permission of the archive, our wiki intersects with the journal *Alcheringa/Ethnopoetics*. While *Alcheringa/Ethnopoetics* is rich as a source for ethnopoetic stories, chants, poems, and other oral verbal art, the journal is limited by space, the physical constraints of the print medium, and the conventions of the literary journal. Viewed today, we recognize it omits cultural information that might be valuable for teachers and students.

EXAMPLES

An undergraduate student Hayley Brown was the lead author in developing context for "Praises of Bantu Kings," appearing in *Alcheringa* 1.1. The fifth of the series of freely translated poems begins:

> I love.
> I overrun the country.
> I am awarded lands
> I was scornful of their goats & sheep.

The lead author of the wiki entry on these poems conducted bibliographic research to locate their prior publication in *Royal Praises and Praise Names of the Lunda Kazembe of Northern Rhodesia* by Jaques Chileya Chiwale; she then presented the transliterations from *Bemba* and *Luba* and Chiwale's literal translation into English to compare with the free translation above.

Luba:

Nkonda bilo,
Wakondele ubuleyi nebutombo,
Mutunda mwabilwa Ntanda,
Bashele babilwa mbushi ne mikoko.

Bemba:

Newayemwa,
Ukupoke fyalo mukucimfya,
Neupelwa ifyalo na bantu,
Abanandi bapelwa imbushi ne mikoko.

I love
To seize the country by force,
I who am given lands and people,
Whereas others are given goats and sheep.

Even with no training in the languages of northern Rhodesia (now Zambia), she begins to enter into the linguistic complexity of oral history in a contested, post-colonial land. She also shares the narrative context for the poems, writing "after Nkuba and his brother were murdered, Nacituti gifted Mwata Ilunga the land and rivers of Shilal and begged the ruler to stay in the area to also rule over their land so that she and her family would not be slaughtered as her son had been. Mwata Ilunga then sang his own praise song, something that was customary for rulers to recite under special circumstances such as these." This poetry is memorable as art but also reminds that song and poetry can be political acts and part of history. Other students looked at poems from Quechua that had been translated into English through Spanish or explored more recent scholarship on the Mayan *Rabinal Achí*.

Even a less advanced class can be invited to contribute meaningfully to a collaborative, scholarly wiki. If the students are less prepared to work with the multilingual complexity of such texts, a group might take a role in less challenging but equally important editorial tasks. They might build a glossary of indigenous, colonial, and postcolonial place names; or construct a cross-referenced list of poems with parallel themes using content tags; or develop a current reference bibliography for an entry; or develop a list of links to relevant community websites, maps, and language learning resources.

Conclusion

The teaching of diverse oral poetries via digital tools and participatory student scholarship allows us to acknowledge the past and also learn some of the language—the words, songs, stories, jokes, and prayers of others—who lived here before, and who live here and elsewhere now. In addition to land acknowledgements, I would like to see our profession teach students of English to pronounce words in Navajo, listen to and transcribe sermons, or analyze speakers reciting toasts or playing the dozens. And if those students come to our English classes with heritage experience of other languages and traditions, I would like them to know that those stories, poems, and legends deserve to share the stage with the poetry of the standard syllabus.

Further Reading

The anthologies *Shaking the Pumpkin* (3rd ed., Station Hill Press, 2014) and *Technicians of the Sacred* (3rd ed., U of California P, 2017) represent an additional corpus of oral poetry. John Foley's *How to Read an Oral Poem* (U of Illinois P, 2002) gives a reader-friendly approach to the variety of oral practices, both more accessible and less dogmatic than the classic *Orality and Literacy* by Walter Ong (30th anniversary ed., Routledge, 2012). Scholarly and polemical, Dylan Robinson's *Hungry Listening* (U of Minnesota P, 2020) makes a crucial argument about how concert music institutions admit "indigenous content" but not "indigenous structure," where Native American performers and music are "fit" into a classical context (6) with that structure left in place. Joan Jensen's edited collection *Travels with Frances Densmore: Her Life, Work, and Legacy in Native American Studies* (U of Nebraska P, 2015) offers a partly sympathetic account of early ethnographic collection. Julia Novak's *Live Poetry: An Integrated Approach to Poetry in Performance* (Brill, 2011) expands attention from oral tradition to performance in video and live events such as poetry slams. Two other scholarly texts, Peter Middleton's *Distant Reading: Performance, Readership, and Consumption in Contemporary Poetry* (U of Alabama P, 2005)and Charles Bernstein's *Close Listening: Poetry and the Performed Word* (Oxford UP, 1998) together explore how orality and performance suffuse even the culture of print poetry.

Many selections in *Alcheringa* ultimately grew into book projects. Of note are *Breath on the Mirror* (U of New Mexico P, 1997) and *Popol Vuh* by Dennis Tedlock (Touchstone, 1996), *Powerhouse for God* by Jeff Titon (U of Tennessee P, 2018), and *Yaqui Deer Songs* by Larry Evers and Felipe Molina (U of Arizona P, 1987). Tedlock's *Spoken Word and the Work of Oral Interpretation* (U of Pennsylvania P, 1983) and Dell Hymes's *In Vain I Tried to Tell You* (U of Nebraska P, 2004) are appropriate for the scholar seeking a more formal understanding of oral poetics. Brian Swann's *Coming to Light* (Vintage, 1996) includes many well-transcribed oral poems and stories. Leslie Silko's *Storyteller* (Penguin, 2012) makes a literary performance of the importance of oral story in culture, as does her *Ceremony* (Penguin, 2006).

Ethnopoetics.org hosts an in-progess wiki that teachers and students are welcome to join. Audio recordings of oral poetry can be found via Ubuweb.com in a collection curated by Jerome Rothenberg as well as Pennsound (www.ubu.com/ethno/soundings.html). The OYSI School project by Chilean poet and artist Cecilia Vicuna (oysi.org) emphasizes "the value of orality, art and poetry as multidimensional vehicles to expand knowledge for the future," and includes a range of audio-visual materials with an emphasis on Spanish and indigenous languages of the Americas. Ojibwe.net links oral traditions with language learning, observing that "[o]ne component of a living language is [that it] is not only spoken fluently, but also used creatively" with an emphasis on contemporary song and children's education. There are surely other resources. One hopes that contributors to the Ethnopoetics.org will help to identify them and share them with appropriate audiences.

Notes

1. Listening is a literal practice—since this art has oral origins—and because a practice of ethnopoetic listening and transcription can remind us of the difficulties of hearing well, the layers of richness that are not apparent in one session, in the variations attendant on the ears of a community of listeners.

Works Cited

Ethnopoetics Wiki. wiki.ethnopoetics.org. Accessed 17 May 2024.

Kalish, Jon. "How Two Visionaries Linked Jewish and Indigenous American Culture." *The Forward*, 17 May 2024, forward.com/culture/613717/jerome-rothenberg-charlie-morrow-indigenous-culture.

Quick, Catherine. "Ethnopoetics." *Folklore Forum*, vol. 30, no. 1/2, 1999, pp. 95–105, hdl.handle.net/2022/2324.

Robinson, Dylan. *Hungry Listening: Resonant Theory for Indigenous Sound Studies*. U of Minnesota P, 2020, www.upress.umn.edu/book-division/books/hungry-listening.

Rothenberg, Jerome, and Javier Taboada. "An Omnipoetics Manifesto." *Poems and Poetics*, 4 Oct. 2023, poemsandpoetics.blogspot.com.

———, eds. *The Serpent and the Fire: Poetries of the Americas from Origins to Present*. U of California P, 2024.

Rothenberg, Jerome, and Dennis Tedlock. "Statement of Intention." *Alcheringa / Ethnopoetics*, vol. 1, no. 1, fall 1970, p. 1, wiki.ethnopoetics.org/doku.php?id=alcheringa:1-1:statement_of_intention.

Tedlock, Dennis. Back cover. *Alcheringa* (New Series), vol. 4, no. 1, 1978.

Tedlock, Dennis, and Jerome Rothenberg. *Alcheringa: Journal of Ethnpoetics*. 1970–1980, jacket2.org/reissues/alcheringa.

Vendler, Helen. "Ha—Mine Soul—I Say 'Alas' and I Say 'Alas' and 'Alas' and 'Alas'!" *The New York Times*, 30 Dec. 1973, www.nytimes.com/1973/12/30/archives/america-a-prophecy-a-new-reading-of-american-poetry-from.html. Review of Rothenberg and Quasha's anthology, *America a Prophecy*.

18

Against Mastery

Working Through the Desire for Order
in Teaching M. NourbeSe Philip's *Zong!*

JESS A. GOLDBERG

> The stories on board the *Zong* that comprise *Zong!* are jammed together—"crumped"—so that the ordering of grammar, the ordering that is the impulse of empire is subverted.
>
> —M. NourbeSe Philip, "Notanda"

How do we teach a literary text that explicitly resists the very possibility of *meaning* itself? M. NourbeSe Philip's 2008 book *Zong!* presents us with this challenge as it undercuts at every turn its own attempt to "un-tell," in the poet's words, a horrific story of slavery.

Philip's poetry takes as its occasion the 1781 *Zong* Massacre, in which about 133 enslaved Africans were thrown overboard a slave ship ostensibly to save a dwindling water supply. Throwing enslaved people overboard in order to protect the overall "success" of the transatlantic voyage was not an uncommon practice on slave ships, but this particular instance garnered considerable attention in its own historical moment and continues to do so today because of the ensuing legal battle. The trial, *Gregson v. Gilbert*, was not a murder trial because the law did not recognize enslaved Africans as persons. Instead, the trial was an insurance case. The owners of the ship claimed that the underwriters were liable for the monetary value of the jettisoned Africans, defined as cargo, while the insurers argued that the ship's decreased water supply was due to errors of the crew, meaning, to them, the jettisoning of cargo was unnecessary. Philip uses the text of *Gregson v. Gilbert* as the source for *Zong!*; she rearranges the words of the legal record to craft poetry that recognizes that "where the law attempts to extinguish be-ing, as happened for 400 years as part of the European project, be-ing trumps law every time" (200).

There is a wealth of resources on anti-racist teaching available for readers, so I will not be discussing general strategies for teaching about slavery here, except to say that in choosing to teach about traumatic historical violence, any teacher is obligated to take seriously the ways that differently positioned students will experience encountering the material. This is of course not to say that we ought not teach about traumatic or painful histories, but that we (1) remember not to reduce the history of *people* to only a history of trauma or violence, while we (2) make room in class for students to choose how to respond to the pain of the history under study—in the case of racial chattel slavery in *Zong!*, this could mean Black students, specifically, though no teacher is ever in a position to predict ahead of time how any student will respond to any text, no matter what we think we know about anyone's individual identity. In teaching *Zong!*, I discuss with my students excerpts from published interviews with Philip as well as moments in the book when she recounts the pain of the writing process, and we analyze "the archive" of slavery and the law through affective as well as historical terms. That is, we as a class work through how Philip describes how it *felt* to research and write the book, how it *feels* to read the book, and how history is a force that is felt by us in the present, though differently by each of us. In fact, my first question to students on day one of discussing *Zong!* is "How did it feel to read this poetry?"

It is imperative for any instructor who wishes to teach texts about slavery to provide students with the necessary historical background and to be trained to facilitate anti-racist class discussions that challenge students to critique dominant cultural narratives about slavery while also making space for the heaviness of studying systemic murder, sexual violence, and exploitation. In this chapter I focus on how I have taught one particular book, *Zong!*, which asks students to struggle with experimental poetic form while learning about and processing the sheer ubiquity of mass murder in chattel slavery, and the connection between slavery and contemporary institutions such as insurance and banking as aspects of what Saidiya Hartman names "the afterlife of slavery." My essay will narrate the first class session of a unit on *Zong!*. The session asks students and instructors to confront our own desires for *order* in the classroom when confronted with the disorder of Philip's unruly text. Ultimately, I gesture towards ways we might eschew flat, linear narratives of healing, reparation, or closure in studying historical atrocity in favor of sitting in the discomfiture of mourning the irrecoverable as a form of what Christina Sharpe calls "wake work."

When I told colleagues I would be teaching Philip's *Zong!* in two of my lower-level courses, I was cautioned that the text would be too difficult for students less robustly trained in close reading, let along the history of Atlantic slavery. With this in mind, I designed both courses—"Intro to Literary Analysis" and "Neo-Slave Narratives"—to scaffold lessons that prepared students with background knowledge on slavery and practice with close reading. In "Literary Analysis," the *Zong!* unit followed a unit on Walt Whitman's *Drum-Taps* (1865) that included lectures and essays of literary criticism on the role of slavery in the US Civil War, and then I assigned short public history articles on the *Zong* Massacre itself. In "Neo-Slave Narratives," by the time we got to *Zong!*, students had already read Frederick Douglass, Harriet Jacobs, Toni Morrison's *Beloved* (1987), Fred D'Aguiar's *Feeding the Ghosts* (1997), about the *Zong* Massacre, and Hartman's 2008 essay "Venus in Two Acts." The background knowledge on slavery was necessary for the content, and the practice with close reading (in the form of both in-class and out-of-class zero-stakes to graded exercises) was necessary for the form of the poetry. All of this preparation leads up to students being asked to read the first sections of the book, "Os" and "Dicta," on their own.

I always begin the first session on *Zong!* by asking students to freewrite for five minutes about what reading *Zong!* was like for them. I clarify that I am *not* asking for them to analyze the text but to reflect on their feelings and readerly experiences. I then have them exchange their writing with someone next to them and silently read each other's accounts. Finally, I ask everyone to read their own reflection aloud simultaneously. The ensuing conversation reflecting on what it was like participating in the cacophony of reading directs students to thinking about the difficulties of polyvocality alongside the difficulties of being intimidated by poetry that refuses to offer up discernable sentences of text or obvious figures of meaning as beacons of interpretation. This exercise orients us towards thinking about the importance of confusion itself as both an object and method of analysis. *What must it have felt like to have been lost at sea, not knowing the destination?* one student asked in one of these class sessions as we discussed feeling confused and what that might have to do with the book itself. While I would caution against the impulse to try to identify with the experiences of the enslaved since this impulse runs up against the fact that "empathy is double-edged," because, as Hartman writes, the logic of substitution that structures the act of empathy contains the potential to obliterate the other in the process of inserting the self into the experience of the other (*Scenes* 19), I don't mention this on day one so that the students can see where this thread of thinking leads them.

Instead, we turn to poems, beginning with "Zong #11"[1]:

Zong #11

        suppose the law

                is

not

        does

not

        would

not

        be

not

suppose the law not

        —a crime

suppose the law a loss

suppose the law

suppose

Nomble Falope Bisuga Nuru Chimwala Sala

I ask three students to read the poem aloud, one at a time. In every class in which I have done this so far, each student has read left to right, top to bottom, sometimes reading the title and sometimes not, and very rarely does a student read the names inserted as seeming paratext on the bottom of the page. Yet, the poem begins by conjuring a hypothetical, "suppose the law," and then offers by way of its scattered form a series of possible readings: suppose the law/is/a crime, suppose the law/ does/a crime, suppose the law/would/be/a crime, suppose the law/is/not/a crime, suppose the law/does/not/a crime, suppose the law/would/not/be/a crime, or suppose the law/would not be/not/a crime. After these individual readings, I ask that we all, myself included, read the poem aloud together. I never read left to write and top to bottom, but rather I read down columns, crafting phrases out of the words on the page. And every time, so far, I notice the way my reading disrupts my students. Some of them stop altogether; some of them noticeably contort their faces; some of them interrupt themselves to try to mimic me. We then unpack as a group what just happened. And often, students articulate feeling like they had to follow me, because I am, for them, the "authority" on the text in the room, and that they thought they were wrong so they wanted to hear my "correct" way to read the poem. We then reflect on how in the face of uncertainty, what many of them were looking for was an authority to tell them what to do. They were seeking law and order, not merely metaphorically but in a deeply important way that indexes the extent to which carceral epistemology operates as a governing logic of the ordering grammar of the law that Philip identifies in this chapter's epigraph as the impulse of empire.

What does it mean to seek order, to discover the rules, for and in a text whose occasion is the obliteration of enslaved peoples as enforced by a law that "orders" humanity into subjects and objects, those worthy of protection and those whose lives are unmournable? What does it mean to confront this question without refusing to engage the poetry that gives it form? That is, it would be all too easy to claim, as a twenty-first-century reader, that (1) it is impossible to understand the experiences of those aboard the *Zong* so we ought not try, or, on the other hand, to claim—against Philip's own self-account of her writing—that (2) the text somehow recovers the supposedly lost voices of the enslaved as a form of reparation fulfilled.

These two types of "easier" claims often surface in a later stage of the *Zong!* unit. This later stage of the unit, I admit, is kind of a pedagogical setup on my part that invites these "easier" claims.

On the day scheduled for discussing the section "Ventus," I walk into class late, closed book in hand, and immediately hiss "Shh, not so loud—the bell!" This silences the class and draws attention to me, and then I open my book and begin reading aloud:

Figure 18.1. Scanned reproduction of the first page of "Ventus." *Source*: M. NourbeSe Philip, *Zong!*, p. 79. Used with permission.

```
                                           sh h
                                  not so
       loud did nt the                     bell ring oh
                         oh my
                  ass
                       hot                          apes
           all sing                                 sing
                    they sang le       sang el
                           song le         song sing
                    again                              my goat bag of
                                  palm wine
                         dance             dance they sing my
                               ass
           lips gape oh          oh sad tune
                       sing again           they groan not
                            so loud
              when did we decide    desire            le sang
                             pain         oh oh
                       they ma ma mai
                                         with no
              notes                 tears they
                           sit moi je                  am they
                    lie
       over                     them
                        the sun sow          the seven
                                    seas
                 with            aves                 of am
                      & ash sing              him oba
                              him
                                         ask tiki tiki
              fo me                 the ship            heaves
                        sing i say                to
                                          &
                             fro           groans
       the oba sobs again         the din of my
                         own my very
                                         own dying
                              negroes a pint
              of gin the candle              flame s and a hey
                                          hey ho once              an
                              am
                      died             dead
```

I proceed to read all of the "Ventus" section, using my voice to form the letters into words and the words into sentences through which discernable narrative threads emerge, even if only partially. In this performance, I read faster than Philip does when she performs *Zong!* live as part of an intentional projection of a confident assertion of the text's narrative cohesion; I am knowingly performing mastery of the text against the intentions of the author. At the end of "Ventus," I snap the book shut and give the students the following directions: "Break up into three groups. By the end of class, each group has to give a presentation on the chunk of *Zong!* that we've read thus far." Then I sit in the corner and refuse to speak for the rest of class. (It is important to note that this lesson comes about halfway through the semester, so I have worked hard to establish a community of trust in the classroom before this, and my students will recognize my actions as an intentional pedagogical performance.) Each time I've done this, the students have broken themselves into groups, kept an eye on the clock, and devised presentations on the fly. At the end of class I thank them for their work and tell them we'll talk about the exercise next time.

In our next class meeting, I ask students about the experience of the previous class. What was it like listening to me read? When did they realize what I was doing? What was it like trying to put together a group presentation on the fly? What do they think they learned about *Zong!* and about literary analysis in general from the activity? How do they feel? The follow-up conversation has differed drastically between classes, but every time the idea of mastery comes up. Here is one term in which the content and form of *Zong!* come together. And I should emphasize here that while I am sketching daily lessons in broad strokes, much of the details of our class conversations on *Zong!* are devoted to technical close reading of aesthetics, form, and technique. The poetry is not—and, I would argue, *should not be*—merely a screen against which we project a lesson about the historical facticity of slavery. The poetry matters *as* poetry—as language that struggles with itself *as language*, not as a portal of access to historical knowledge. Attending to form is especially important precisely because *Zong!* is especially challenging to readers. And in presenting us with a challenging experimental form, it is tempting to read the text in a quest to *find* a meaning and then to take pride in demonstrating an understanding of the book and the history it reconfigures. It is tempting to act as masters of the historical knowledge we have supposedly *found* in the poetry. But one point I have in mind for the unit, I tell students by the time we get to Philip's essay "Notanda" at the end of the book, is to push against conceptions of *mastery*, both in terms of literally holding power over others and in epistemological terms.

That is, how might *Zong!* challenge us to relinquish the internal desire and structurally imposed academic requirements to demonstrate mastery of a body of knowledge or technical methodology (like that highly disciplined method I love so much, close reading)? Further, how do these challenges confront teachers like me who assign *Zong!* in the first place—How does my pedagogy undo the very "lessons" it is trying to teach? After all, both of these class activities mobilize my performance of mastery to take advantage of my actual authoritative position over my students (I grade them!) in order to, in a way, manipulate them into confronting discomfort that I see emerging through the text's poetics. How am I, to use Philip's word as she reflects on her relationship to *Gregson v. Gilbert* in writing *Zong!*, "contaminated" by the very concept I am trying to undo?

It would be all too easy for me to end this chapter with a ribbon tying together what I think we should "accomplish" as a "learning objective" (a "destination"?) by the end of a unit on *Zong!* But instead, I end here with questions, and with the proposition that when we teach poetry about historical atrocity, perhaps we would do well to stew with our students in the discomfiture of confusion, in the tension of confronting our own impulses to "master" knowledge of the past through literature, in the fantasy of any desires in the room to see the triumph of progress and how such fantasies reproduce the ongoing violence of atrocity's legacy. I want to suggest that reading aloud together, not to arrive but to listen, when paired with intentional metareflection, attention to formalist analysis, and historical context, may be a method of slow pedagogy that allows us to think the difficulty of experimental form as we sit with the difficulty of the enormity of history's wounds.

Further Reading

As a celebrated contemporary poet, Philip's texts have been widely discussed by scholars and reviewers. In addition to essays in scholarly journals and literary and art magazines, for teachers interested in strengthening their knowledge of the text and its contexts, there are a number of sources I would recommend.

First, I strongly encourage teachers to read Christina Sharpe's *In the Wake: On Blackness and Being* (Duke UP, 2016), which elaborates models of complex analysis that grapple with the foundational violence of antiblackness while simultaneously refusing to reduce Black subjects to sheer abjection in order to open thought towards avenues besides thin frameworks of inclusion or the impossible task of recovering what cannot be recovered. With equal emphasis, on the point of impossible recovery, I direct readers to Saidiya Hartman's essays "The Time of Slavery" (*The South Atlantic Quarterly*, vol. 101, no. 4, fall 2002, pp. 757–77) and "Venus in Two Acts" (*Small Axe*, vol. 26, 2008, pp. 1–14)—both of which I often assign in my courses. For ways of thinking about race and law in the humanities, readers can look to Hartman's *Scenes of Subjection: Terror, Slavery, and Self-Making in Nineteenth-Century America*, cited above, and Alexander Weheliye's *Habeas Viscus: Racializing Assemblages, Biopolitics, and Black Feminist Theories of the Human* (Duke UP, 2014). And for a powerful study of experimental poetics that explicitly discusses *Zong!*, I recommend Anthony Reed's *Freedom Time: The Poetics and Politics of Black Experimental Writing* (Johns Hopkins UP, 2014). Finally, for readers looking for historical background, two books that are incredible resources for both teachers and students are James Walvin's *The Zong: A Massacre, The Law, and the End of Slavery* (Yale UP, 2011) and Stephanie Smallwood's *Saltwater Slavery: A Middle Passage from Africa to American Diaspora* (Harvard UP, 2007), both of which highlight the circum-Atlantic scope of chattel slavery.

Notes

1. Poem reproduced with permission of M. NourbeSe Philip.

Works Cited

Hartman, Sadiya V. *Scenes of Subjection: Terror, Slavery, and Self-Making in Nineteenth Century America*. Oxford UP, 1997.

Philip, M. NourbeSe. *Zong!* Wesleyan UP, 2008.

19

Future-Facing Archives
Phillis Wheatley Peters and the Intertextual Poetic Past

Sarah Nance

Tucked in the opening pages of Phillis Wheatley Peters's only published collection, *Poems on Various Subjects, Religious and Moral* (1773), is the often reprinted "On being brought from AFRICA to AMERICA." The eight-line poem—significantly briefer than any that precede it—addresses Wheatley Peters's own enslavement and American chattel slavery. This poem, which Honorée Fanonne Jeffers calls the most "(in)famous poem" that Wheatley Peters wrote (171), opens with a line that many students—mirroring long-standing conversations by literary scholars and historians—flag as potentially problematic, coerced, or indoctrinated: "'TWAS mercy brought me from my *Pagan* land," the speaker explains (Wheatley 1). And yet, as Jeffers points out, "Phillis Wheatley Peters is much more than that" (185).[1]

Following Jeffers's lead in work such as her 2020 poetry collection, *The Age of Phillis*, I examine here the possibility of framing the legacy of Wheatley Peters for students as part of an extended, future-facing archive, one which builds on the work of early Black writers to draw throughlines to our current moment. This approach allows students to understand intertextual and intertemporal connections, using the contours of these strategies to build their own sense of poetic lineage across time and place.

In fall of 2019, I started a new, full-time teaching position and, after a scheduling shift, was unexpectedly assigned to teach the American literature survey course to English majors. While in my graduate program, I worked as part of a large team that redesigned the English major curriculum, so I was familiar with the long-standing debates surrounding survey courses and "American" literature as such. I decided the best thing to do in these circumstances was to frame the course itself as directly attending to these questions: "Becoming American," the course was titled, "(Re)reading as Cultural Formation." Arranged more or less chronologically, the innovation of the course was not its order but instead its focus on the way writers read and reread, asking students to note when ideas, people, texts, and authors were recycled, rearticulated, revised, or repurposed. I had some intentional pairings in mind, overtly placed on the syllabus—Jimi Hendrix's version of Francis Scott Key's "The Star-Spangled Banner," Adrienne Rich writing on the poetry of Anne Bradstreet—but the most extensively paired texts of the class happened to be culled from my own current reading, where I had just finished poet Tiana Clark's 2018 collection, *I Can't Talk About the Trees Without the Blood*. In it, Clark includes four poems, each titled "Conversation with Phillis Wheatley," with an accompanying number: 1, 2, 7, and 14. Her work had reminded me of Kevin Young's *For the Confederate Dead*, which includes the poem "Homage to Phillis Wheatley," with its Wheatley-esque subtitle: "*Poet & Servant to Mr. John Wheatley of Boston, On Her Maiden Voyage to England*." With this constellation of texts in mind, I placed their poems alongside Wheatley Peters early in the course to help suggest for students how this "(re)reading" might take place and, with any luck, setting up an approach for the rest of our reading that semester.

 Within these paired texts, students saw art using art to explain itself, the long line of literary history appearing as more of a tangled web than anything remotely linear. As one student wrote in an essay examining Clark's references to Wheatley Peters, "I chose Clark's piece because of obvious comparisons to Wheatley. . . . Yet, as I started writing, it became less clear what that comparison was meant to be." The perceived success of my American literature course spun on the axis of that sentiment: if I could get students to trouble the tidy progression of literary history, to question the notion of literary lineage, to complicate the palimpsest that emerged from the readings on the syllabus, I felt as though I had given them a useful tool for understanding literary studies, American culture, and humanistic thought.

 My approach questioned how to expand traditional delineations of literary history, reframe memory, and forge a future-facing archive that connects past and present. Engaging with the alternate archival chronology created alongside the poems of Clark and Young allowed my students a more comprehensive understanding of the questions raised in Wheatley Peters's poetry, particularly in "On Being Brought." As I sketch out possible contours this work might take, I hope it is evident that this approach is not limited to survey courses—indeed, many programs are moving away from survey courses for both practical and pedagogical reasons (case in point, my own institution changed its English major curriculum a few years after I initially taught this survey). Although mixing texts across time productively challenges the strict chronological development that survey courses so often use, the core philosophy of the exercise would be at home with a wide variety of classes and topics. I model the approach here with Wheatley Peters specifically because, in the classroom setting described above, pairing historical accounts of her poetry and its changing critical perception over time with a contemporary intertextual method allowed my students to understand the larger "archive" of Wheatley Peters as expansive, extending through literary history. In particular, pairing Wheatley Peters with other Black poets who directly reference her poetic and historical influence suggests for students the development of literary discourses surrounding race, class, and gender that maintain important traction in our current cultural moment.

To start, reading through a network of poetry commenting on other poetry helps acclimate students to productive uncertainty: nuance, paradox, open-ended questions. Writers like Young and Clark respond to the ambiguity of Wheatley Peters's work with what seems, at times, like further ambiguity—no easy answers for questions that confound. Students noticed that Young opens his poem "Homage to Phillis Wheatley" with a statement that underscores his own sense of uncertainty: "There are days I can understand / why you would want to board . . . some ship / and sail" (1–4). In these four lines, Young establishes a shared understanding, but also implies that there are some days he *doesn't* understand her desire to sail, as his subtitle narrates, "On Her Maiden Voyage to England."

Clark's poems capture that sense of vacillation as well, and students were quick to jump into a board exercise—easily adaptable to small discussion groups as well—where they listed clear, concrete images we could hold onto, and those that were more slippery. Some descriptions or metaphors, of course, spanned both categories; in one instance from Clark's first "Conversation" poem, she describes the "moving hyphen" in the term "African-American." This "dash," she writes, "exposing the break"

(16–17). In discussion, students explored what a "break" in identity might look like, both for Wheatley Peters and themselves. Using Clark's configuration, we can track how this hyphen "mov[es]" throughout Wheatley Peters's poetry, noting how different images help complicate the uncertain relationship between self and culture in early America.

In addition to working through images, initial investigations into stylistic choices and the artistic practice of imitation allow students to start mapping lines of poetic inheritance across time. I asked the class to examine the structure, format, word choice, and other formal features at play in Young and Clark's work, and to compare what they noticed to Wheatley Peters. What looks the same? What looks different? How do these stylistic strategies relate to other texts we're reading in the course? How might some of these strategies have different effects in the 1770s versus the 2010s and 2020s? What lineages do these poets reimagine and how obvious is that to the everyday reader?

In Young's poem, students recognize the hallmarks of Wheatley Peters's own style in his use of elevated diction, unexpected capitalization—"Civilization's / Cold seat"; "Republic's / Rough clime"; "a sense no Land can / give"—and mode of address: he refers to Wheatley Peters as "My Most Excellence" (5–6, 15–16, 49–50, 40). These details, of course, help reinforce Young's use of "homage" in the title of his poem: a "work of art or entertainment which incorporates elements of style or content characteristic of another work, artist, or genre, as a means of paying affectionate tribute" (*Oxford English Dictionary*). Although the capitalized words mimic the unsolidified typography of early America, the attention to word-level detail through an *OED* exercise helps students understand nuance, especially in the use of meaning-laden nouns like "clime" or "sense" (as in Young's examples above) or, for Wheatley Peters in "On Being Brought," "mercy," "soul," or "die," or her memorable array of modifying language: "benighted," "sable," "scornful," and "diabolic." Tracing numerous meanings in the *OED*'s definition of each word helps build on the sense of uncertainty already discussed and drives home the point that language holds a multitude of meanings—and that some of those meanings are temporally or contextually bound. This exercise works particularly well as an individual exploration first, then together in groups.

Once students have worked through some of the initial issues of form and content, they might—depending on the structure and level of the course—be ready for more involved research-based, skill-building activities. As with the *OED* exercise, historical and cultural contexts can help students grasp the political and social interventions the poems make.

As Wheatley Peters's "On Being Brought" makes clear, her poems often navigate sites of cultural conflict. Whether showcasing friction between Africa and America, class structures, or political powers, part of the work being done by contemporary writers like Young and Clark is to likewise plumb the depths of such encounters, giving students an apt jumping-off place for further research. Using newspaper databases such as the American Antiquarian Society Historical Periodicals Collection, American Periodicals (1740 to 1940), and African American Periodicals (1825 to 1995), students can do basic searches—such as Wheatley's name—to map how class, gender, race, and nationality are represented across American periodical history (for a free database, see "Chronicling America" from the Library of Congress). Although students may benefit from writing up their findings and integrating their research alongside close readings, conducting part of this activity together as a class can help students harness the excitement of archival research as they narrate and pool their findings.

A final iteration of these activities brings the findings of historical research into play—and I mean quite literally that this assignment can be a form of play. After navigating periodical archives, students can try their hand at entering (and expanding) the archive themselves. One of the most compelling aspects of Clark's conversation poems is that they treat Wheatley Peters as a interlocutor, someone who can be directly addressed. Although this strategy is common in poetry, the overtness of this move stands out to students: the titles, after all, each include the word *conversation*. Students find Clark's poems notable in the way they suggest an ongoing and lengthy dialogue (numbered as they are, 1, 2, 7, and 14), markedly missing parts in the progression. Clark's strategy throughout is to create the feel of a living discourse, one which places our contemporary moment side by side with that of Wheatley Peters. She offers a vision of potential archival recovery—even if imagined—and of female writing communities, as evidenced in her final "Conversation" poem, a "recovered letter from Obour Tanner," who lived in Rhode Island and was, as Clark points out in her notes, "Wheatley's only known correspondent of African descent" (21, 105). Directing students to imagine and create their own conversations allows them to find freedom within constraints: real people (you can provide a list or let them choose) and real histories from their research dictate aspects of the conversation, but students formulate how their own voices fit into the dialogue and, importantly, what form the dialogue takes.

These strategies, I hope, suggest a wide array of pedagogical possibilities for pairing poems across a long historical lineage. Perhaps most important are the benefits of this kind of broadly archival reading: students can use these discussions of form, content, race, class, gender, and context to better understand the political stakes of poetry and the larger, ongoing conversations that are a part of poetics writ large, both historically and now. Furthermore, they can begin to see themselves as part of this archive and understand the genre of poetry as part of a larger cultural formation, one that is continually expanding.

Further Reading

Others have envisioned the afterlives of Wheatley Peters, including Robert Hayden in his "A Letter from Phyllis Wheatley" (*Collected Poems*, Liveright, 1996), Alice Walker (*In Search of Our Mothers' Gardens*, Mariner, 2003), June Jordan ("The Difficult Miracle of Black Poetry in America or Something Like a Sonnet for Phillis Wheatley" in *Some of Us Did Not Die*, Basic/*Civitas* Books, 2002), and lauren woods (*Poems on Various Subjects . . . [A Portrait of Wheatley in Six Parts]*, "Public Works," en.calameo.com/read/005809913acbf07903efc). Wheatley Peters's archive is also literally expanding; see Wendy Raphael Roberts, "'On the Death of Love Rotch,' a New Poem Attributed to Phillis Wheatley (Peters): And a Speculative Attribution" (*Early American Literature*, vol. 58, no. 1, 2023, pp. 155–84).

For archive-expanding pairings, I propose letting the texts themselves dictate the potential reading list. Young's book, for instance, opens with anther reference, a poem titled "Elegy for Miss Brooks" for Gwendolyn Brooks; Terrance Hayes's *American Sonnets for My Past and Future Assassin* (Penguin, 2018) refers to Wanda Coleman's use of the same form.

Notes

1. Jeffers advocates for including Wheatley's married name—Peters—rather than solely the surname of her enslavers.

Works Cited

Clark, Tiana. *I Can't Talk About the Trees Without the Blood*. Pittsburgh UP, 2018.
Jeffers, Honorée Fanonne. *The Age of Phillis*. Wesleyan UP, 2020.
Wheatley, Phillis. *The Collected Works of Phillis Wheatley*. Edited by John Shields, Oxford UP, 1988.
Young, Kevin. *For the Confederate Dead*. Alfred A. Knopf, 2008.

20

Cultivating a Culture of Enjoyment in the Poetry Classroom

Rachel B. Griffis

Pedagogies that unsettle white supremacy often reveal the lifeless and joyless state of a classroom informed by this ideology's directives. Nevertheless, joy itself is understudied as a feature of pedagogy that subverts racism and prejudice while proactively nourishing the hearts and minds of students. Tema Okun includes "objectivity" and a "sense of urgency" in a list of characteristics of white supremacy culture originally created for the organization Dismantling Racism Works (8, 2). The former, Okun argues, is an issue because it cultivates "impatience with any thinking that does not appear 'logical' " and "the belief that emotions are inherently destructive, irrational, and should not play a role in decision-making," while the latter is problematic given that it "makes it difficult to take time to be inclusive" and to "encourage democratic and/or thoughtful decision making" (2, 8). These two characteristics tend to represent the teaching practices of some poetry teachers, who, in the words of Billy Collins in "Introduction to Poetry," attempt to "tie the poem to a chair with rope / and torture a confession out of it" (58). Whereas Collins notes the inherent violence committed against a text by approaching it with a "sense of urgency" and confidence in the "objectivity" of one's reading methods, this approach needs to be studied further as a problematic practice of white supremacy culture. This chapter, then, argues that reading poetry for enjoyment is a powerful anti-racist practice and describes teaching methods that develop students' capacity for humor and admiration, which contribute to a culture of enjoyment in the poetry classroom. These practices challenge the competitive and dogmatic culture of white supremacy and ultimately participate in humanizing reading practices as well as education more broadly.

In *Teaching to Transgress* (1994), bell hooks illuminates the ways in which white supremacy culture lurks in task-oriented, consumeristic approaches to education when she compares her experiences at schools before and after racial integration. At her all-Black school, she remembers that going to school "was sheer joy. I loved being a student. I loved learning. School was the place of ecstasy—pleasure and danger. To be changed by ideas was pure pleasure" (3). In contrast, at her integrated white school, "knowledge was suddenly about information only. It had no relation to how one lived, behaved. It was no longer connected to antiracist struggle" (3). By communicating that the reason to pursue knowledge was for "information only," and not to find essential intellectual and spiritual resources for life, the white school expresses the values of white supremacy culture that Okun illuminates with her insightful list. Native American philosopher and activist John Mohawk concurs with hooks's critique of her integrated white school when he notes, "schools teach people how to more successfully compete for affection. They teach how to reach careers with increased amounts of money and/or control," and "[t]he culture, the system, the way of life are presented as unchangeable, mandated by God, history, and charts of progress" (264). Mohawk, in turn, draws attention to the ways white supremacy culture persists in Western education when he suggests that the values are largely unquestioned because of the way they are "presented as unchangeable" (264).

To challenge these particular values of Western education, I create lessons to help students enjoy poetry alongside traditional lessons focused on textual analysis and close reading. I incorporate humor into my poetry lessons by showing students imitation poems of works I assign and then facilitating an activity wherein the students write their own imitation poems and present them to the class. Some of my favorites include a series of poems that imitate the work of William Carlos Williams, found on the popular website *McSweeney's*. I show my students a version of "This is Just to Say" by Julie Vick, which draws attention to the speaker's avoidance of responsibility for stealing another person's breakfast. Reading this particular imitation poem illuminates the dark humor of Williams's poem, demonstrating—in a lighthearted way—the speaker's perspective, which is an interesting combination of entitlement and smugness. After laughing with my students over this poem and others, then they write imitation poems of their own with the following goals in mind: to represent an aspect of the speaker of the poem and to exaggerate the poem's topic in a humorous way. When students select "This is Just to Say" for their own imitation poems, I encourage them to keep the title as is, but to change other aspects of the poem—such as the plums to their roommate's favorite cereal or to their best friend's significant other. As students share their poems with the class, they make each other laugh and connect with one another over the common human experience of encountering and coping with the entitlement of another person.

Drawing on Daniel Lavery's *Texts from Jane Eyre: And Other Conversations with Your Favorite Literary Characters* (2014), I also lead class activities that involve students translating a poem (or group of poems) into a text message exchange, which often results in moments of laughter and enjoyment in the classroom. In *Texts from Jane Eyre*, Lavery writes creative and hilarious text message exchanges between characters in novels as well as between writers and people in their lives (such as Emily Dickinson and a family member who wants her to leave her house for an evening). Similar to the imitation poems, these text messages exaggerate a character's or writer's qualities and thus deepen the reader's understanding of a literary work through humor. When I am teaching poetry, I show my students an example from Lavery's book featuring a poet. Given that we study the carpe diem poem, beginning with Andrew Marvell's "To His Coy Mistress," followed by different responses to and iterations of Marvell, I have developed an activity wherein students write text message exchanges between Marvell's speaker and other poets. Through the course of a poetry unit, my students will read T. S. Eliot's "The Love Song of J. Alfred Prufrock" and Gwendolyn Brooks's "We Real Cool," both of which take up the carpe diem concept in ways that respond to, extend, and challenge Marvell's "To His Coy Mistress." On different class days, therefore, my students will write a text message exchange between the speaker of Marvell's poem and Eliot's, and later, between the speaker of Brooks's poem and Marvell's. I instruct my students to use creative and humorous ways to exaggerate the perspective of each speaker, which often results in Marvell's speaker taking on the persona of an irresponsible dreamer. Additionally, my students tend to emphasize Prufrock's indecisiveness. One group of students, for example, developed a text message exchange between Prufrock and

Marvell's speaker in which Prufrock was obsessing over the question, "Do I dare to eat a peach?" and Marvell's speaker implored Prufrock to forget about the disturbing texture of his peach before he loses his virginity to a worm in the grave (1113). Writing these text message exchanges gives my students the opportunity to laugh with each other as they are brainstorming ideas and then composing conversations together. Further, they genuinely seem to enjoy performing their text messages for the class and making their classmates laugh as well. These lessons are not meant to replace traditional activities focused on textual analysis but rather serve to extend them so that students take joy in learning and relate what they are learning to how they live, as hooks suggests is a worthwhile end of education. In a course wherein twelve class days are devoted to poetry, I will plan three or four lessons guided by the pedagogy of enjoyment I have described in the examples above.

To give students the opportunity to develop their capacity for admiration, I require them to keep commonplace books during the poetry unit of an introductory course. By teaching students to admire poetry, I hope to subvert the deleterious effects of what Kathleen Fitzpatrick describes as "the utilitarian practice designed to extract The Answer from a text" (98). Fitzpatrick explains, "students may have a point when they complain that too many of their classes destroy the pleasure of reading for them," and she consequently argues that "focus[ing] just a bit less on mastery and more on connection may have benefits for our work with our students, pressing us to consider the ways we instruct and develop lifelong enthusiasts" (97, 86). Accordingly, my commonplace book assignment encourages students to connect with texts on a personal level as they consider what they admire and why. For this assignment, students must collect a certain number (usually ten to fifteen) of passages of poetry that they admire, favor, or simply wish to remember. I encourage students to organize the passages intentionally—for example, they might be organized according to passages that contain beautiful imagery or lines they find thought-provoking or humorous. They submit the collection of passages with images, creative fonts, and other elements that make their commonplace books aesthetically pleasing. They also write a short reflection on what they have learned about their taste in poetry, particularly what they find beautiful or admirable.

The commonplace book is a very popular assignment and students normally go above and beyond the requirements as they put them together. However, every semester I assign the commonplace book, I initially receive questions from students that demonstrate their discomfort with an assignment that does not require them to find "The Answer." As Mohawk insightfully argues, the values of white supremacy culture "are presented as unchangeable, mandated by God, history, and charts of progress," and my students consequently struggle with understanding an assignment that is ill-suited to an objective grading method and moreover encourages them to draw upon their emotions to complete (264). I send emails and have conversations with students before and after class that assure them that the parameters for their selection of passages is only that they admire and appreciate them and can find a way briefly to articulate why. I also use written instructions as an occasion to explain the philosophy behind the assignment. I refer to Wendell Berry's argument that "[t]he thing being made in a university is humanity," and state that being a human entails the freedom to enjoy and admire what we love in contrast to a philosophy that demands tangible, and usually monetary, outcomes (77). Students' initial discomfort with this assignment, in my view, demonstrates the need for more pedagogical techniques in the poetry classroom designed specifically to cultivate a culture of enjoyment.

Overall, these assignments and activities reinforce the idea that education—and life itself—should not be unequivocally focused on finding answers, accomplishing tasks, and producing results that can be commodified. Instead, when students are encouraged to laugh at and admire poetry, they learn that finding enjoyment in their endeavors is not only a worthy end of life but a way they can resist white supremacy culture.

Further Reading

Poetry teachers will benefit from reading Tema Okun's "White Supremacy Culture" (whitesupremacyculture.info, 2020) in its entirety. She lists several characteristics that illuminate the ways white supremacy culture underlies Western assumptions and practices, which should be applied to education. John Mohawk's "Western Peoples, Natural Peoples: Roots of Anxiety" in *Thinking in Indian* (Fulcrum, 2010) similarly observes the characteristics and values of white supremacy culture and makes explicit how they function in schools. Both bell hooks's *Teaching to Transgress: Education as the Practice of Freedom* (Routledge, 1994) and Kathleen Fitzpatrick's *Generous Thinking: A Radical Approach to Saving the University* (Johns Hopkins UP, 2019) articulate theoretical considerations for educators seeking ways to subvert the status quo in their classrooms and to cultivate more humane environments in their work with students. Regarding practical resources for teaching poetry, I encourage teachers to review *McSweeney's* website for a variety of humorous responses to literary texts as well as the minefield of clever and enjoyable conversations in Daniel Lavery's *Texts from Jane Eyre: And Other Conversations with Your Favorite Literary Characters* (Henry Holt and Company, 2014).

Works Cited

Berry, Wendell. *Home Economics*. Counterpoint, 1987.

Brooks, Gwendolyn. "We Real Cool." *The Norton Introduction to Literature*, Shorter 12th Ed., edited by Kelly J. Mays, Norton, 2016, p. 745.

Collins, Billy. *The Apple that Astonished Paris*. U of Arkansas P, 1988.

Eliot, T.S. "The Love Song of J. Alfred Prufrock." *The Norton Introduction to Literature*, Shorter Twelfth Edition, edited by Kelly J. Mays, Norton, 2016, pp. 1110–13.

Fitzpatrick, Kathleen. *Generous Thinking: A Radical Approach to Saving the University*. Johns Hopkins UP, 2019.

hooks, bell. *Teaching to Transgress: Education as the Practice of Freedom*. Routledge, 1994.

Lavery, Daniel. *Texts from Jane Eyre: And Other Conversations with Your Favorite Literary Characters*. Henry Holt and Company, 2014.

Marvell, Andrew. "To His Coy Mistress." *Metaphysical Poetry*, edited by Colin Burrow, Penguin Books, 2006, pp. 198–99.

Mohawk, John. "Western Peoples, Natural Peoples: Roots of Anxiety." *Thinking in Indian: A John Mohawk Reader*, edited by José Barreiro, Fulcrum, 2010.

Okun, Tema. "White Supremacy Culture." *White Supremacy Culture*, 2020, www.whitesupremacyculture.info/uploads/4/3/5/7/43579015/okun_-_white_sup_culture_2020.pdf.

Vick, Julie. "William Carlos Williams Poems for Introverts." *McSweeney's*, 17 Sept. 2018, www.mcsweeneys.net/articles/william-carlos-williams-poems-for-introverts.

Williams, William Carlos. "This is Just to Say." *The Norton Introduction to Literature*, Shorter 12th Ed., edited by Kelly J. Mays, Norton, 2016, p. 829.

21

Reframing Modernism

Creative Composition and the Analysis of Modernist Poetry at an HBCU

CANDIS PIZZETTA

Over the years, I noticed that while students could grapple successfully with high modern poetry, their first reaction to reading Wallace Stevens's "Thirteen Ways of Looking at a Blackbird" (1917) or Marianne Moore's "The Paper Nautilus" (1923) or to wading into the Vorticist manifesto *Blast!* (1914) or Mina Loy's *Feminist Manifesto* (written 1914, published 1982) was bemusement followed closely by an expression of the belief that modernist poetry and poetics were too alien for them to grasp on their own. While navigating the complexities of high modern poetry poses challenges, it also presents opportunities for intellectual growth. Instead of positioning myself as the sole interpreter of these texts, I encourage students to engage directly with the material, leveraging their critical thinking skills. In this essay, I explain how I promote direct engagement through a creative exercise that asks students to construct found poems. This assignment fosters independence and allows students to explore modernist poetry from multiple perspectives, including their own.

If students are initially unenthusiastic when reading high modernist texts, mostly written by white poets, their initial reluctance does not signal a lack of openness to poetry in general. At the historically Black university where I teach, the students and I tackle modernism in one undergraduate poetry course and in an undergraduate twentieth-century literature survey course. Both courses include Harlem Renaissance poetry and prose essays by Harlem Renaissance writers as well as texts by more contemporary writers of color. With both contemporary, postmodern poetry and Harlem Renaissance poetry, students quickly became fully engaged. I could understand the students' affinity for more contemporary poetry, but I noticed that the messages of the Harlem Renaissance poets, while those of another era, another generation, had far more resonance with the experiences of Black students in the Black community in a racially divided United States than did the poems of the white poets of the same era. For instance, students demonstrated a profound sympathy with W. E. B. DuBois's concept of "double consciousness" in Sterling Brown's Slim Greer poems (1930 to 1933) and the call in Alain Locke's essay "Enter the New Negro" (1925) for a new racial identity free of white cultural influence. This deep comprehension among students of color stems not solely from a shared racial background or previous exposure to the historical contexts of the Harlem Renaissance. Rather, their daily experiences with implicit bias and cultural bifurcation in contemporary America enable them to engage deeply with the themes presented. They are fully capable of critiquing and appreciating literature from diverse cultural backgrounds, but they show particular interest in works by Black authors because these works resonate with their experiences and struggles, reflecting ongoing issues similar to those addressed by movements like Black Lives Matter and artists such as Tupac Shakur in "Changes" (recorded 1992, released 1998) and Joyner Lucas in "I'm Not a Racist" (2017). This connection does not suggest a diminished ability to analyze and value poetry from different cultures. In fact, using the found poetry exercise, we can further enhance students' engagement with high modernist poetry, enabling them to explore and appreciate these works in a manner that is both insightful and personally engaging.

The poetry of the Harlem Renaissance resonates deeply with the everyday experiences of Black students, showcasing a rich tapestry of themes and narratives. In contrast, white modernist poetry often navigates different terrains that might not directly reflect the lived realities of students. Through found poetry, students explore modernist themes creatively, allowing them to bring their personal insights to the forefront. This method is not about bridging a gap but about enriching the literary dialogue. It empowers students to engage with all texts on their terms, appreciating the diverse literary contributions without assuming that any single perspective holds more value. Incorporating found poetry as part of a classroom strategy opens possibilities for students to see and make links to their experiences. Found poetry is an act of composition that involves selecting, reframing, and transforming text from existing sources to express new meanings and insights. The poet curates words and phrases with a creative vision, arranging them in such a way that they reveal unexpected relationships and invite fresh interpretations. This verbal collage manipulates the structure and context of the original words and breathes new life into the borrowed text, proving that the creation of poetry can occur within the confines of preexisting words. Outside of the classroom, the exploration of found poetry has had something of a moment in the twenty-first century. As highlighted by Michael Leong in his essay "Conceptualisms in Crisis: The Fate of Late Conceptual Poetry" (2018), this technique has provided a unique platform for writers of color. Leong specifically discusses how he, and others like him, use found poetry to engage in political critique and address their own experiences with racial trauma. This perspective is vital, but it's important to clarify that such experiences and reactions to racial trauma are deeply personal and vary widely among individuals, including BIPOC students. In our classroom, by analyzing modernist themes through the creation of their own texts, students are encouraged not just to study the poets and their works but to explore and express what these themes might signify in their own lives, acknowledging that each student's engagement will be influenced by their unique perspectives and experiences.

Although instruction in the courses I lead involves very little lecture and a great deal of student-led and student-centered activity, the poetics of high modernism presented a challenge for fully engaging students. I began experimenting with pedagogy to create an opportunity for the students to identify the social constructs inherent in their interactions with the text. Instead of leading students to "read" the modernist texts as I read them, I encourage them to find an idea or meaning related to their own experience and then to use that experience to guide their reading of the modernist texts. The course structure foregrounds the Harlem Renaissance writers as the first texts we engage with from the early twentieth century, thereby decentering white modernists and demarginalizing the Harlem Renaissance texts. Although in selecting readings for the course I still guide the process by choosing specific texts for the syllabus, when we move from the Harlem Renaissance readings to the white modernists, students select for themselves which texts from the syllabus they will draw upon to create their found poems. As I worked to refine this approach over several semesters, I came across Monica Prendergast's explanation of her process for adapting found poetry to the exploration of the concepts in an academic review of literature. Prendergast argues that found poetry can better align the dense academic prose with "the transitory, ephemeral, and affective nature of performance" than can a traditional literature review (369). As a researcher in drama education, Prendergast has published widely on the intersections between drama education and performance studies, focusing on how theory can enhance student learning. Although Prendergast's use of found poetry had a very different focus than my application in teaching modernism, that one phrase resonated deeply with me as an instructor who was trying to connect students with modernist poetic practices. Prendergast's description of the nature of performance seems to echo the very nature of the college experience for undergraduate students, which is, in many ways, "transitory, ephemeral, and affective." Their time on campus, their exposure to a wide variety of subjects, and their varying degrees of intellectual and emotional engagement with the subject matter involve affective as well as academic response.

As students embark on a comprehensive exploration of twentieth-century literature, which aligns with the learning outcomes of both the survey course and the twentieth-century poetry course, our survey includes a wide array of voices and perspectives, including a segment where we will analyze a manifesto by a white poet. The inclusion of a white poet's manifesto in our curriculum is designed to broaden the scope of literary analysis, not to prescribe a required connection with white literary traditions. By examining diverse literary voices, including those that may not directly reflect their own experiences, students gain a comprehensive view of the twentieth century's literary landscape. This critical engagement enlarges their awareness of various literary influences and the evolution of literary movements. The exercise is designed to encourage critical engagement and analysis—inviting students to critique, question, and explore the manifesto's relevance (or lack thereof) to their own experiences and the broader literary canon. It offers an opportunity to examine how white imagination and experiences have been historically centered in literature and to discuss the implications of this focus. The goal is to empower students to confront and critique these narratives, thereby enriching their understanding of literature's diverse and multifaceted nature. In approaching this exercise, it has been vital to create a space where all students feel comfortable expressing their perspectives and where the variety of student experiences is recognized as a valuable part of the learning process. We seek to approach all texts, including the white high-modernist manifesto, with a critical eye, agreeing that engagement does not equate to endorsement but is rather part of a broader educational endeavor to consider and critically evaluate the complex landscape of twentieth-century literature.

After students have read the manifesto and a poem by the same poet, they work in groups to identify a theme or concept related to the essay from the white modernist as the focus of their found poems, and then identify an essay from a Harlem Renaissance writer to put in conversation with the white modernist essay. This group discussion generally takes an entire class period as students reread essays, pull examples from poems, and review their notes, arguing for or against pairing authors. Over the next week, students work as individuals to pull text from the essays, from a poem by each of the essay authors, and from two contemporary texts of their choosing, selecting words and phrases that they will use in their poem about the agreed-upon concept. Essential to this process is that each group must identify a concept without input from the instructor, which shifts responsibility both for the interpretive and the creative process to the students. However, not having to reflect the original poems' and essays' exact messages in their own writing, instead layering their analysis of those texts with words and concepts from other texts, establishes a safe intellectual space for students to investigate and share their perceptions of the modernist texts.

In our exploration of modernism and its key figures, we include writers like William Carlos Williams as one of several representative figures whose work exemplifies the movement's innovation and breadth. Alongside Williams, we discuss John Dos Passos, who is of Portuguese ancestry, Mina Loy, with her mixed Jewish and English background, and Jean Rhys, a Dominican writer who bridges Caribbean and European literary traditions. These authors, like Williams, whose heritage includes Martiniquan and Puerto Rican roots, challenge the simplified categorizations of literary history that have traditionally highlighted "dead white men." Introducing these writers as key figures in modernist literature highlights for students the nuanced ways in which race, ethnicity, and personal history inform an author's work and influence the movement at large. By including such diverse voices in our study, we invite a critical examination of modernism that goes beyond its surface narratives, encouraging a deeper appreciation for the complex identities and diverse influences that contribute to twentieth-century literature. This approach allows us to question and expand our construction of what constitutes the modernist canon, enriching our engagement with the texts and their contexts.

For instance, in one recent pairing of William Carlos Williams's lecture "The Poem as a Field of Action" (1948) and Sterling Brown's lecture "A Son's Return" (1973), students identified the following statement on writing from Brown's speech: "My standards are not white. My standards are not black. My standards are human" (17). Their understanding of that viewpoint informed their reading of Williams's essay, especially his claim that "the objective is not experimentation but man. In our case, poems! . . . The poem is what we are after" (291). Some students from the group saw the two statements as an expression of a similar commitment to creative practice while others saw a wide gulf in the experiences of the two authors, with Williams free to concentrate on the creative process while Brown, despite his claims to the contrary, still had to address racialized expectations when he wrote. As the students indicated in their later reflection essays, the emphasis on finding meaning rather than identifying the "correct" ideas was both freeing and overwhelming. Working as a group to narrow down possible concepts to serve as the focus of their poems allowed them both peer feedback on their ideas and a sense that they were calling upon similar cultural experiences in their reading of the texts.

After composing their found poems, students discuss the intended focus of their poems and workshopped final revisions. That class discussion is followed by a short reflection essay, in which they are asked to assess the creative process and reflect upon how concentrating on the found poem changed their interpretation of or interaction with the white modern texts. This process owes a great deal to Samina Hadi-Tabassum's essay on her use of found poetry to examine social justice issues in a graduate literacy course. Hadi-Tabassum shares a variety of techniques for creating found poetry, most of which I have adapted in the survey courses, and she explores the value of found poetry for engaging students in discussions of current events, which is similar to the role it plays in our undergraduate literature classroom where students interpret and compare the cultural messages from a framework of their own making. By focusing on the creation of the poems, the students can reflect on the primary texts and their meaning without approaching the discussion as merely preparation for a future exam. From the standpoint of student learning, the process of seeking and synthesizing texts for the found poems provides a break from explicit instruction and learning. Instead, the activities related to organizing ideas and writing the poems involve implicit learning and open what is known as an incubation period during the creative process. The incubation period enhances the unconscious work by shifting the focus to a different activity, in this case writing poetry to better apprehend the conceptual framework that the modernists describe (Gilhooly et al.). Interestingly, the incubation period also allows for the creative process to lead to new connections or the perception of hidden associations between concepts, texts, and contexts (Aslan et al.). The found poems that result reflect the richness of the students' differing experiences, what Judith Willison calls "the wisdom of students" in her essay on empowering students of color (914).

Further Reading

For more on various techniques for creating found poetry around social justice issues, see Samina Hadi-Tabassum's "Found Poetry: Building Bridges in the Classroom" (*Michigan Reading Journal*, vol. 49, no. 3, 2017, pp. 20–29) as a case study for adopting found poetry for the classroom or Judith Willison's "Supporting the Success of Students of Color: Creating Racial Justice through Student Activism" (*Transformative Dialogues: Teaching & Learning Journal*, vol. 9, no. 2, 2016, pp. 1–18) as an example of student activism using found poetry. Also, for a discussion of adapting found poetry to academic inquiry see Kathleen Galvin and Monica Prendergast's *Poetic Inquiry II: Seeing, Caring, Understanding: Using Poetry as and for Inquiry* (SensePublishers, 2015) along with Prendergast's "Found Poetry as Literature Review" (*Qualitative Inquiry*, vol. 12, no. 2, 2006, pp. 369–88) in which the authors demonstrate how found poetry can distill and re-voice a wide range of concepts. Andrew David Gitlin and Marcie Peck's *Educational Poetics: Inquiry, Freedom, & Innovative Necessity* (Peter Lang, 2005) addresses the need for innovative pedagogy through empowering author-learners in the classroom.

For a glimpse into how the creative process can impact learning, see Andrew Allen and Kevin Thomas's "A Dual Process Account of Creative Thinking" (*Creativity Research Journal*, vol. 23, no. 2, 2011, pp. 109–18), Ken Gilhooly, George Georgiou, and Ultan Devery's "Incubation and Creativity: Do Something Different" (*Thinking and Reasoning*, vol. 19, no. 2, 2013, pp. 137–49), and Simone Ritter and Ap Dijksterhuis's

"Creativity—The Unconscious Foundations of the Incubation Period" (*Frontiers in Human Neuroscience*, vol. 8, 2014). For discussions of the pedagogical value of found poetry adapted to other disciplines, see Hub Zwart's "What Is Nature? On the Use of Poetry in Philosophy Courses for Science Students" (*Teaching Philosophy*, vol. 37, no. 3, 2014, pp. 379-98), Kirti Sawhney Celly's "Creative Writing in Marketing Education: Poetry as an Innovative Pedagogical Tool" (*Marketing Education Review*, vol. 19, no. 1, 2009, pp. 65-71), and Robert Ostrom, Michael Gotesman, and Juanita C. But's "Poetry in Biology: Enhancing Science Education with Creative Writing" (*Teaching College-Level Disciplinary Literacy*, edited by Juanita C. But, Palgrave Macmillan, 2020).

Works Cited

Aslan, Clare E., et al. "Cultivating Creativity in Conservation Science." *Conservation Biology*, vol. 28, no. 2, 2014, pp. 345-53.

Brown, Sterling A. "A Son's Return: Oh, Didn't He Ramble." *A Son's Return: Selected Essays of Sterling A. Brown*, edited by Mark A. Sanders, Northeastern UP, 1996, pp. 1-21.

Gilhooly, Ken J., et al. "Incubation and Creativity: Do Something Different." *Thinking and Reasoning*, vol. 19, no. 2, 2013, pp. 137-49.

Hadi-Tabassum, Samina. "Found Poetry: Building Bridges in the Classroom." *Michigan Reading Journal*, vol. 49, no. 3, 2017, pp. 20-29.

Leong, Michael. "Conceptualisms in Crisis: The Fate of Late Conceptual Poetry." *Journal of Modern Literature*, vol. 41, no. 3, 2018, pp. 109-31.

Prendergast, Monica. "Found Poetry as Literature Review." *Qualitative Inquiry*, vol. 12, no. 2, 2006, pp. 369-88.

Williams, William Carlos. "The Poem as a Field of Action." *Selected Essays of William Carlos Williams*, edited by William Carlos Williams, Random House, 1954, 280-91.

Willison, Judith, et al. "Supporting the Success of Students of Color: Creating Racial Justice Through Student Activism." *Transformative Dialogues: Teaching & Learning Journal*, vol. 9, no. 2, 2016, pp. 1-18.

22

Whose Voice Matters?

Reading Aloud Across Language and Ability

Eileen Sperry

When one imagines teaching poetry, the first image that jumps to mind might be something out of a movie: a student solemnly standing to recite Keats while the rest of the class listens in quiet reverence. Even if our classrooms and our students share little else with that nostalgic fantasy, for those of us that do teach poetry, the practice of having students read aloud often still remains central. *Of course* we ask our students to read aloud in class; we were asked to read aloud as students, so (as with so much of teaching), it feels only natural. And yet, as with so much of teaching, just because our professors did it doesn't mean it's necessarily still worth doing. If we want to move beyond that outdated vision for what the poetry classroom can or should look like, we need to return to the basics of our pedagogy. We need to ask, for instance, what we might lose when we ask our students to read aloud. In what follows, I want to suggest that reading aloud cannot be our only, or even our primary, tool for introducing students to poetry. When we center the aurality of the text above all else, we send a clear message to our students about whose voice matters—and whose might not. For many—especially multilingual, Deaf, or hard-of-hearing students—reading aloud can reveal and exacerbate power inequities in the classroom, widening the fractures of ableism and linguistic prejudice.

Certainly, there has been no shortage of compelling arguments offered in favor of reading aloud in the classroom. Some are historicist: poetry originates in oral traditions long before it enters the written record, and so voicing a poem allows students to tap into that prehistory, imagining themselves alongside Cædmon or the Homeric poet. Moreover, reading aloud forces students to consider the sonic dimension of the text. Poetry, we tell our students, is sound and rhythm, signifying everything. How else, we might ask, will they sense the galloping of Tennyson's "Charge of the Light Brigade" (1854)? How else will they feel the crackling fire of Hayden's "Those Winter Sundays" (1966)? For many, reading aloud remains "a communal, nearly sacral event for heightened speech, investing the poet with the transformative power of the *vates*," the *Princeton Encyclopedia of Poetry and Poetics* entry on "performance" notes; many "continue to believe that poetry achieves its body only when given material form, as sound, in the air, aloud" (1018). We tell our students that they need to immerse themselves in the embodied knowledge of performance to get the full meaning of the text.

Likewise, despite generations of disagreement about whose voice, exactly, the poem captures, teachers of poetry have long argued that reading poetry aloud helps students bring that voice to life. The Romantics argued that the poet was, to paraphrase Wordsworth, a person speaking directly to their peers, pouring out the essence of their subjectivity. Years later, the New Critics argued that the speaker was a character, a persona crafted for readers to interpret. More recently, critics have argued that poetry can also offer what Roland Greene has called a "ritual" dimension. Like a collective prayer or oath, the poem can offer a script for the reader's own thoughts, bringing them in line with its prescribed actions. While these arguments differ significantly in their account of whose the lyric voice is, they reconverge on what reading aloud provides: to give a poem your voice is to become the vessel that brings it to life. Susan Stewart argues that "the work of poetry is to counter the oblivion of darkness . . . to make visible, tangible, and audible the figures of persons, whether such persons are expressing the particulars of sense impressions or the abstractions of reason or the many ways such particulars and abstractions enter into relations with one another" (2). Poetry is the vehicle of intersubjectivity, she writes, a way to encounter our shared humanity. And for as long as we've read poetry, that encounter—the communion and creation poetry offers—has been ascribed to the act of reading it aloud.

But while reading aloud may be a standard practice, it is not a neutral choice—not politically, and not pedagogically. To ask a student to take on the voice of the poem is, in a very real way, also asking them to put aside part of their own. I came to this realization quickly one semester in a course I was teaching on early modern English lyric. I assigned the students a performance project: they were to record themselves reading one of the course texts, modeling their work after several other performance videos we'd watched in class. After I circulated the assignment, one student, a young Puerto Rican woman, came to me with a concern. The poem she wanted to perform was Richard Crashaw's "On the Wounds of Our Crucified Lord" (1646). Crashaw's baroque seventeenth-century English Catholicism guides the poem as it winds its way through Christ's body, transforming the wounds of crucifixion into mouths, eyes, and roses. She loved the poem, she told me; as a Catholic, the imagery felt familiar and new at the same time, and she wanted to use her reading to explore how Crashaw's faith differed from her own.

But, she said, she kept running into issues with the language. A native Spanish speaker, she was struggling to put together a performance of Crashaw's poem she felt confident in. While the imagery and faith of the poem felt so intimate and so familiar, she told me, reading aloud only seemed to push the text further away. Her struggle wasn't rooted in literacy or comprehension; we had discussed the text extensively in class, and she had had little trouble following the poem's complicated conceits. Instead, it was the act of articulation that was bothering her. She told me that it just didn't *feel* right, didn't feel like it was capturing the spark she had felt reading the poem on her own. She confided that she felt like her own mastery of English just wasn't up to par for a poem like Crashaw's and wondered if there was another approach she might take.

In what I had intended to be an opportunity for students to get closer to the texts, reading aloud had instead created a sense of alienation. This was because reading aloud privileges fluency: it insists that speaking and hearing are requisite abilities in the study of poetry and that absent those abilities, a reader cannot ever access the full truth of the poem. And while able-bodied poets and scholars have only recently begun to acknowledge this, Deaf poets and disability theorists have long recognized that poetry pedagogy relies on a normative model of able-bodied experience, one that inevitably excludes a number of students and writers. Deaf poet Rachel Kolb writes that her introduction to poetry came from such a space of alienation, of feeling excluded from the inner mysteries of poetry. "*Listen for it*: with those words, a good half-dozen high school English teachers and, later, college professors explained how I should approach meter," Kolb recalls; "I did not. How could I?" Kolb and critic Julian Gerwitz, writing together, go on to note that by centering reading and listening as foundational critical practices, poetry pedagogy has come to rely on the ear not only as a metaphor for mastery—having "a good ear" for poetry—but as a very real and material gateway for participation in literary culture. "To new students of poetry, however, the ear and related aural expressions, such as 'listen for it,' are today primarily bywords for *ability*," Kolb and Gerwitz write. "The metaphor of the ear is tied to this unintended emphasis on particular kinds of ability and has the unintended consequence of creating a sphere of *inaccessibility* in the way poetry is read and discussed."

I offer these two examples of alienation—the non-native speaker and the Deaf poet—because both reveal the same potential problem with reading aloud. The danger implicit in such an assignment is that the poem begins to displace the reader in the power hierarchies of the classroom. Reading a poem aloud elucidates crucial dimensions of the text, but it also centers the text, asking the reader to adapt their voice, their ear, to fit it, rather than the other way around. Greene argues that the ritual dimension of lyric—the dimension he argues most demands to be read aloud—necessarily involves a power imbalance between text and reader. He writes, "In performance it may be not only compulsory but coercive discourse, for the nature of lyric's ritual dimension, simply stated, is to superpose the subjectivity of the scripted speaker on the reader, and that substitution can entail a kind of violence" (5–6). Particularly for English-language learners and students of color, forcing them to adopt the voice of the author can echo a message they hear so often outside the classroom: that their own voices don't measure up to those of their (affluent, white, English-speaking) peers. Likewise, if we make reading and aurality the price of entry into the study of poetry, we may be telling students who are Deaf, hard-of-hearing, or have selective mutism that the poetry is not for them. Poet Meg Day, speaking with other Deaf and hard-of-hearing poets, writes that

> Hearing folks don't want you to just play with sound, they want you to play with sound in majors & minors, chords & harmonies. Even what we call dissonance in a poem is a certain kind

of bending, a certain kind of agreement with the way hearies process sound. I've memorized rhymes. I know where in the mouth you like your vowels to match. It's a lot of labor & who gets to enjoy it? Who benefits? Whose poetics are erased? I'm done with that. ("Roundtable Discussion")

Centering sound, Day argues, centers only one model of poetics, forcing those outside it to adapt or abandon ship. Why, she argues, must Deaf students or poets adapt to a hearing standard of poetics? Is hearing a poem the only pathway to understanding?

Rather than continue to emphasize reading aloud as the only or even primary avenue to understanding, we as poetry instructors should work first and foremost to guard our students' voices, ensuring that they are valued with equal or greater weight than the voice of the text. When my student approached me with her concerns, I considered my goals for the assignment. What I wanted was for students to develop a deeper sense of connection with the poem—to get to know it from the inside. I realized that reading aloud was one way, but by no means the only way, for my students to accomplish that. And so, we came to a new agreement. She wouldn't read the poem as written, but would instead create a new, bilingual translation that blended Crashaw's original with her native dialects. The resulting video was earnest, emotional, and an unqualified success. Importantly, it captured what the student had wanted all along: the movements between English and Spanish, original and translated, echoed her own relationship with Christianity, which, in turn, echoed the long history of the colonial presence of the Catholic church. The poem was now a text in which faith was both familiar and distant, native and foreign; the student spoke back to, even as she was asked to speak for, forces of historic political violence. After watching the project, I wondered: would this student have been able to explore this dynamic of her experience if I had insisted on the original prompt? If I had prioritized the poem's integrity, instead of the student's own voice?

This essay is not a polemic against reading aloud. Done thoughtfully, these exercises still have a place in our classrooms; they still often have a place in mine. But these are not our only options, and they cannot not be the only avenue we offer students for exploring the mechanics of poetry. Reading assignments can and should be balanced with student-directed, student-centered assignments: translations, adaptations, multi-modal interpretations. In US-based classrooms, we can ensure that the linguistic diversity of our students is regarded as an asset, and not an impediment, for the study of poetry. After working with my student, I rewrote that assignment as one that imagined performance more broadly, allowing students to think across media and language to reimagine their relationship with the text. But the work of inclusion also stretches beyond assessment. We need also to be more intentional with the language we use to define poetics in our classrooms; we can go beyond sound to think about rhythm, shape, space, time, and the countless other senses poetry touches. "Becoming more inclusive in our metaphors and our vocabulary for talking about poetry does not mean stripping away the richness and texture of our critical vocabulary," Gerwitz and Kolb remind us. "Rather, it points to the possibilities of expanding it." The more modalities we offer our students for encountering poetry, the richer their relationships with the texts will be. More than anything, we can design courses and assignments that place the students—and their voices—at the center of our classrooms.

Reading aloud isn't going away any time soon. Susan Burch writes, "Poetry has been traditionally an auditory art form. Rhyme, alliteration, and meter have always been meant for the appreciation of the ear, if only the internal ear. But," she continues, "poems never have been simply words. They are extensions of the self, the exploration of thoughts, moods, and feelings, even whole philosophies and cultures. Poetry demands a heightened sense of language and an appreciation of the psychological universe behind its linguistic structure" (120). What better way to offer our students a heightened sense of language than to encourage them to take hold of their own language—to allow the poem to become an extension, not of the poet's voice, but of their own.

Further Reading

For more on Deaf poetics and pedagogy, consult Kolb and Gerwitz's essay, "An Ear for Poetry," written for *Poetry Foundation*. *Poetry International* hosted and published two critical roundtables—"Roundtable Discussion on Poetics and Disability" and "Roundtable Discussion on Deaf Poetics"—that feature Deaf and hard-of-hearing poets on performance and Deaf poetry. Other sources include the disability poetry anthology, *Beauty is a Verb* (Cinco Puntos Press, 2011), edited by Sheila Black, Michael Northern, and Jennifer Bartlett.

For more on anti-racist and inclusive pedagogies, particularly as they relate to multi-lingual students, consult A. Suresh Canagarajah's *Resisting Linguistic Imperialism in English Teaching* (Oxford UP, 1999) or April Baker-Bell's *Linguistic Justice—Black Language, Literacy, Identity, and Pedagogy* (Routledge, 2020). Relevant shorter pieces include "Revealing the Human and the Writer: The Promise of a Humanizing Writing Pedagogy for Black Students," by Latrise P. Johnson and Hannah Sullivan (*Research in the Teaching of English*, vol. 54, no. 4, May 2020, pp. 418–38) and "Upending Colonial Practices: Toward Repairing Harm in English Education," by de los Rios et al (*Theory into Practice*, vol. 58, no. 4, July 2019, pp. 359–67).

Works Cited

Burch, Susan. "Deaf poets' society: Subverting the hearing paradigm." *Literature and Medicine*, vol. 16, no. 1, 1997, 121–34.

Day, Meg, panelist. "Roundtable Discussion on Poetics And Disability." *Poetry International Online*. www.poetryinternationalonline.com/roundtable-discussion-on-poetics-and-disability. Accessed 21 Apr 2023.

Greene, Roland. *Post Petrarchism: Origins and Innovations in the Western Lyric Sequence*. Princeton UP, 1991.

Kolb, Rachel R., and Julian Gerwitz. "An Ear For Poetry." *Poetry Foundation*, 8 Sept. 2015, www.poetryfoundation.org/articles/70264/an-ear-for-poetry.

Brogan, T. V. F., et al. "Performance." *Princeton Encyclopedia of Poetry and Poetics*, edited by Roland Greene et al., Princeton UP, 2012, pp. 1016–20.

Stewart, Susan. *Poetry and the Fate of the Senses*. U of Chicago P, 2002.

23
Reimagining the Poet's Procedure
Imitation as Literary Analysis

Lizzy LeRud

This essay introduces a classroom activity that uses imitation as analysis, asking students to reimagine a poet's procedure for writing a given poem or a set of poems and inviting them to try out the procedure for themselves. Of course, imitating another writer's poem is nothing new to creative writers. This activity grew out of a myriad of exercises I have encountered both in creative writing workshops and literature classrooms that formalize one of the ways that writers read: when we appreciate another writer's work, we figure out how to copy a technique or adapt it, experimenting with ways of writing similarly. To serve the students in my literary studies classrooms, my approach amplifies the analytical in this mode of appreciation, getting students to dwell more on the figuring-out part and less on to the imitation itself. While imitation exercises may be at home in a creative writing classroom, this activity is designed for literary studies, for an environment that emphasizes strategies for reading as much as, or more so than, those for writing.

But really, why settle for a divide between creative writing and literary studies in the first place? In 2009, disciplinary historians Mary Ann Cain and Gerald Graff bemoaned that New Critical divisions between creativity and critical thinking had played out in institutional separations, a detriment to all (230, 271). More recently, Kimberly Quiogue Andrews observed that it is still a benchmark of the successful creative writing program to operate independently of an English department, sustainable on its own (2). Yet, as Andrews argues, there is a profound connection between the writing of poetry—perhaps more than other genres—and the labor of textual criticism, "a spectrum of interdependence between them," that grew up responsive to the ways modern and contemporary poets gauged their proximity to or exclusion from academic spaces (15). In their "anti-handbook" for creative writers, Steve Westbrook and James Ryan similarly argue against a longstanding impulse in creative writing studies to differentiate writing praxis from scholarship on literature: "being creative does not mean avoiding critical inquiry" (9). Following Andrews, Westbrook, and Ryan, this essay begins at the intersection of these two productive sites for studying poetry and poetics—the creative writing classroom and the literature one—finding there the tools for building something new.

The goal of this classroom activity is for students to reimagine the poet's process for writing a poem, setting that process out on paper as a set of instructions another writer may follow to imitate the original poet. To write such a set of instructions, students must engage closely with elements of form—considering how a writer constructs the craft elements of a poem, including grammar, typography, images, metaphors, allusions, and more—while considering too the poet's intellectual environment and historical context, ultimately placing themselves imaginatively in the mindset of a poet creating a text. After students compose their instructions, they switch instruction sets with another group, trying out each other's work and writing a poem together in class. At the end of the class meeting, we critique the process, an opportunity for examining what we discovered by inhabiting the writer's process ourselves.

This hands-on, collaborative project is easily adapted to a wide range of texts and writers, but I find that it works especially well when used to study poets interested in inventing new forms and techniques. In such cases, students must rely most closely on the text at hand to guide their instruction-writing process rather than any previous lessons on prosody and traditional forms. Still, this activity also helps students explore the contours of conventional poetic forms while examining the complexities of varying those formats.

The experimental American Sonnets by Black Los Angeles poet Wanda Coleman are ideally inventive and linked to a long formal tradition, pushing students to reassess their understandings of the sonnet to fully engage Coleman's innovations. Always an independent poet, Coleman's career was marked by exclusion from academic spaces, an exclusion that troubled her: she always wished for and knew she deserved more attention from academic critics. But as a single parent working to support a family, she was unable to complete her college education, studying poetry instead in the home workshops of local poets like Diane Wakoski and Clayton Eshleman and practicing her craft in the city's spoken-word venues, like Beyond Baroque and The Bridge. Working outside the academy meant that other forms of public recognition, like poetry prizes, mattered greatly to Coleman, and she won numerous awards for her poetry, including the Lenore Marshall Prize and a Guggenheim Foundation fellowship. Indeed, Coleman specifically designed the American Sonnets project to appeal to awards committees: noticing that, in the 1980s and 1990s, fellowships and grants often went to traditionalists rather than experimental writers, she began developing a "jazz sonnet," responsive to the sonnet's long history but formally free, improvisatory, and rhythmically changeable. Her sonnets didn't win her the awards she intended them for, but she nevertheless completed a masterful sequence of one hundred sonnets. They bear witness to the joys and sorrows of urban Black life during the Reagan and Bush administrations. They offer a trenchant critique of the era's exploitive capitalism and systemic racism, a paean to Black womanhood, and they are bitingly funny.

Before a class on Coleman's sonnets, I warn students that these are no ordinary sonnets. To help them as they read, I ask students to consider the ways these sonnets resemble other sonnets and to look for differences, too. I tell them that Coleman's language is difficult; she's a highly inventive poet who frequently coined new words, and her poetry is densely allusive. I also tell my students that Coleman sometimes used derogatory language including the n-word and other racial slurs, and while she was a staunchly anti-racist writer who used such language with care, some readers may still find these words upsetting. In our discussions of these poems, we are thoughtful in taking up these terms that can and should disturb us, as they raise special ethical, intellectual, and emotional challenges. Finally, I tell students that when we meet in class, we will talk more about Coleman's politics, personal history, and unusual writing process, and they will get a chance to try writing an American Sonnet themselves.

In class, I begin with an interactive mini-lecture before the imitation exercise, giving students knowledge to build on as they begin to assess the poem's construction. I play a recording of Coleman reading American

Sonnet 100 (available online; see below for resources), and we briefly discuss the poem. For American Sonnet 100, we focus first on its numerous allusions: its star-studded poetry landscape with references both old and new, from Shakespeare and Erato to the "black and luscious" lyrics of a "gangster poet's" work. We discuss formal elements, too. I briefly remind them that conventional sonnets are distinguished by, among other things, their rhyming pairs, and I show them how Coleman embedded seven rhyming couplets in American Sonnet 100: breast/jest, phrase/glaze, floor/galore, queens/sputterings, light/delight, fruit/brute, and kill/will cascade diagonally across the poem's landscape. Comparing Sonnet 100 to a few other American Sonnets, I ask students why Coleman might choose to fixate on the couplet here, and they begin thinking about how this final American Sonnet's numerous couplets recall the couplet concluding a Shakespearean sonnet, as if Sonnet 100 is a resounding concluding point on Coleman's sequence overall. It is, we decide, Coleman's way of celebrating the milestone achievement of one hundred sonnets, flaunting her chops in the face of those who underestimated the uncredentialed poet.

Once students are prepared to consider both the content and craft of Coleman's sonnets, we turn to the imitation exercise. Grouping students together in twos and threes, I give them a blank sheet of paper with these instructions at the top:

> How would you guide someone to write their own American Sonnet? In the space below, reimagine Wanda Coleman's procedure, identifying in order the steps that you think she may have taken to compose each sonnet. For this task, you may choose either a single American Sonnet as your model or you may direct someone how to write an American Sonnet in general. Be prepared to share your work with others who will try out your procedure today in class.

By approaching the poems through this framework, students are encouraged to name elements of a poetic process. Basically, this task helps us gather data: students do not necessarily need to state why the poem does what it does, they just need to try to point to it. Too often we jump to interpretation too quickly, missing out on the intricacies of poetic constructions. One benefit of this assignment is the way it gets us to slow down and consider a given poem holistically but in detail.

Inevitably, student groups will approach the same poem quite differently. For example, one group's reimagined procedure might start to enumerate the poem's essential structural elements (*your poem should be roughly 12–15 lines; don't adopt a rhyme scheme but you may incorporate occasional, unexpected rhyming sounds . . .*) while others will begin by prescribing a mindset (*you have just completed an epic masterwork that proves your genius once and for all. Start by thinking about how you might add swagger to your evident status as a poet . . .*). When students exchange their work and try out another group's instructions, they start to notice what might be missing from any one set of instructions, acknowledging the immense complexities of Coleman's work.

Writing from their peers' procedures requires another dimension of focused reading as students imaginatively inhabit the mindset of a poet. Students may feel uncomfortable writing a poem together—especially in a literature classroom—but the process reminds them that the texts printed in books, anthologies, and on webpages began with a blank page, a fresh idea, and the will to create. Ultimately, this part of the class's process is an occasion for joy. When students start building poems responsive to each other's direction, their voices get louder, they giggle, they commend each other on the right word, they get into it.

I conclude the activity with a discussion about the process: I invite each group to describe the instructions they received, explain how they differed from the instructions they composed, and read the poem they created. After the poem recitations, we might finish with questions such as:

- Which procedural tasks worked well? Which ones captured something important about this poem?

- What procedures were apparent but difficult to name? What elements of this poem aren't defined by rules and processes?

- You've spent a lot of time analyzing these poems as American Sonnets: what's your takeaway? Why do you think Coleman wanted to write these as "American Sonnets"? What's gained by identifying these poems by a shared type or form?

After a classroom project like this one, students will be ready to think further about the intersections of poetic forms and a poet's material conditions. They are better prepared to consider the nuances of a writer's historical circumstances—how a Black urban writer like Coleman, working outside of standardized Creative Writing Studies models, sets herself at projects like the American Sonnets—as well as the procedures writers take to produce a text itself, the evident formal elements of any given American Sonnet, say. In addition to making students better readers of poems, this activity also prepares them to think critically about the ways readers write about poems. From here, students could productively pivot to further discussions about prosody, comparing the ways poets describe their poem's procedures to the ways readers describe what they see. They will be prepared to acknowledge the limits of any one perspective on a poem as well as the delightful chaos of describing what we read.

Further Reading

While there are many examples of other imitation exercises for both literature and creative writing classrooms, readers interested in bridging between literature and creative writing methods will especially appreciate Rob Pope's *Textual Intervention: Critical and Creative Strategies for Literary Studies* (Routledge, 1995). My approach in this essay was shaped especially by two scholars at the University of Oregon who I was fortunate to work with as a graduate student: Lara Bovilsky and Geri Doran. Doran elegantly linked writing prompts to specific poems for her creative writing students, and Bovilsky delighted literature students with a final paper assignment prompting them to imitate a course reading and then write about why their imitation worked.

Readers curious to learn more about Wanda Coleman might start with Terrance Hayes's edition of her selected poetry, *Wicked Enchantment* (Black Sparrow, 2020), her collected American Sonnets, *Heart First Into This Ruin* (Black Sparrow, 2022) with its introduction by Mahogany L. Browne, plus scholarship by Krista Comer, Tony Magistrale, Jennifer Ryan-Bryant, and a special issue of *Hecate* dedicated to Coleman's work (vol. 40, no. 1, 2014). Coleman reads American Sonnet 100 in Bob Bryan's documentary, *The Wanda Coleman Project*.

For guidance on teaching texts that use the n-word and other modes of hate speech, see Koritha Mitchell's podcast episode, "The N-Word in the Classroom: Just Say NO" (*The C19 Podcast*, Season 2, Episode 6), and her website, www.korithamitchell.com/teaching-and-the-n-word.

Works Cited

Andrews, Kimberly Quiogue. *The Academic Avant-Garde: Poetry and the American University*. Johns Hopkins UP, 2023.
Cain, Mary Ann. " 'To Be Lived': Theorizing Influence in Creative Writing." *College English*, vol. 71, no. 3, 2009, pp. 229–41.
Graff, Gerald. "What We Say When We Don't Talk about Creative Writing." *College English*, vol. 71, no. 3, 2009, pp. 271–79.
Westbrook, Steve and James Ryan. *Beyond Craft: An Anti-Handbook for Creative Writers*. Bloomsbury Academic, 2020.

24

From Stifling to Expansive

Reimagining Poetry Teaching and Learning with *The South African Poetry Project*

SOORIAGANDHI NAIDOO, TONI GENNRICH,
AND EUNICE PHIRI

As a team of teacher educators and a practicing teacher who are members of *The South African Poetry Project* (ZAPP), we have been involved in research and workshops with English First Additional Language (EFAL) teachers and learners. For many South African learners, English is not their Home Language, but it is used as the Language of Learning and Teaching (LoLT) from grade 4. These children take EFAL rather than English Home Language in secondary schools. Poetry is not generally taught at the grade 12 level because teachers view it as more difficult than other genres of literary texts. In our work with ZAPP, in schools where poetry is selected, many EFAL teachers have expressed that their lack of confidence stems from feeling overwhelmed by the assessments that focus on unrelatable content and literary concepts in the prescribed poems. Recently, there has been a move to decolonize curricula that has led us to consider what pedagogical approaches can help debunk some of the myths that abound regarding the teaching of poetry, especially in a tradition that is grounded in a colonial and apartheid past. Thus, although this essay draws from our experiences in training teachers in the specific context of South Africa, our findings can be applied, more broadly to readers who work in teacher training and, more specifically, to those who work in English education and are interested in applying postcolonial and anti-colonial theories as well as teachers working with English language learners who come from predominantly English speaking and non-English-speaking populations.

In our experience, one of the myths perpetuated in some schools is that poetry is beyond the grasp of EFAL learners. This notion seemingly emanates from beliefs, systems, and practices that position teachers as being the primary source of information, what Freire calls the *banking concept of education* (53). Another contributing factor is the view that knowledge is static, with clear right and wrong answers that can be found in texts.

We suggest two reasons why the myths, concepts, and practices outlined here go unchallenged in poetry classrooms. First, teachers have deeply ingrained ways of teaching poetry which are difficult to shift. This is because they are entrenched, not only in the teachers themselves but in the *fields* (Bourdieu 66) in which they work. Teaching *habitus* is structured by one's personal history and many teachers teach in the ways that they have been taught (Gennrich and Janks 457). During apartheid, teaching and teacher training adopted an authoritarian, indoctrination approach and this is what many EFAL teachers have experienced. Second, in South Africa the Department of Basic Education (DBE) currently provides a teaching plan which is misconstrued by some teachers as obligatory. The deadlines, syllabus demands, and teaching to the goal of assessment cause teachers to be reluctant to explore alternative poetry methodologies for fear of "wasting" time needed to cover the syllabus.

In this essay, we reflect on a workshop held in a South African township high school in a peri-urban area, where one of us, Eunice, was the Head of Department of English. Learners at the school come from socioeconomically disadvantaged households and they speak a range of South African languages, with Sepedi being dominant. Eunice has run a poetry club at the school since 2016. This club creates a space where learners write, perform, and share ideas.

Eunice arranged the workshop, which was attended by a subject advisor, secondary school teachers, and learners at the school. It ran for four hours and included different poetry lesson presentations and performances, demonstrating various ways of teaching poetry. It used a central theme celebrating Women's Day, a South African public holiday, commemorating the 1956 women's march to the Union Buildings, Pretoria, over the apartheid government's oppressive pass laws. The teachers and the subject advisor present were sufficiently interested to shift from being observers to participating in the group activities with learners. Not only that, but after this workshop they continued to collaborate with the ZAPP team as they also attended a follow-up teacher workshop willingly and enthusiastically, hinting at a shifting mindset about the value of teaching poetry.

We argue that EFAL learners have the potential to think critically and respond emotionally when learning about poetry. We challenge the view that poetry is difficult and should be structurally analysed, dissecting the poem line by line. The key practices used in this workshop included encouraging learners to ask questions of the text, focusing on the multi-modal elements, and integrating poetry with history. The workshop also challenged the myth that poetic devices such as rhythm, rhyme, and metaphor are difficult for EFAL learners by helping them to connect these tools with their cultural experiences.

We focus on one workshop section, presented by a contemporary South African poet, writer, educator, and fellow ZAPP team member, Phillippa Yaa de Villiers. Phillippa read the epic poem *Tongues of their Mothers* by Makhosazana Xaba (2008) and the audience responded warmly to her powerful performance that lifted the words off the page and created an authentic, emotional experience. This poem is a tribute to the unsung women of South African history who have been obscured in history told by men. Phillippa welcomed African cultural experiences into the learning space, helping learners to identify the rich *cultural capital* (Bourdieu 124) they have to draw on, by linking elements such as rhythm to the African drum, an integral part of the cultures that bring us together.

The two aims of this lesson demonstration were to help participants recognise that knowledge is uncertain and that some things are unknowable and, secondly, to demonstrate that learners should actively drive their own discovery, drawing on their *funds of knowledge* (Moll et al. 133) to make sense of the poem. To do this, Phillippa put the learners into groups and gave each group a stanza of the poem to work with. She invited them to construct their own questions in groups, independently of any help from facilitators or teachers. For example, in response to the lines about Sarah Baartman, "It will borrow from every single poem ever written about her, / conjuring up her wholeness: her voice, dreams, emotions and thoughts," (Xaba 25) learners asked, "Did everyone respect her dreams and aspirations?" In response to the stanza referring to Nandi and "her choice not to marry" (Xaba 25) learners asked, "Why would she choose not to marry?"

In an email, Phillippa told us about her thinking while planning this section of the workshop, "I wanted them to get used to the idea of not having all the answers . . . to stimulate their curiosity by finding out what they didn't know. I wanted them to ask the questions and be confronted by a teacher who didn't know the answers, and to then talk through how we would find the answers." She wanted to create a space for conversation and interaction by using social pedagogy. Phillippa looked for ways to help unleash the learners' potential by establishing what is referred to as a *community of inquiry* (Garrison et al. 88). Learners engaged in a self-directed interrogation of what they thought was important to help them understand the poem. They raised questions about why they thought a historical person, Sarah Baartman, was othered or why, in South African history we know about Griffith Mxenge but know nothing of his wife, Victoria, or why Gatsha Mangosuthu Buthelezi is well known, yet we have not heard of his mother, Princess Magogo Constance Zulu. In a context where these EFAL learners do not take history as a subject, the exercise gave them a chance to think across the curriculum, to experience what could sometimes be perceived as stifling content as relatable.

This conversational, questioning approach positions knowledge as dynamic. By challenging the power relationships in the poetry classroom we emphasized that meaning comes about through co-creation and co-construction. Instead of establishing rigid, predetermined answers about the poem, what evolved were ideas that stimulated learners to look for and discuss answers themselves. The focus of the lesson shifted from the norm of a technical analysis of the poem, looking for *correct* answers to one where learners were positioned as researchers.

Afterwards, Phillippa encouraged learners to engage in a voluntary self-reflection exercise based on their workshop experiences. She invited them to be creative in their responses, using any form they chose. This contrasts with some post-classroom activities where teachers set questions or tasks that focus on assessment *of* learning rather than assessment *for* learning and *as* learning. The learners' reflective responses suggested that there was some transformation and disruption in their assumed identities and their attitudes to poetry. Responses reflected a shift in how they perceived themselves (the self) in relation to the teacher (the other) as well as in relation to poetry (material) and time (context). For example, some of them responded by saying, "[it] shows us another side of poetry"; "fascinating world of poetry"; "before I had a foolish mentality. . . [there was] no need to read other poets." Others stated that they were "listening," "enjoying," and "actively doing," and these responses contest the view that EFAL learners are passive and disinterested in poetry. Some responses focused on how the workshop had given them "self-belief and respect" and " . . . unlock[ed] the potential I had." Instead of alienating them from poetry, the workshop was described as a "bonding session." Since we encouraged them to use their mother tongue, one learner wrote, "[it] made me realise I have neglected my mother-tongue." Another wrote, "[I was able to] think out of the box," as he seemed to recognize his potential to engage in critical thinking. We see these diverse responses as positive indicators that learners' engagement with poetry can become an embodiment of their lived experiences. Instead of using a deficit model to position EFAL learners in the poetry classroom, we should consider alternate, more expansive strategies that are inclusive of both the affective and cognitive domains. We believe that this is how the teaching and learning of poetry can serve as a just sociocultural imperative.

Teacher educators and practicing teachers should aim for strategies that deconstruct and reconstruct how teachers and learners position themselves as they work together to understand the poems, realising that there might be different understandings and perceptions. Teachers and teacher educators need to consider alternative approaches which challenge learners to read critically such as allowing them to exercise their right to ask questions of the texts for themselves. Encouraging learners to research what is unknown should be used as leverage to afford them the opportunity to think expansively about possible answers. The emphasis in teaching poetry should shift from the *banking model of education*, focusing on predetermined answers to a problem-posing strategy in which learners "develop their power to perceive critically *the way they exist* in the world *with which* and *in which* they find themselves" (Freire 64) and, in this way recognise how they are part of a transforming reality. Second, incorporating self-reflection exercises facilitates the identities and voices of the learners. This empowers both teachers and learners to read, interpret and enjoy poetry in more creative spaces (imagined or real). Third, inviting learners to draw on their cultural capital and welcoming their cultures and languages into the classroom enables learners to become active agents in their learning processes in ways that promote lifelong learning practices. We believe that teaching poetry in all classrooms can encourage creativity in inspiring learners' own writing and performance of poetry and recognizing the power in words. To overcome the perception that poetry is a difficult genre to teach and learn, poetry should be included as a core content area in the training of all teachers. Furthermore, poetry should also be considered in all subject training, not only in the training of language teachers. Teacher trainers need to model the position that teachers do not have all of the answers—learners can be empowered or scaffolded into ways of looking for answers for themselves.

The approaches shared here can assist in demolishing some of the systemically and historically entrenched poetry pedagogies. We encourage teachers and those involved in training them to be mindful of their specific sociocultural contexts and to consider how they can draw on these contexts to disrupt any stifling spaces to create expansive spaces that accommodate diverse perspectives.

Further Reading

To learn more about Phillippa Yaa de Villiers, visit poetryarchive.org/poet/phillippa-yaa-de-villiers. For a more expansive reading of ZAPP's contribution towards alternative pedagogies we suggest the article coauthored by Phillippa Yaa de Villiers, Louis Botha, and Robert Maungedzo, "Research That Is Real and Utopian: Indigenous Knowledge as a Resource to Revitalize High School poetry" (*Decoloniality in/and Poetry*, special issue of *Education as Change*, vol. 24, 2020, which provides a range of articles that can be retrieved from unisapressjournals.co.za/index.php/EAC/issue/view/324).

Works Cited

Bourdieu, Pierre. *The Logic of Practice*. Stanford UP, 1990.
Freire, Paulo. *Pedagogy of the Oppressed*. Penguin, 1996.
Garrison, D. Randy, et al. "Critical inquiry in a text-based environment: Computer conferencing in higher education." *The Internet and Higher Education*, vol. 2, no. 2, 1999, pp. 87–105, doi.org/10.1016/S1096-7516(00)00016-6.
Gennrich, Toni, and Hilary Janks. "Teachers' Literate Identities." *International Handbook of Research on Children's Literacy, Learning and Culture*, edited by Kathy Hall, Teresa Cremin, Barbara Comber, and Luis C. Moll, John Wiley & Sons, 2013, pp. 456–68.
Moll, Luis C., et al. "Funds of knowledge for teaching: Using a qualitative approach to connect homes and classrooms." *Theory into Practice*, vol. 31, no. 2, 1992, pp. 132–41.
Xaba, Mkhosazana. *Tongues of their Mothers*. UKZN Press, 2008.

25

Transgressive Teaching and Subverting Censorship in the Dual-Credit Classroom

Ronnie K. Stephens

bell hooks tells us that "[t]he classroom remains the most radical space of possibility in the academy. . . . Urging all of us to open our minds and hearts so that we can know beyond the boundaries of what is acceptable, so that we can think and rethink, so that we can create new visions" (12). Though I encountered this statement years into my teaching career, the prevailing sentiment has guided my approach to education since my first year in the classroom. Let us not pretend that our classrooms are the same as they were even three or four years ago. The teaching profession has long endured ire and judgment, both from the public and from legislators, but teaching today requires educators to navigate stressors ranging from health risks to police presence on campus to increasingly restrictive legislation around curriculum.

At the center of the storm are our students, most of whom enter the classroom desperate to feel seen, respected, and valued. Anti-ethnic and anti-LGBTQIA+ legislation makes that increasingly difficult for public K–12 educators, who are vulnerable to consequences from district employers and potential lawsuits from the state. Though legislative efforts to censor curricula in higher education are, to date, less common, South Dakota, Idaho, Oklahoma, and Iowa have all passed laws which effectively restrict educators at public higher education institutions from including certain topics or theories in the classroom. On the surface, these laws extend to all state employees, but the language makes clear that higher education institutions are the intended target. Nonetheless, college instructors have both the ability and responsibility to meaningfully address the very issues that state legislation seeks to prohibit, particularly with the aid of well-selected poems that inform and invite debate around the most relevant issues of our time.

It is impossible to understate the urgency of unsettling the classroom. During the 2021 to 2022 academic year alone, as many as thirty-eight states passed legislation to greatly restrict curriculum material. Cathryn Stout and Thomas Wilburn compiled an interactive map for Chalkbeat that tracks all states with legislation or pending legislation that prohibits references to racism and white supremacy in public education. Jamie Gregory, writing for the Intellectual Freedom Blog, compiled numerous digital and print forms being circulated by districts to empower parents to report violations of anti-ethnic and anti-LGBTQIA+ legislation. At the time of this writing, Mississippi Governor Tate Reeves has signed a bill to ban instruction that refers to racism and systemic racism as fixtures in American nationhood, arguing that such sentiments "[run] counter to the principles of America's founding" (Reeves 00:00:36–00:00:38). He subsequently declared April Confederate Heritage Month and Genocide Awareness Month, but failed to acknowledge the systemic eradication of Indigenous peoples or the slave industry as genocidal practices in American history. Granbury Independent School District (GISD) Superintendent Jeremy Glenn, echoing numerous school leaders and lawmakers across the country, described students who challenged his order to remove books from the high school library as radical leftists who support pornography in the classroom (Granbury 03:02:36–03:05:04). Against this backdrop of intentionally polarizing rhetoric and prohibitive legislation, educators can and should attempt to inform students about the most pertinent issues of their time and ensure authentic representation in the classroom.

Given the threat of professional consequence for public educators, dual-credit instructors are uniquely positioned as college educators who can subvert these restrictions for high school students and better prepare them to enter adulthood as informed citizens. Dual-credit courses, also known as dual enrollment courses, offer an opportunity for high school students to earn high school credit and college credit concurrently; in most situations, contracts between colleges and local school districts explicitly state that dual-credit courses mirror the rigor and content of traditional college courses. This provides a unique and essential space inside high schools where college instructors can directly subvert attempts to censor or whitewash curricula. Poetry is a particularly effective entry point for addressing relevant and difficult sociopolitical themes, both methodologically and practically, for educators across the curriculum.

Engaging with poetry may appear tangential for many dual-credit instructors, as most are tasked with teaching core curriculum courses where poetry is typically out of place. This necessitates a reframing of poetry as more than high literature with limited accessibility or applicability. Poems are, in fact, cultural artifacts that concretize the human condition across nearly all cultures and historical moments. Students are able to practice every key skill inherent to research, critical inquiry, and textual analysis through rigorous engagement with poetry. The urgency and immediacy inherent to the digital publishing age also means that poems are very likely to be both a product of their times and a window through which students can discuss contemporary issues. Scholarship over the last decade highlights the broad applicability of poetry in academic pursuits ranging from neuroscience and psychology to palliative care and social work. There is substantial scholarship to suggest that poetry is, for many historically marginalized groups, the preferred genre for writing as resistance. Including poetry in any core course, then, is far from tangential; in fact, it is strong pedagogical practice, and it may help respond to the often glaring omission of authentic representation in textbooks. Dual-credit instructors can make meaning of historical events and cultural movements by juxtaposing traditional artifacts like newspapers and diary entries with poetry, then highlighting relevance to current sociopolitical moments through analysis.

Dual-credit instructors rarely have the opportunity to select their own textbooks, as districts often negotiate these choices with college officials ahead of the academic year. They also navigate numerous firewalls and internet restrictions within their respective districts. While these firewalls purport to prevent students from accessing inappropriate content, many districts also filter out websites that are overtly political or address themes related to the LGBTQIA+ community. Unsettling the classroom, then, requires frequent and strategic supplemental readings that work to center diverse experiences, as well as diverse voices. History professors, for example, may consider including the poetry of Jane Johnston Schoolcraft to supplement instruction on Manifest Destiny or Frances Ellen Watkins Harper to broaden students' understanding of intersectionality and suffrage following the Civil War. Psychology instructors may supplement clinical or technical readings around various mental health conditions with poems that address those conditions experientially, such as selections from Shira Erlichman's *Odes to Lithium* (2019) or poems from Andrea Gibson that directly address the physical and emotional realities of living with Lyme Disease. Supplementing the textbook does not just broaden student understanding; it also centers the voices and experiences of the communities that restrictive legislation seeks to censor, an essential aspect of transgressive teaching.

One method for subverting the current poetry canon is through comparative analysis. With this method, students might engage oft-anthologized poets like Emily Dickinson and Walt Whitman, for instance, alongside less familiar poets pulled from the archives of nineteenth-century Black and Chicanx newspapers. Presenting contemporaries to further student understanding is a core academic strategy, yet the deliberate pairing of canonized poets with underrepresented voices expands the conversation about the sociopolitical climate of nineteenth-century America without overtly impressing any single ideology on students. Similarly, educators might present highly anthologized sonnets alongside contemporary sonnets by poets like Danez Smith, Franny Choi, Terrance Hayes, and Natalie Diaz, all of whom engage the form masterfully while also pushing against it to critique social inequity and historical injustice. Students who critically engage the nuanced alterations of the sonnet form present in contemporary sonnets by authors of color not only generate a keener understanding of poetry but also begin to understand how poets engage form deliberately to create additional layers of meaning. Instructors can add another element to conversations of form by introducing contemporary poets who co-opt traditional forms to comment on sociopolitical issues and identity politics, like Fatimah Asghar in "Microaggression Bingo" (2016) or "Script for Child Services: A Floor Plan" (2018).

Another pedagogical practice that is essential to increasing representation and visibility in the classroom is the intentional inclusion of translingual poetry and poetry written outside White Mainstream English (WME). Failure to represent multiple Englishes within the classroom risks alienating students and subconsciously elevating WME as a standard or superior form of English. Textbooks and anthologies highly prioritize WME as the norm, making poetry a convenient and effective opportunity to counterbalance such standardization with diverse forms of English. Seeing their language represented in literature not only encourages students to engage but also works to validate their voices as legitimate and valuable in a classroom setting. Gloria Anzaldúa perfectly captures the importance of translingual poetry in her hybrid genre book, *Borderlands* (1987):

> When I saw poetry written in Tex-Mex for the first time, a feeling of pure joy flashed through me. I felt like we really existed as a people. In 1971, when I started teaching High School English to Chicano students, I tried to supplement the required texts with works by Chicanos, only to be reprimanded and forbidden to do so by the principal. He claimed that I was supposed to teach "American" and English literature. At the risk of being fired, I swore my students to secrecy and slipped in Chicano short stories, poems, a play. (59–60)

While I do not advocate for swearing our students to secrecy, dual-credit instructors can make use of their freedom to supplement textbooks by incorporating poems from authors who write outside WME. This may include poems that engage non-English languages, or poems that utilize variations of English other than WME. Asking students to critically analyze translingual writing is an opportunity to address internal biases while also rigorously engaging how language impacts responses to literature. Outside literary analysis, incorporating translingual poetry across the curriculum increases representation, subverts the prioritization of WME as a default lens for academic discussion, and recenters the lived experiences of historically marginalized individuals.

Erasure poetry offers a unique opportunity for instructors to have students create their own poetry, conduct research and communicate findings, and analyze the choices that poets make in creating erasure poetry. Mai Der Vang combines several types of erasure in her collection *Yellow Rain* (2021), which uses declassified government documents about a phenomenon that contributed to thousands of Hmong refugee deaths. Vang specifically employs erasure to subvert the official narrative put forth by the United States in the 1980s, redacting information and revising released documents to center and validate the experiences of Hmong refugees during sustained conflict and genocidal efforts from Laos and Russia. In addition to using erasure to create a counterpublic that challenges the official state narrative, Vang also subverts the dehumanization of Hmong people evident in clinical reports, using erasure to rehumanize them and insist that readers see them as wholly dynamic individuals with histories and lineages. Tracy K. Smith's "Declaration" (2018) is another excellent resource for students, as the poet creates an erasure poem from the Declaration of Independence to critique the systemic racism infused in American politics from its very inception.

Combining digital archives with erasure poetry adds a layer of complexity while also increasing representation for various cultures. Students can engage primary source documents from pivotal moments in history like the Chicano Movement, the Harlem Renaissance, global conflicts, and others. Rather than crafting traditional research papers, students can use erasure and redaction to recenter the narrative on those themes and peoples they find most important to the event. Psychology instructors might consider utilizing archived notes or treatises on various mental health conditions and proposed treatments as source texts for erasure poetry, challenging students to mine these documents and create poems that center the experience of the patient. They might then engage in discussion about the tendency for mental healthcare to emphasize suppression and conformity over expression and individuality, which will help frame dialogue around the weaponization of mental health to further marginalize transgressive individuals in society.

Ultimately, the restrictions and prohibitions imposed on public educators today are not new or unique. They are, however, one of the most immediate and pervasive issues affecting our students. Countless studies have expressed the long-term mental and emotional trauma associated with a lack of representation in the classroom. Legislation that seeks to further erase people of color and/or LGBTQIA+ people from the curriculum will perpetuate increasing rates of mental health crisis and suicidal ideation among young people. Isolation and alienation in the classroom will also continue to exacerbate feelings that academia is an inherently White pursuit, discouraging historically marginalized students from entering higher education. Educators who fail to subvert attempts to minimize the experiences and realities of diverse student populations tacitly condone censorship and the trauma it inflicts on our students. Dual-credit instructors have the opportunity to support the high school students in their classrooms through intentional representation, visibility, and language. Transgressive teaching does not need to be difficult. It can start with a poem.

Further Reading

Two of the most important and informative texts that inform my pedagogy are *Sister Outsider* by Audre Lorde (Crossing Press, 1984), and

Teaching to Transgress by bell hooks (Routledge, 1994). *Sister Outsider* includes "Poetry is Not a Luxury," which I consider essential reading on the function of poetry for disenfranchised voices. Other essays direct the nuances of identity formation and intersectionality that speak to some of the most important issues our students face. *Teaching to Transgress* argues for teaching as radical practice and is, for educators, the most directly applicable book from bell hooks, one of the most important voices in Black feminism and pedagogical practice. More recently, *Linguistic Justice* by Ashley Baker-Bell (Routledge, 2020) addresses the importance of decentering WME as the standard in classrooms through a combination of theory, reflective practices and pedagogical strategies.

Several books that directly address the place and function of poetry in the sociopolitical climate have proven remarkably informative for curriculum development. *A Sense of Regard: Essays on Poetry and Race*, edited by Laura McCollough (U of Georgia P, 2015), compiles dozens of short essays that seek to define poetry outside the canon, speak to the pressures of assimilating to WME in poetry, and question how poetry both reflects and reinforces cultural norms. Caroline Levine's *Forms: Whole, Rhythm, Hierarchy, Network* (Princeton UP, 2015) takes an impressive and in-depth look at how forms and structures act as social commentary, offering methods of critical analysis that use form as a means of understanding and contextualizing meaning. *Can Poetry Matter?* by Dana Gioia (Graywolf Press, 2011) remains an essential collection of essays that speaks to the necessity of continually engaging poetry and argue for its relevance across disciplines.

Works Cited

Anzaldúa, Gloria. *Borderlands/La Frontera: The New Mestiza*. Aunt Lute Books, 1987.

"Granbury ISD School Board Meeting—January 24, 2022." YouTube, uploaded by Granbury Independent School District, 24 Jan. 2022, www.youtube.com/watch?v=BZx6V7.

hooks, bell. *Teaching to Transgress: Education as the Practice of Freedom*. Routledge, 1994.

Reeves, Tate. "Governor Reeves Takes Action Against Critical Race Theory." Facebook, uploaded by TaterReeves, 14 Mar. 2022, www.facebook.com/tatereeves/videos/governor-reeves-takes-action-against-critical-race-theory/771428113837269/.

26

The Florence Poetry Collective

Death Row as a Site of Poetic Production
and Expressive Sovereignty

JOE LOCKARD

Death Row provides a determinative and barbarous social context for writing poetry.[1] Twenty-seven US states, the federal government, and the US military retain capital punishment,[2] and these prison units, spread across the country, house people who the US judiciary deems worth only killing. Death Row poetry asserts the opposite, a right to live. The act of writing a poem, story, or essay affirms that life continues despite condemned status. Death Row writing usually does not speak directly to death sentences or awaiting execution, for that would be permitting executioners an early victory. In refusing to become death-bound subjects, poets represent affirmation of a vital, living subjectivity that refuses and rejects the state's claim against their lives.

Arizona retains the death penalty, although executions have been suspended since the 2014 torture-execution of Joseph Wood that took almost two hours of chemical injections (CBS News: 60 Minutes). There are currently 110 people on Arizona's Death Row. A previous, politically ambitious Republican attorney general campaigned for speedy executions of twenty-one prisoners whose appeals had run out (Arizona Attorney General). In the words of one editorial commenting on Arizona's "campaign for death," capital punishment is "a politician's plaything, not a means of achieving justice" (*Los Angeles Times*). A new Democratic governor, supported by a new attorney general (Channel 12 News), issued a 2023 executive order to review implementation of capital punishment (State of Arizona). The current governor, Katie Hobbs, and attorney general, Kris Mayes, both take the position that capital punishment is the law and they will enforce the law, but that a moratorium is necessary in order to determine the best means of killing people.

Prior to this administrative abeyance, from September 2019 to March 2020, when the Arizona state prison system closed due to COVID-19, I conducted a weekly poetry workshop at the Death Row Unit of Florence State Prison.[3] This required special permission from the Department of Corrections, Rehabilitation and Reentry that I was able to obtain because I had spent nearly a decade teaching poetry and literature in other units at Florence State Prison. There was no educational programming in the Death Row Unit.

Institutional trust is necessary because Death Row attracts less than desirable sorts, from the morbidly curious, to people searching for long-distance romances, to publicity-seeking evangelical missionaries eager to claim a converted soul. My motivation was exactly what it had been from the outset years ago: a belief that education is a fundamental human right, inseparable from our humanity. Human rights need to be enacted, not simply cited in rhetoric. Teachers who go to where there is limited or no education available enact and expand a fundamental right. In a political era denominated by neoliberal commodification of education, it becomes a radical act to provide free education as a human right and make it available to those denied education as a matter of public policy.

Arizona's Department of Corrections, Rehabilitation and Reentry provides no educational programming on Death Row beyond basic literacy classes mandated by federal law. Arizona state law prohibits public finance of education on Death Row (Arizona Revised Statutes 31-240[C]).[4] Lifers and Death Row prisoners are the only population denied public education in Arizona by black-letter law. This legal provision marks people on Death Row or serving life sentences as beyond the pale of humanity and education.

However, this prohibition does not cover volunteer teaching. In consequence, our poetry workshop was the only available educational opportunity for people in this small unit. We held class inside the unit because Death Row's isolation from the general prison population is so complete that the yard would have to be closed and other prisoners cleared before condemned prisoners would be allowed to cross to attend class in the regular classrooms. Death Row is its own world and the collective's self-creation reflected that insularity.

Collectively and along with prose production, this poetry constitutes a literature of witness against capital punishment in the United States. Support for and publication of Death Row poetry contributes to public recognition of the unacceptable cruelty of judicial murder by means of toxic injections or poison gas. When Theodor Adorno posited a modern confrontation in a dialectic of culture and barbarism, he wrote famously "To write poetry after Auschwitz is barbaric. And it corrodes even the knowledge of why it has become impossible to write poetry today" (34). Yet we wrote poetry next to the execution chamber where the state of Arizona sought to use hydrogen cyanide—the same gas as the Zyklon B used at Auschwitz—to kill its citizens (*The Guardian*). Adorno's dictum may be best understood as poetry representing an aesthetic countervailing force against a violent, cruel, and vicious society. An execution chamber emblematizes that barbarism. If Adorno is read literally, then we disproved his words on the impossibility of poetry with each poem we wrote.

Florence Poetry Collective Workshop

We were a small group. The weekly workshop attracted eight writers, about a tenth of those housed in this lower-security section of Death Row. A graduate student MFA candidate and I functioned as conveners. We used a present-and-comment mode of workshopping, where writers brought their handwritten work for a first reading and comment, then we commented again the next week on a typed version. We held successive rounds of comment until the writer was satisfied, or at least sated, with their poem. We emphasized positive, supportive comments to encourage development of ideas and language in drafts of a poem. Cheers and clapping accompanied the reading aloud of poems.

After three months, the workshop group decided unanimously to call themselves the Florence Poetry Collective. One of the writers proposed the name and the rest adopted the suggestion immediately. Their next decision was to publish a journal based on their work. It included workshop poetry, writing from another workshop in the South Unit of the same prison, and artwork from a member of the Collective. The editorial process was collective and democratic, finished just prior to the prison system closure. Per agreement, the Death Row supervising officer reviewed galley proofs of the journal, without changes being made. All contributors signed agreements to publish their work. We published a limited-edition journal with an eponymous title. The Department of Corrections controlled in-prison distribution. Each contributor received two copies of the journal. Our agreement with the Department forbade posting the journal online so as to avoid offending the families of murder victims.

While due to privacy considerations I cannot discuss teaching moments or specific poems from the workshop, we can discuss some general principles for poetry workshops in prisons, whether in general populations or segregated units such as Death Row.

The first principle is respect for incarcerated writers. Disrespect due to criminal convictions or past actions has no place in a prison classroom. Students in prison have already been judged: they do not come to a classroom to be judged again. Incarcerated students must be treated equally as high school or college students. Those incapable of separating their work as teachers from the work of the judicial and penal systems have no business in a prison classroom. Respect for writers and the effort of writing is part of this foundational principle. Workshop criticism functions best when it is friendly, good-natured, and positive. The question is not "what is wrong here?" but "what could be better here?"

In prison, a few short, handwritten poems on dirty paper may be the memories of another life and of immense sentimental meaning to a writer who has left behind a destroyed life. For older poets who have spent most of their lives in prison, their poetry is the legacy they hope to leave as their mark in the world. For younger poets, writing may be a means of gaining respect in a prison's social hierarchy, particularly through commissioned poems—for example, a love poem in exchange for commissary goods. Writing conditions in jails and prisons can be exceedingly trying: overcrowding, lack of privacy, counts and lockdowns, minimal amounts of paper (paper is rationed due to security and potential use in fire attacks), and golf pencils for writing (another security issue). A few prisoners with clerical jobs may be able to submit typed poems; the rest submit handwritten work. By whatever means these writers produce poetry, writing becomes a means of psychological resistance against the conditions of daily existence. Respect is due not only for the person but for the challenging conditions of poetic production.

A second principle is respect for voice. Many incarcerated writers have had limited education and this is apparent in their writing. An expressive voice and its experience are more important than technical writing issues that can be improved in drafts. Voice changes over the course of a workshop. Often new poets arrive with an understanding of poetry as resembling saccharine rhymed verses on Hallmark cards. One of the first exercises we do is to rewrite prose as a poem in order to understand and define a poem, and especially that there is no requirement to write rhyming lines. This altered understanding of what a poem can be and its relationship to prose helps less experienced writers develop a voice of their own rather than imitate preconceived ideas of a poem. A poem is not a sacred text: we learn to sharpen our voice by working and reworking a poem, draft after draft, until we find no further room to develop the poem's idea. This rewrite cycle, often at first foreign to incarcerated students who stand and read their poems repeatedly from the photocopied weekly handout, helps identify the characteristics of each writer's voice. In the social submersion of incarceration, where people lose their public voices, respect for voice is of paramount importance.

A third principle is that everyone at the table has something to teach and we are all learners. While I can speak to poetry as a seasoned teacher and critic, I know little about life inside and the stories of what brought people to prison. I am a learner as much as a teacher. I can provide knowledge, organizational leadership, and institutional legitimacy for the class, but we are all equals sitting around the circled tables. Participants lend their own perspectives and stories to interpreting the writing, without theoretical framing. The nominal subject of the class is creative writing: the real subject is words that emerge from different lives. We teach each other; we learn from each other.

Finally, a poetry workshop in prison is a site of expressive sovereignty. Incarceration means state control of the details of life, including daily schedule, work, clothing, food, prescribed behaviors, associations, and much more. A workshop organized on principles of democratic education, one where participants set the agenda with their writing, provides one of the few occasions and places in prison life where people exercise collective control of their space and time. The strict disciplinary hierarchy disappears for the duration of the workshop class. There is a temporary sense of freedom and relief from disciplinary control. Once established, that freedom to speak and be heard creates an attraction that binds workshop participants and brings them back together each week. The Death Row poetry collective organized its own additional group readings on the cell block, contravening an administrative directive that education classes were not to serve to organize students. Poetry served as a means to attain a subterranean sovereignty based on shared words and thoughts.

Poetry provides affirmation of humanity in the face of widespread public belief that people on Death Row are monsters. Poetry voices opposition to dehumanization and a means of expressive sovereignty where the state has determined that the lives of people have meaning only for judicial killings. So, we arrive at the final point: what is the role of teachers once we leave Death Row? The response is simple. Go beyond organizing and teaching a writing class: we must protest against capital punishment and assert the right of condemned people to live.

Further Reading

Death Row writers in the United States have produced a coherent body of poetry that affirms their humanity in the face of its negation by the state. Death Row anthologies dedicated primarily to poetry include Julie Zimmerman, *Trapped under Ice: A Death Row Anthology* (Biddle Pub. Co., 1995), Donald Hall, *The Human Zoo: A Death Row Poetry Collection* (Poundstone Press, 1997), and Kristen Lukiewski and Reina Takahashi, *Thirty-four Kites: A Collection of Work from Men on Pennsylvania's Death Row* (Carnegie Mellon UP, 2008). The *Florence Poetry Collective* (2020) edition described in this chapter was privately printed and is not available for distribution.

Single-author poetry volumes include Johnny Duane Miles and Tio MacDonald, *Learning Curve* (East Oakland Times, 2019); Eugene Broxton, *Innocent on Death Row: Poems* (2017); Kenneth E. Foster Jr., *A Voice from the Killing Machine: A Trilogy of Poems* (2017); Julius Darius Jones, *Juwels from Death Row* (2015); and Beunka Adams, *Delirium—A Mind on Death Row* (2010).

Death Row writers such as Kenneth E. Foster, Jr., Bill Harding (Art of San Quentin), Alphonso Howard, and others, publish on websites put up by outside friends or supporters. The Minutes Before Six website, which began in 2007 as an online journal from the Texas Death Row, now includes writings and art from hundreds of incarcerated people and has dedicated sections for Death Row essays, poetry and art from across the United States (Minutes Before Six).

For description of a university-based writing project that produced large amounts of poetry from the Penitentiary of New Mexico's long-term solitary confinement units, see Joe Lockard and Sherry Rankins-Robertson, "The Right to Education, Prison-University Partnerships, and Online Writing Pedagogy in the US" (*Critical Survey* 23, 2011, 3:23–39).

Notes

1. The author thanks students at the Death Row Unit of Florence State Prison for their insights and poetry. This essay contains no direct quotations from workshop students. It limits discussion of the workshop in order to maintain privacy and comply with human subject requirements.

2. The Death Penalty Information Center maintains an up-to-date website that lists states that permit capital punishment. See deathpenaltyinfo.org/state-and-federal-info/state-by-state.

3. Florence State Prison and its historic Central Unit, opened in 1908, closed in 2022. The Death Row Unit transferred to nearby Eyman State Prison.

4. The language of this law creates a curious loophole that enables educational access for people serving so-called Methuselah sentences extending hundreds of years. For example, one student of mine, a former graduate student sentenced to 340 years for voyeurism and possession of child pornography, was able to attend the poetry workshop because technically he did not have a life sentence and had a release date.

Works Cited

Adorno, Theodor. *Prisms*. Translated by Shierry Weber Nicholsen and Samuel Weber, MIT Press, 1983.

Arizona Attorney General. "Attorney General Brnovich Files Motions to Move Forward with Executions for Two Death Row Inmates." 6 Apr. 2021, www. https://www.azag.gov/press-release/attorney-general-brnovich-files-motions-move-forward-executions-two-death-row-inmates

Arizona Revised Statutes 31-240(C).

Art of San Quentin. www.artofsanquentin.com/blog/voices-from-the-row-an-exhibition-of-poetry-and-art-from-san-quentins-death-row-held-at-the-poetry-society-in-london-july-2018. Accessed 6 Mar. 2023.

CBS News: 60 Minutes. "The Execution of Joseph Wood." 10 July 2016, www.cbsnews.com/news/execution-of-joseph-wood-60-minutes-2.

Channel 12 News. "AG Kris Mayes Halts Executions, Wants Arizona to Review Capital Punishment Protocols." 20 Jan. 2023, www.12news.com/article/

news/local/arizona/attorney-general-kris-mayes-halts-executions-until-arizona-reviews-capital-punishment-protocols/75-877a4ff3-1d86-4257-b6b2-0737d8052c81.

Foster, Kenneth. lilacduville.com/essays-and-poems-by-kenneth-e-foster-jr. Accessed 6 March 2023.

Guardian. "Arizona 'Refurbishes' its Gas Chamber to Prepare for Executions, Documents Reveal." 28 May 2021, www.theguardian.com/us-news/2021/may/28/arizona-gas-chamber-executions-documents.

Hofmann, Klaus, "Poetry after Auschwitz—Adorno's Dictum." *German Life and Letters*, vol. 58, no. 2, Apr. 2005, pp. 182–94.

Los Angeles Times. "Arizona's Attorney General Wants to Finish His Term with a Rush of Executions." 12 Apr. 2021, www.latimes.com/opinion/story/2021-04-12/arizona-death-penalty-brnovich-barr-trump.

Minutes Before Six. minutesbeforesix.com/wp. Accessed 6 March 2023.

State of Arizona. "Establishing a Death Penalty Independent Review Commissioner." Executive Order no. 5, 20 Jan. 2023, azgovernor.gov/office-arizona-governor/executive-order/2023-05.

Part 2 Cluster

Project-Based Learning

27

Engaging Poetry

The Review as Critique and Conversation

VICTORIA CHANG AND DEAN RADER

In 2021, we began writing a regular collaborative poetry review column, "Two Roads," for the *Los Angeles Review of Books*, in which we discuss collections of contemporary poetry in a dialogue format. Over the past couple of years, we learned from various instructors that they often use these reviews in class as models of how two poet/critics think through the way poems work. While we had not necessarily thought of these columns as pedagogical tools, we were excited to discover their utility. So, for this volume, we decided to shift our focus a little bit but keep the same two-lens camera, shaky as it may be.

Dean Rader: Hi, Victoria!
Victoria Chang: Hi, Dean!
Dean: I'm eager to jump into our first collaborative essay. Maybe I'll begin by saying a few words about the title and about why we both think reviews are important in a classroom setting.

We both believe the review—especially the poetry review—does some very important pedagogical work. This is true when professors have students read reviews as a way into a book of poems but also when we ask students to write reviews, a process we will discuss in greater detail later.

One reason I like assigning reviews in poetry classes is that it liberates the poem from the shackles of *analysis* where it seems to be trapped in the dreaded "Landscape of Hidden Symbolism," where only the most intrepid and most prepared dare enter. Instead, a well-written review places a poet's work in the more interactive territory of discourse. Reviewers are often practitioners themselves, and I have found that poets reviewing collections of poems approach the text as a fellow poet, as opposed to a critic. There is often a sense of exchange, interaction, and engagement between reviewer and poet. Reviewers tend to enter books as living things, thriving, pulsing, groping; full of ambition and shortcomings. Not unlike ourselves.

One way reviews accomplish this is through authorial voice. One of the hurdles most of my literature students crash into when writing a standard MLA-cited literary analysis is what voice to use. They try to adopt this grad student-professor persona who speaks in lofty tones and deploys obfuscating Latinate phrases. They seem to think that effective or persuasive writing requires an "authorial" or "professorial" tone. What I appreciate about the review as a form is how the reviewer's voice sounds more like a human's and less like a cyborg's. Writing as a "critic" rather than a "scholar" tends to loosen things up. Reviewers somehow adopt a different subjectivity; there is usually more uncertainty, there are more frequent questions and puzzling. And, most importantly, a reviewer generally lets the reader know if a book is—in the parlance of our students—"good" or "bad," which is really what they are most interested in anyway.

One last note here: there are almost no examples of MLA-based writing used anywhere but in scholarly journals and college classrooms. In contrast, it is really easy to point to newspapers, magazines, websites, and blogs to demonstrate how well reasoned, thoughtful, insightful reviews actually reach readers and initiate dialogue. And for me that notion of dialogue—dialogue between a student and a text, between a reader and a review—is really what it is all about.

Victoria: Excited to get going here. I like what you are saying about the review as a form of dialogue with the text. I think about reviewing and criticism in a poetry classroom as a way to subvert and upend traditional poetry pedagogy and discourse. When I think about the review, I think about two ways it can support the poetry classroom: one, having students read poetry reviews that others have written, and two, having students write poetry reviews as part of their own education, as well as making contributions to the great poetry dialogue and discourse.

I'll spend less time talking about the first, but I think that bringing reviews into the classroom is an interesting way to supplement discussions on poetry books, particularly a way to think about and discuss the ways in which reviewers frame their own thinking about books. Sometimes these discussions can veer into talking about assumptions of the critic, as well as the venue where the review is published. I can't help but think of Helen Vendler's review of the Penguin anthology that Rita Dove edited in 2011. The review was called "Are These the Poems to Remember?" and was published in the *New York Review of Books* on November 24, 2011. So much of what Vendler says is outright racist and Dove responds to Vender's review in the December 22, 2011 issue. Any contemporary poetry review could also be unpacked in a classroom setting as students discuss the assumptions (and sometimes the problematic assumptions) behind each review.

In terms of the second usage of poetry reviews in the classroom, I know that both you and I (and many other faculty that I personally know) often assign students to write poetry reviews. I assign poetry reviews nearly every term that I teach for several reasons. I think closely analyzing a book, a group of poems, a poem, or even a line, can help a student think through aspects of the line, the poem, a book, etc. I always say that this, hopefully, in turn, will allow the student to more objectively analyze their own poems when that time comes because they will have internalized critical thinking about other people's poems.

I also assign students a poetry review writing assignment each term because I think that criticism can always be widened in terms of representation. I encourage my students to review books by smaller presses, marginalized poets in terms of race, gender, class, region, aesthetics, etc. Literary journals and other publications seem to be on the lookout for new reviews all the time. As part of my classes, I also encourage my students to send those reviews to such journals for possible publication or I submit the reviews myself to journals I may have contact with.

I wonder if you have further thoughts on any of the things I just discussed?

Dean: You know me; I always have further thoughts.

What got me interested in reviewing—and using reviews in my classes—was the very thing you mention above: the desire to subvert the way mainstream (and largely Anglo) critics were writing about Indigenous American poetry. To me, Native poetry was being treated too much like ethnography. Too often, readers and teachers approach work by people of color thinking they are interacting with or experiencing *culture*—this is particularly true for Indigenous literatures. I kept getting annoyed that critics who were willing to talk about the craft of, say, T. S. Eliot or Louise Glück were still reading Indigenous poetry through the lens of "message" or "theme." Why does John Ashbery get to be an artist and be taken seriously for his formal innovations while excellent and inventive poets like Orlando White and LeAnne Howe do not? My goal early on as a reviewer was to make a case for Indigenous writers as artists—not just protectors of the oral tradition.

Reviews have an edge over traditional literary criticism here because of their immediacy. Reviewers don't have to worry about research, covering scholarly ground, or theoretical frameworks. Reviews can focus on the text at hand, and in so doing, they tend to make the experience of textual engagement feel human, interactive, lived, relevant. To illustrate, I want to quote a long passage from part of one of your sections of our review of Douglas Kearney's *Sho* (2021). Kearney is an African American poet who loves puns, wordplay, and all forms of experimentation. I think you are brilliant here:

> In the poem, "Eulogy for a Pair of Kicks," there's the playful meditation of a pair of shoes juxtaposed with violence, loss, and societal degradation. Playfulness and gravity have equal weight in Kearney's poems, so much so that the reader might need to read the poems numerous times to catch the complex layering. The poem, as the title says, is a eulogy, praise for something that has died—in this case, a pair of shoes. There's already humor in the title of the poem (and grief) and the poem begins slyly with an apostrophe to God:

> *Almighty Lord, give unto me two pair*
> *of wings to hie them unto Thee on high!*
> *Permit these worn gums take the sky.*
> ¤
> O my soles!
> Where'er your tread pressed
> the rugged earth's crust,
> there you bore me home.
> Now, I walk bare and alone.
> God have mercy,
> let be blessed

what shod me,
now, unbound for rest.

>   Note the pun of "O my soles!" which is a pun for "soul" and could also be a play on the singular (as shoes are in pairs). Just in one stanza, there's so much sound play of "tread" and "pressed" and "crust," along with alliteration of "bore" and "bare" and the slant rhyme of "home" and "alone" which also has assonance of the "o" sound.
>   And as I said earlier, the poem traverses between the humorous and the serious throughout. Those of an older generation might chuckle at the "Brown bustered tot you untied!" which is a reference to Buster Brown shoes and the character, but even here, "Brown bustered" has a double meaning with the inverted syntax so that the child is a person of color. In fact, there are sly references to color throughout this poem. Another example is: "Slick winter slips you black tracked!" instead of "back tracked" or "your canvas coke-white / as Death's icy cheek—" Note that "white" is associated with "Death" (instead of black) and leads fluidly to the speaker praying for the well-being of the dead shoe, hoping the shoes can make it to heaven, mated. This final color association with white is the associative pivot point of the poem as it barrels toward its ending. (Chang and Rader)

I just want to point to how pedagogical you are without being didactic. I love how you begin by prepping us for what to expect (the way most of us do in the classroom), then you walk us through some of the key formal components of the poem, before moving on to thematic issues. You help us love the poem for how it is put together, and you help us appreciate the larger argument it is making. I also appreciate how regularly you talk about the work the poem is doing rather than the poet.

I appreciate how writing reviews enables the writer to *be a writer* by giving us the freedom to go micro then macro with the speed and alacrity of a volta. By this I mean, reviews facilitate correspondence; they are an embrace of writing. Writing about writing foregrounds *writing*. In a well-written review, the reviewer gets to talk in broad, global terms about poetry or fiction or the novel or the book—and their role in society—but also is able to get into the weeds to discuss line breaks and alliteration and white space, and rhythm, and pacing. As a reviewer, you get to write about both craft and content, both medium and message.

Victoria: Yes, true, you do always have more to say! And I love what you say here about your experience with Native poetry. What's fascinating about this is that I know for me (and I can only speak for myself), sometimes I feel like no matter what I do, I can't win in a white supremacist system and structure. If I don't write "about" my own experiences as an Asian American (specifically a Chinese and Taiwanese American woman), then white critics won't be interested in my work at all. When/if I do, however, then I get pigeonholed into being an Asian American poet, and today, it actually gets thrown back at me as "identity politics." And even more so, it's nearly impossible to get a book of poems "covered" by a white critical establishment that likes to write reviews on white writers so if my book is covered, I should somehow be grateful for the sometimes sloppy criticism and lack of a nuanced reading. I only bring in my own experiences here because I don't like to speak for other communities or other people and can't presume to know how they might feel.

In terms of what you mention, thanks for bringing in this example. I can't take credit for this mode of thinking and criticism, though. This stems from the traditions of the "annotation" which is how I was trained during my MFA program at Warren Wilson. Also Francine Prose wrote about the idea of "reading like a writer" which I think the concept of annotations emerges from. An annotation is simply a brief (usually one or two pages single-spaced) analysis of someone else's writing (book, poem, essay, passage, etc.) through the lens of "craft." I don't necessarily have a problem with the word *craft*, just how narrow its elements have been in the past. For example, craft for poetry can go beyond just line breaks and sound, to also include how a poet writes about race (in my opinion). The purpose of an annotation is to help the writer read with the goal of improving their own writing. One might focus an annotation or a review on any aspect of a book that intrigues the reader. There are hundreds of things to write about in even one book, but noting patterns is a way to start. One could, for example, note how an author's sentence structure is mostly fragmented and hypothesize about why. Or how the use of a longer line with caesuras operates in the frame of the book's subject matter. The key to coming up with ideas is to take notes while reading.

While I've read a lot of poetry criticism over the years and admire certain elements and the ways in which the critics have thought through and presented their analyses, I definitely come to criticism from my own background writing a lot of annotations. We also use annotations in the low-residency program where I work, Antioch University's MFA Program, where students are required to turn in two annotations per packet (each student must submit five packets per term). Over a period of two years, that's a lot of critical writing and thinking! Because of my own training, I tend to go deep into the text, seeing the text for what it is instead of wishing the text were something else. I do try hard and bring my thinking higher up as well, meaning, I try to think about the poet's work within history, a larger cultural context, as well as tradition, but again, going back to what we were talking about earlier, I definitely think my ideas of tradition are broader than other people's naturally.

Dean: Agreed. I think of form as an ethic. Not just an aesthetic. Joy Harjo likes to tell a story about a time someone asked why she plays the saxophone since it is not an Indigenous instrument. Her reply was: "It is when I play it."

I think about that a lot. English is an instrument of colonization, oppression, and marginalization, but not necessarily and not always. One of the things you and I discuss all the time (and one of the reasons we started "Two Roads") is how, for so many decades, talking about poetry almost always privileged the singular artistic genius. It was typically a monologue about a monologue. I like to think our collaborative reviews do to poetry criticism what Harjo's playing does to the saxophone or what Kearney's poems do to "poetry." They puncture precious and mythical notions of authority and creation.

This is one reason I like assigning collaborative poetry assignments and collaborative review assignments. Reading is always collaborative, and to me, teaching is collaborative. The University of San Francisco, where I work, is one of the most diverse campuses in the country. I have had students in my classes from five different continents, all at the same time, with radically different ideas about god, language, culture, and expression. People sometimes talk about the classroom as a contact zone, but to me, in a class of twenty students, there are twenty different contact zones. Recently, I was teaching some Terrance Hayes poems, and in my class were a Filipina student who identified as a lesbian, a Chicano student who identified as straight, an African American male student who identified as queer, a Middle Eastern student, a Chinese student, an Asian American student who was gender fluid, and fifteen other students with their own complicated (and ever-shifting) identities. So, teaching a Terrance Hayes poem about race and Wallace Stevens required me to think hard about power, hegemony, and authority, but it also required each of these students to think about these things as they made comments about the poem and as they responded to each other. Creating assignments that foreground community-based responses, that focus on dialogue, helps dismantle the linearity and exclusivity of a top-down approach to poetic engagement, and I think makes reading and responding to poetry (and all written texts) more inclusive.

For example, in my poetry classes, I always assign collaborative projects. My favorite is the collaborative sonnet. For this, I put students into pairs and require them to write two poems—one conventional sonnet and one more experimental. For the traditional sonnet, I generally recommend they use the form that Simone Muench and I relied on in *Suture* (2017)—our collection of collaborative sonnets. In our book, the first line of every sonnet is taken from a previously published sonnet by a well-known poet such as Rita Dove, Pablo Neruda, Wallace Stevens, or Adrienne Rich. After that first line, Simone and I take turns writing the opening quatrain. Then, we pass it back to the other who writes the second quatrain and completes the octave. Then it goes back to the person who started the poem, who generally writes a tercet. Then it returns to the second person, who finishes the poem.

I have found that this assignment generates the best work of the semester. I suspect this is because most people are capable of writing two interesting stanzas. One of the hardest things is writing a flawless poem from beginning to end—especially a flawless sonnet. But, without the pressure of having to write a perfect poem, it is amazing how creative students can be. Plus, you never want to let your collaborator down. Greatness rises to the surface.

Similarly, I often require my students to write collaborative reviews. Sometimes these are a dialogue (like our "Two Roads" column) and sometimes I ask them to write as a collective "we," which forces students to work and write as a unit. In this latter model, they have to find common ground, which is always easier and more rewarding than they think. Again, I think that collaborating on writing reviews highlights how interactive reading, at its core, really is. Also, working through a book with a partner can be a lot more fun that staring into the literary abyss all by yourself. Collaborative assignments remind students we are in this together!

Victoria: So much here! I appreciate what you say about collaboration. In fact, I think of the classroom as a collaboration. But I know that I didn't grow up in that kind of educational system. I also love the specific example that you give with your particular students. We're not particularly young, yet we're not extremely old either, and so while we have quite a bit of poetic knowledge, I think we still have so much to learn from the people before us and the people after us. I think of myself as a hinge to my students, instead of a gavel. A hinge connects things together for a larger purpose while a gavel is dogmatic and authoritative. I like to ask questions and take a more query-based approach in my teaching instead of feeling like I'm bringing in knowledge and providing it to the student. I tell my students that I am learning from them too and oftentimes during my time with students, I will ask them for feedback about even how I am teaching and ask for their suggestions. I do believe learning is their experience, and I want them to feel like they have agency.

I always feel like whatever it is that I do in my life, it's always better when I'm collaborating with someone else.

Dean: Like now?
Victoria: Like now.

Further Reading

For more examples of collaborative reviews, see our column, "Two Roads: Poetry Reviews in Dialogue" in *The Los Angeles Review of Books* (lareviewofbooks.org/sections/two-roads-poetry-reviews-in-dialogue). You might also take a look at "Introduction: Generations and Emanations," in *Speak to Me Words: Essays on Contemporary American Indian Poetry*, edited by Dean Rader and Janice Gould (U of Arizona P, 2003, pp. 3–20). For scholarly takes, see Nicholas J. Rowland, Jeffrey A. Knapp & Hailley Fargo, "The collaborative book review as an opportunity for undergraduate research skill development" (*Higher Education Research & Development*, vol. 39, no. 3, pp. 577–90) as well as Lisa Ede and Andrea Lunsford's classic study, *Singular Texts/Plural Authors: Perspectives in Collaborative Writing* (Southern Illinois UP, 1990). For literary examples of collaboration, take a peek at *They Said: A Multi-Genre Anthology of Contemporary Collaborative Writing*, edited by Simone Muench, Dean Rader, Sally Ashton, and Jackie White (Black Lawrence Press, 2018).

Works Cited

Chang, Victoria and Dean Rader. "Two Roads: A Review-in-Dialogue of Douglas Kearney's 'Sho.'" *The Los Angeles Review of Books*, 4 Aug. 2021, lareview ofbooks.org/article/two-roads-a-review-in-dialogue-of-douglas-kearneys-sho.

Dove, Rita. "Defending an Anthology." *The New York Review of Books*, 22 Dec. 2011, www.nybooks.com/articles/2011/12/22/defending-anthology.
Vender, Helen. "Are These the Poems to Remember?" *The New York Review of Books*, 24 Nov. 2011, www.nybooks.com/articles/2011/11/24/are-these-poems-remember.

28

City, State, and Self
A Collaborative Book Project

JAMES INNIS MCDOUGALL

When I first started teaching poetry, both as a literary genre and as creative writing, I was very much at the center of the class. In retrospect, my focus should have been on student writers as poets and academics and not on myself as a poetry curator. While the exercises, imitations, and assignments yielded some truly wonderful creative and academic work, I felt that these courses were a simulacrum of literature classes I took as a student and the syllabus was a mask I was wearing to cover up my imposter syndrome. I knew that I needed to improve my teaching by shifting the center of the course to student writing.

After reflecting on my first foray as an instructor in the poetry classroom, I decided to commit to a collaborative class project similar to my academic writing courses; for example, I require collaborative proposals in my research writing for sciences classes, and the creation of edited collections and essay anthologies in my freshman writing classes. I learned through experimenting in these classes that project-based learning turns the classroom into a platform for community building, where students have to actively incorporate a process approach to a collaborative project. The emphasis on "doing" that comes with project-based learning fosters communities of practice and speaks to my pedagogy ideals, informed by Paulo Freire's notion of discourse communities and Dewey's pragmatism.

Dewey believed education occurs through practice and "knowing the world as inseparable from agency within it" (Legg and Hookway). In addition to the transferrable skills that come with creating a collaborative book project, this approach allows me to play with ideas that have been formative for me as teacher—Deleuze and Guattari's "line of flight," and Derrida's notion of "play." The results have been encouraging and so I have been committed to using a class poetry book for poetry courses to develop a community of writers and create an active classroom.

The course project involves producing a book that features poems and criticism, edited and assembled as an electronic and printed volume. Such class projects involve multiple steps that require students to develop different skills to master team management, presentations on course readings, project planning, creative and critical writing, contributions to writing workshops, and participation in an editorial process that challenges students to engage with form, poetics, and sentence-level details. This process allows practical consideration of critical and theoretical issues; for example, by proofreading classmates' poems students become engaged in examining the significance of linguistic accuracy, the function of extralinguistic aspects of writing, and how the sequencing of lyrical poems can build narratives and themes. In order to give the book project a particular shape, the assignment revolves around writing about place in poetry as an act that accounts for the dynamism and multiplicity of a locality. I ask students to examine theories of poetic composition by working together in their local off-campus environments to write and analyze their poetry. The class design comes from my reading of Deleuze and Guattari's ideas of flows and captures in terms of two major assemblages: the institution and student production. My course and syllabus power features of an educational bureaucracy through which students follow a vector towards their own assemblages and, ultimately, their own book. In Deleuze and Guattari's terms, my class, which is coded through the syllabus, is deterritorialized through the student project, the line of flight, and reterritorialized as a book. The project mimetically asks students to consider how space is deterritorialized and recoded through writing, editing, compiling, and curating, which collectively constitute a line of flight—a dynamic passage through semiotic regimes as opposed to being above or outside of them; that is, space communicates something into the poem only through the experience of being in that space, and even if only in an imaginary or virtual sense (Deleuze and Guattari 204). Channeling coursework into a book project allows for creative writing and academic analysis of poetry to include nontextual aspects of the craft, including tactics for compiling content, observing reader responses, circulating texts, and managing editorial processes. In a practical sense, students work on four kinds of writing—poetry, academic writing, routine business writing, and literary criticism.

The first iteration of the course, a creative writing class, was named after the core project, "City, State, and Self." The project framed poetry in at least three ways: ecology, semiotics, and collaboration. "City" corresponds to ecology as poetry represents locations, the interpenetration of life and environment; temporality, cycles of beginning-middle-end; history, spaces framed by competing rhetorics, mythologies, and events. "State" refers to both the semiotics or meaning of place, and to the emotional and intellectual state of the poet's encounter with a place. Poems serve as sign systems, including coding, codes, interference, decoding, and feedback; the combination of the graphic, musical, intellectual, and emotional aspects of poetry; systems of rules, limits, and regimes of capture that poetry employs—the state is a state of being, as well as a sovereign sign system. "Self" represents the poetic subject, which paradoxically is a site of interpenetration, a node in a collaborative network, and an agent of collaboration. The class project situates poetry as a communal event, where the production of poetry as a published cultural artifact is grounded in a process, shaped by an audience, and informed by encounters with both the local environment and other texts.

The course asks students to create a collaborative poetic abecedary of the university's local environment. After students form groups, they work together to identify shapes in the environment that appear to have features of letters in the English alphabet that have been assigned to their group. They cannot use actual letters that may appear on signs or buildings, and they must work together to read the city. Students then take digital photographs of these alphabetical apparitions. The images serve as illuminations for the first letter of poems about their encounters with the local environment. Each group is given a set of poetic forms to experiment with—forms that they will then have to teach the class using assigned poems alongside their project drafts. Students use the wiki function on the course management system to create reference materials for the class on rhetorical terms and concepts, poetic forms and meter, and ideas from literary theory on composition, poetry, and literary movements. Figure 28.1 provides an example of an entry for the letter *F* by Wanyu Gan. In this poem, the student's illumination is a set of plastic fish, bearing an *F*

Figure 28.1. An entry for the letter *F* by Wanyu Gan. *Source*: "Plastic Beauty Floats through Frustrated Days," written for the assignment "City, State, and Self" in Introduction to Poetry, Sichuan University–Pittsburgh Institute, 2021. Used with permission. *Note:* In the class's publication, the student editors chose to follow the Chinese naming convention of putting the Romanized surname all in capital letters in front of the given name.

"Plastic Beauty Floats through Frustrated Days" by GAN Wanyu

rustrated these days,
I walk among crowds of people,
Under the gray sky.

Suddenly a school of fish,
Floating strips of colorful plastic, form a
Line by Chengdu's Jin River walk.

Compared to the sky,
These fake fish floating by are full of plastic vigor in
Limpid water, in a city, dark.

Maybe in the frustrations of daily life,
Beauty does not lack,
As much as finding its form and folly.

shape in her mind. The image informs the content of the poem and leads her to experiment with alliteration with *f* sounds as she describes the state of the subjective voice during an encounter with colorful, plastic fish while walking in central Chengdu. I love her closing *f* word, *folly*, as a trait of beauty as well as her tension between earnestness and irony through the repeated use of "plastic" found in her environment as providing beauty but also degrading it with "plastic vigor," which creates a complex idea of artificial lifelessness and something that is malleable.

Students work collaboratively, compiling their writings and creating a critical introduction comparing their work to class readings. They analyze their work through theoretical texts explored during the term. The process creates scaffolding, allowing students to learn about form, analyze poems, and develop a critical vocabulary. Students then curate their writings. The curation process reinforces course materials. For example, one aspect of the project is that it engages with poetry's visual element, allowing me to introduce a concrete poem like Jonathan Williams's "Three Ripples in the Tuckaseigee River" (1985), a meditation on semiotics and the cultural history of naming, as well as George Herbert's "Easter Wings" (1633), and Apollinaire's Calligrammes (1918). I could bring together Gwendolyn Brooks's poem "In the Mecca" (1968) with Hart Crane's *The Bridge* (1933) to represent how urban design, development, and decay shape people's lives. The assignment allows for contemplation on the ethics of an individual's connection to their local environments. From anonymous Lowlands border ballads to the Himalayan highlands of Agha Shahid Ali's *A Country without a Post Office* (1997), from Audre Lorde's Chicago to Robert Frost's New England, students can see how different poets connect politics and philosophy to place. The connection between people and where they dwell have led thinkers like Gloria Anzaldúa, Gaston Bachelard, and Martin Heidegger to turn to poetry to articulate the relation between place and the practice of everyday life. Our readings highlight the heteroglossia of place, revealing the local as a site of overlapping polylocalities with competing vernaculars where discourses collide. The focus on local environments puts student work in conversation with poems by Gary Snyder, Jamaal May, Robinson Jeffers, Yusef Komunyakaa, W. S. Merwin, William Blake, and Joy Harjo, among others who have been documenting our complex and interpenetrated relationship with our environments. Students read Charles Baudelaire, Amiri Baraka, Allen Ginsberg, Frank O'Hara, and John Yau to study how the transversal of urban environments shape the content and form of their poetry. These poets' states are informed by the semiotics of place.

The class project asks students to think about poetry in terms of play. They must represent a thing in its absence, using the city's ABCs as signatures of the city's everyday life. In *Writing and Difference*, Derrida writes: "Free play is always an interplay of absence and presence, but if it is to be radically conceived, free play must be conceived of before the alternative of presence and absence; being must be conceived of as presence or absence beginning with the possibility of free play and not the other way around" (294). Poetry serves as the element of play that "must be conceived." It is the play that happens between fixedness of representation. It is the play in the third string of a guitar bent at the twelfth fret changing a G to an A note. It is the A note hidden in the play of the G. It is the minor chord with the discordance that serves as a bulwark against the bleaching harmonization of the majoritarian language, which in the US is the "adult-white-heterosexual-European-male speaking a standard language" (Deleuze and Guattari 105). Poetry as play finds a way to derive discourse that is "found neither in language A, nor in language B, but 'is language X, which is none other than language A in the actual process of becoming language B'" (Deleuze and Guattari 106). The "'A' not 'A'" is poetry's ability to take language and turn it into rhythm, negative space on the page, or another text from another poet from another place. These deterritorializations are as crucial as concepts like stanza forms, rhetorical tropes, and feet names. Therefore, the assignment starts with semiotics and, paradoxically, the defamiliarization of language. Students then have a fresh pallet for representing their environments, states of being, and themselves.

I have offered this class several times in different countries. Each iteration of the course has been highly successful. Students demonstrate competencies in using different forms of poetry to engage with the world. They built strong bonds with each other. They learn to trust each other's judgment while developing a vocabulary for talking about poetry. Students create reference materials for the class, critique their own work, and use academic writing to pair their classmate's work with the poetry analyzed in class. They gain editorial skills while learning about multimodal digital composition. More importantly, the project really brings the class together, which can be seen through the joy and pride on the students' faces at the end of the semester when we have a class reading from our contributions to the book, and from the students retelling stories to each other about their adventures in finding their poems.

Further Reading

There are many works on project-based learning for every facet of education. However, the most influential force on my design principles for project-based learning in the poetry classroom comes from chapter four of Deleuze and Guattari's *A Thousand Plateaus* (Minnesota UP, 1980), "November 20, 1923—Postulates of Linguistics." Etienne Wenger's

Communities of Practice: Learning, Meaning, and Identity (Cambridge UP, 1998) has shaped my ideas on the value of collaborative learning and led me to rethink how to assign group projects in the poetry classroom.

Works Cited

Ali, Agha Shahid. *The Country Without a Post Office: Poems 1991–1995*. Penguin, 1997.
Deleuze, Gilles, and Felix Guattari. *A Thousand Plateaus: Capitalism and Schizophrenia*. Minnesota UP, 1980.
Derrida, Jacques. *Writing and Difference*. Translated by Alan Bass, Routledge, 1978.
Legg, Catherine and Christopher Hookway. "Pragmatism." *The Stanford Encyclopedia of Philosophy*, 2021, plato.stanford.edu/archives/sum2021/entries/pragmatism.
Wenger, Etienne. *Communities of Practice: Learning, Meaning, and Identity*. Cambridge: Cambridge UP, 1998.

29

Experimental Indexes

Quantifying Poetic Patterns and Project-Based Reading

NICK STURM

I'm interested in indexes as intellectual tools that efficiently and imaginatively sort complex texts. Atomizing a text, even a book of poetry, into an index inherently produces quantitative information—literary data—that can be visualized in any number of ways, like a bar graph tracking the frequency of a theme. Creating an index might also allow a reader to reflect on and organize the initial flood of associations generated by a literary text. Rather than expecting poems to be distillable into a singular takeaway, an index shows how seemingly unconnected images and ideas are linked. My pedagogical experiments with such projects—like one student who skimmed James Schuyler's *Collected Poems* (1993) to catalog the poet's references to flora and fauna, presenting the resulting data in pie charts complete with a guidebook-like account of each reference—confirmed for me that distant reading processes help students develop surprising and sophisticated arguments. The reason, as Franco Moretti writes, is that distant reading "allows you to focus on units that are much smaller or much larger than the text: devices, themes, tropes—or genres and systems" (48–49). Perhaps one of the oldest distant reading methods, indexing requires one to focus on the smallest units of a text by counting, alphabetizing, categorizing, and cross-referencing words to create a reference tool for using that text as a whole. The process asks students to move between quantitative and qualitative research processes, as well as between distant and close reading, as they skim, reread, sort information, find effective ways to visualize data, and then interpret those visualizations.

Creating an index is also an effective way of introducing students to new approaches to studying poetry as a genre. As my student Rachael writes, "When you analyze poetry, you don't typically read for the statistical patterns, nor do we tend to associate understanding literature with numbers or graphs." But as she learned through indexing a book of poems, "I realized that poetry isn't just the expression of emotions, it is an argument devised around patterns and repetitions." In his book *Index, A History of the* (2022), Dennis Duncan describes the rich history of the index as a tool, including its applications with poetry, such as Alexander Pope's indexes of his eighteenth-century translation of *The Iliad*. As Duncan writes, Pope's "indexes turn the poem into an encyclopedia," a useful pedagogical kernel that reminds us that poems function as storehouses of information that might be used by students in ways other than the traditional analytical essay (189). Like Pope, my students, as indexers, could begin to sort the particulars of potentially any literary text.

Danish poet Inger Christensen's ecopoetic *alphabet* (2000) is an ideal book for indexing. The book-length poem's formal adaptation of the Fibonacci sequence, which inventories an ecstatic and terrifying list-like accumulation of what "exists," offers an intricate and affective introduction to how poetry can communicate at the intersection of the ecological, social, and political. Beginning with the memorable line "apricot trees exist, apricot trees exist," each section of the poem grows exponentially—and alphabetically—to include more and more of what exists in an expanding catalog of the world's beauties and terrors, including atom bombs, bracken, cicadas, dioxin, elms, famine, guns, half-lives, and ice ages (11). Like a post-WWII Book of Genesis set in the atomic heart of the Anthropocene, Christensen's poem operates on both enormous and intimate scales, inviting students to think about a dense, generative set of interlocking questions. Using *alphabet* to create "experimental indexes," as I called the project, allowed students working in groups to explore the book's major themes, which we came up with collectively in class discussion: the human, nonhuman, time, science, and the metaphysical. Such indexes are experimental not only because they approach a text through a thematic lens, which gives a reasonable scope to the project, but also because they are as much a reference tool as they are an in-progress argument.

This indexing project was developed in early 2019 as I was designing a first-year writing and communication course, "The Poetics of Sustainability: Environment and Race," at the Georgia Institute of Technology. Alongside *alphabet*, this summer course would include books by Claudia Rankine and Raúl Zurita and, through a partnership with Georgia Tech's Serve-Learn-Sustain initiative, allow my students to volunteer at an urban farm and visit the Center for Civil and Human Rights. I chose these books because each offers a lyric record of witness to injustice and devastation with both oblique and direct references to race, nationalism, and the environment. Christensen's would be the first book students would read for the ways that it activates these associations. Adapting our program's multimodal pedagogy, I asked students to produce a multimodal document that would function as a well-designed, usable reference tool, including an interpretative introduction and data visualizations.

Students begin by individually responding to written prompts about their experience of reading *alphabet*. This assignment gives them a space to externalize their initial encounter with this challenging text. Coming together as a class, students share their experiences in a high-energy discussion, describing how strange Christensen's poem is but also where they see patterns. We discuss the book's Fibonacci form, its historical references, and how the poem's complexity is generated; for example, we note how the first-person pronoun *I* exists for the first time as soon as "atom bombs exist" (24). The emergence of this speaker, who witnesses and suffers the devastation the poem catalogs, becomes an opportunity for students to reflect on their own capacity to be witnesses, both to the text and to the crises of our own moment.

This discussion primes students to be attentive to individual words and the book's form as they break into groups to begin the indexing process. Using Google Docs, groups compile their raw indexes by splitting the text into equal sections so that each group member can extract words related to their assigned theme. As the index takes shape, there is vigorous debate about how to define their theme's scope. For a group creating a nonhuman index of *alphabet*, words like *apricot* and *eider duck* are easy enough to agree on including, but what about *hydrogen* or *dream*? Similarly, words like *clocks* and *June* are immediately recognizable for an index of time-related words, but through repeated reading students come to see words that signify duration as equally important, such as *after* and *exist*. Such debates are one of the most memorable parts of this assignment for students, which encourage them to think critically and imaginatively about the conceptual capacity within ideas. These debates also prepare students for future conversations about racism, violence, and inequity, that, by introducing discourses around microaggressions and environmental racism, for instance, might challenge their assumed limits to what racism looks like in our society.

Creating a full draft index then requires alphabetizing, noting frequency, double-checking page numbers, and forming relevant subcategories. For example, the nonhuman index requires the subcategory "bird" because *alphabet* refers to fifteen different species of bird in addition to the word *bird* ten times. While a first-time reader might notice that doves appear frequently, students creating this index can now say that "doves" are referenced precisely eleven times—the most common bird in the book. The larger ecosystems and systems of meaning within the text begin to reveal themselves. These observations help students to draft their index's introduction, which describes what their index tells us about *alphabet* as an ecopoetic text. Students also make decisions about what types of qualitative data they want to extract to create visualizations, which will be incorporated into the introduction, and then build those visualizations using easy-to-find online tools. These interpretative introductions are strictly introductory—and speculative—as I want students to identify trends and correspondences while stopping short of making full-fledged arguments. I want them to see indexing as intellectual work unto itself, one in which *a reader becomes a scholar* as they reread, annotate, organize, and prepare a text to be encountered by others. The preparation of the index is finalized as students use the free online platform Canva to layout their index in a traditional two-column style, add relevant visual content for illustrative purposes, design a cover page, and present their written introduction integrated with data visualizations. Downloaded from Canva as a PDF file, these indexes are usually between ten and fifteen pages long.

Though the process of compiling an index might be slightly tedious (the genre and length of *alphabet* means I can require my students to create their indexes with physical copies of the book, later proofing their indexes against a searchable digital copy), the novel ways it encourages students to engage with a text have the potential to reframe their understanding of reading and writing about literature. Forrest, Rachel, Jayden, Aditi, and Rachael write in the introduction to their metaphysical index that the combination of distant and close reading was essential in helping them unpack Christensen's book.

Experimental Indexes | 249

Figure 29.1. Data visualization from nonhuman index by Joshua, Tova, Hannah, Josh, and Leah. *Source*: Provided by the author.

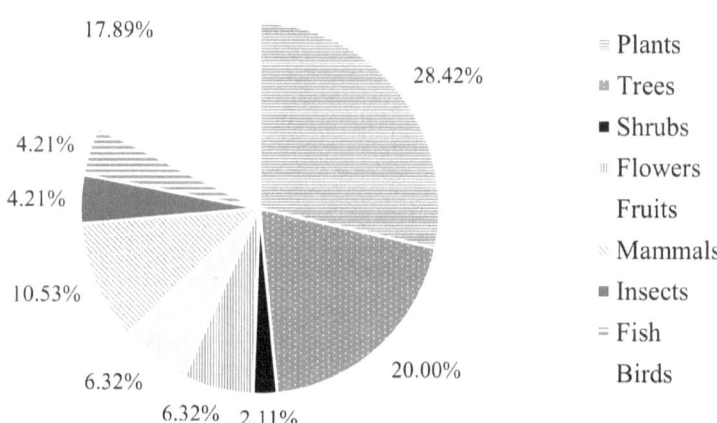

It was as if we had drifted away, above the poem, and were staring at it with a bird's eye view, trying to see a bigger picture even though we couldn't understand what we were looking at. The farther back we got, the blurrier it seemed until suddenly everything shifted into place. We had pulled back so far that we could see everything. Every word had two meanings, literal and literary. Everything could be questioned. Just as the poem evolved from simple phrases to complex memories, our understanding shifted from seeing the literal wasteland of nuclear catastrophe to watching the underlining metaphysical messages develop. . . . While initially we were overwhelmed, after obtaining the larger picture, and then refocusing ourselves to see the individual words again, we were able to appreciate the uncertainty of *alphabet*.

Similarly, my student Joshua writes in his reflection that "As I broke apart *alphabet* into smaller pieces, the written communication barrier I had always felt no longer seemed to haunt me as it did when I tried to process too much of the poem at once." Rather than being overwhelmed by the text, atomizing Christensen's poem gave Joshua more confidence to write about the book's big ideas. Another student, Ryan, confirms that making an index showed him that "the best way to analyze a poem is to make small connections and start to build larger patterns. When you make small connections, it is easier to link ideas together into main themes." Again,

Figure 29.2. Excerpt from nonhuman index by Joshua, Tova, Hannah, Josh, and Leah. *Source*: Provided by the author.

Nonhuman Index of *alphabet*

A

absence, 70, 71
ages, 20 (2), 62 (2)
air, 33, 41, 52, 54, 58, 59, 67, 71, 73
all, 31, 40
alone, 64, 65, 75
anemones*, 60
angels, 47
animals, 44, 49, 54, 58, 76
apple, 35
apricot, 16 (3), 29 (2), 35
    apricot trees, 11 (2),16 (3), 28, 34
    dried apricots, 29
Arctic Ocean, 31, 64 (2)
arms, 52
ash tree, 17
avenue, 58

B

back, 64, 65
background, 38
banks, 44
bark, 42
    barkskin, 42
bat, 22
beach, 46
beaks, 45
bed, 47, 55
beeches, 60
bench, 67
berries, 26

birch, 29, 42, 45 (2), 46, 49 (2)
birch tree, 17
bird, 16, 25 (2), 28, 41, 42, 48, 49, 54, 76
    doves, 14 (3), 21, 23, 26, 41, 57, 69, 70, 71
    ducks, 15
        Eider Duck, 46
    fisherbird herons, 16
    geese, 17
    gulls, 70
    gyrfalcons, 23
    hawk, 41, 58
    lapwings, 36
    nightingale, 63
    ospreys, 16
    owls, 17, 63
    parrot, 41
    ptarmigans, 16
    sparrow, 23, 58, 67
bit, 21 (2), 75, 76
black, 36, 67
blackberries, 12, 39
Black Sea, 65 (2)
blood, 57
bloom,66
blossoms, 21
blue, 20 (2), 29, 32
    bluish, 71
body, 45, 46
bogs, 56
bomb, 23, 30, 40

*Click on underlined terms for additional visuals   4

unpacking the text helped to demystify poetry as a genre and to make students feel like capable, confident readers of a challenging literary work.

My students' familiarity with *alphabet* was on full display when they were volunteering at an urban farm in southwest Atlanta the following week. Their reading of Christensen's poem led us to conversations about environmental racism in the South, and then to a specific historical investigation of the Adair Park neighborhood where redlining and industrial pollution significantly affected Black residents. With their hands in the soil, students were tending a thriving strawberry patch on what used to be a polluted bus maintenance site, aware that, as Christensen writes, "by spraying / fields and forests / we achieve fall and death / in the middle of the most / luxuriant summer" (54). As we were walking through a grove of recently planted fruit trees, our host pointed out a plum tree, an apple tree, and, of course, an apricot tree. My students spontaneously shouted, "Apricot trees exist!" It was hard to convince them I hadn't planned it.

Further Reading

Since working with students to index Christensen's *alphabet*, I've applied the experimental index project to other books, including Bernadette Mayer's *Midwinter Day* (New Directions, 1999) and Joe Brainard's *I Remember* (Granary Books, 2001), which share catalog-like formal qualities that make them ripe for this method. However, I can also imagine students indexing the other books we read in my Summer 2019 course—Rankine's *Citizen: An American Lyric* (Graywolf Press, 2014) or Zurita's *Song for his Disappeared Love* (Action Books, 2010), translated by Daniel Borzutzky—to approach and unpack the inequities and violence these books document. A historical case for the pedagogical value of indexing poetry can be found in Rachel Sagner Buurma's and Laura Heffernan's *The Teaching Archive: A New History for Literary Study* (U of Chicago P, 2021), which includes a chapter on Caroline Spurgeon's 1913 "Art of Reading" course. As Buurma and Heffernan describe, Spurgeon focused on teaching students reading methods that allowed them to unpack a text and "then recompose it into the shapes of their own interpretations and arguments" (37). Spurgeon's course concluded in a culminative project like the one I've given to my students in which they "index a work whose hierarchy would reflect their individual perspective on it" (36). Buurma's and Heffernan's chapter on Josephine Miles's quantitative research of literary texts with her students in the mid-twentieth century is equally inspiring for its emphasis on collaboration. As they write, Miles's work was "collaborative both in the creation of its data and in its vision of sharing the data with other scholars" (161). My own teaching has deeply benefited from this collaborative energy, from a willingness to experiment with multimodality and distant reading, and to imagine how sometimes invisible reference tools like indexes can become primary forms for undergraduate students approaching poetry.

Works Cited

Buurma, Rachel Sagner, and Laura Heffernan. *The Teaching Archive: A New History for Literary Study*. U of Chicago P, 2021.
Christensen, Inger. *alphabet*. Translated by Susanna Nied, New Directions, 2000.
Duncan, Dennis. *Index, A History of the: A Bookish Adventure from Medieval Manuscripts to the Digital Age*. W. W. Norton, 2022.
Moretti, Franco. *Distant Reading*. Verso, 2013.

30

Teaching Anti-Racist Research Practices Beyond Research Papers

Emma Lazarus, Esther Schor, and My First-Year Composition Students

MOLLIE BARNES

"The Ampersand" and Feminist, Anti-Racist Pedagogy

In this essay, I'll discuss an assignment I've created, inspired by Esther Schor's interactive edition of Emma Lazarus's "The New Colossus" (1883) that unsettles traditional writing assignments by prioritizing research practices over research papers, and by emphasizing not just anti-racist subjects but also writing pedagogies and strategies. In my first-year composition courses, we read this edition our first week—and when students make annotated digital editions of texts of their own choosing at the end of the semester, we study it as a model for inquiry-based critical making. For our culminating project, students write a critical introduction, a series of annotations, a bibliography, and a rationale, explaining the rhetorical choices that they make in constructing this research project. I ask students to think of this assignment as a well-researched, well-developed, if deconstructed, analysis that extends the work of a traditional close reading: in the critical introduction, they present an argument supported in the annotations, which should use facts, clips, definitions, images, maps, and links to useful archival materials to enrich their own interpretations.

Figure 30.1. Screencap of interactive edition. *Source*: Courtesy of Esther Schor. Used with permission.

"THE NEW COLOSSUS"
by EMMA LAZARUS
An Interactive Poem
Annotated by Esther Schor

Not like the **BRAZEN GIANT** of GREEK FAME, With **CONQUERING LIMBS ASTRIDE** from *LAND TO LAND*; Here at our **SEA-WASHED, SUNSET GATES** shall stand A mighty woman with a **torch,** whose flame Is the **IMPRISONED LIGHTNING,** and her name **MOTHER OF EXILES.** From her **BEACON-HAND** Glows **WORLD-WIDE** welcome; her mild eyes command The air-bridged harbor that **twin cities** frame. "Keep, ancient lands, your *STORIED* pomp!" cries she With **SILENT LIPS.** "Give me your tired, your poor, **YOUR HUDDLED MASSES** yearning to breathe free, The **WRETCHED REFUSE** of your teeming shore. Send these, the homeless, **TEMPEST-TOST** to *me,* I lift my lamp beside the **GOLDEN DOOR!**"

About the book

Esther Schor — a poet and professor of English at Princeton University — is the author of *Emma Lazarus*, a biography published by Nextbook Press and Schocken Books as part of the Jewish Encounters book series. To learn more, and to buy

I've realized, like many writing studies people, that researched close reading can happen in forms other than five- to ten-page essays that unfold linearly. In fact, essay alternatives are often more accessible ways for students to practice taking intellectual risks with their writing, especially with poetry. I try to remind myself and my students of the root of the word *essay*: to try (ideas on/out). While this assignment is designed for a first-year writing classroom, it's easily adapted to literature surveys and seminars, if teachers adjust for scope (number of annotations, sources, etc.). I've also come to believe that this kind of feminist assignment design—even in a class where the emphasis in composition and literature is on *composition* (not on literature, and not just on poetry) has helped me to think about poetry, with all its beauties and all its urgencies, alongside students who may never otherwise have imagined themselves as serious (or playful!) readers. I'm constantly reminding myself and my students, especially English majors/minors, that we need to shift our focus from learning specific, invented forms, genres, and institutions to studying practices, skills, and habits of mind. Teaching poetry and writing about poetry has prompted powerful growth, both for me and my students. The pedagogical risk-taking that this assignment requires—my students' and, necessarily, as bell hooks argues, my own—is integral to my feminist, anti-racist practices as a teacher-scholar.

Teaching Lazarus's sonnet the first week establishes several scaffolds for course sequences that unfold over the semester, some attending to the "Literature" part of the course, some to the "Composition" part. On one pedagogical level, this sonnet introduces the texts that we read in the first half of the semester. After "The New Colossus" (composed 1883, placed on the statue 1903), we turn to poems/poets that directly and explicitly respond to this sonnet on a literal pedestal: Bernadette Mayer's "The Tragic Condition of the Statue of Liberty" (1987) and Ella Wheeler Wilcox's "Goddess of Liberty, Answer" (1898). We also zoom in and out of cartoons that mock, remake, and unmake Lazarus, generation after generation. On another level, this sonnet functions as an analytical springboard for me to introduce reading practices and tools that we hone when we turn to other poems that remake/unmake/resist sonnets—including Gwendolyn Brook's "kitchenette building" (1963), Sherman Alexie's "Sonnet, without Salmon" (2011), and Tracy K. Smith's "The United States Welcomes You" (2018)—that challenge us to study writing about immigration, displacement, fair housing, and home.

The scaffolded project—as much as the design and instruction of the sonnet sequence explained above—is central to my feminist, anti-racist teaching practices. While most people in composition studies take scaffolding for granted, it is, unfortunately, *not* something many literature professors truly understand or practice in designing literature courses and assignments—even in "writing-intensive" contexts, including first-year composition, or in our alleged *raisons d'être* for our programs and degrees. Ultimately, these differences in prioritizing (or not) and valuing (or not) scaffolded writing widens the perceived space between "composition" and "literature"—not only in general education courses but also in surveys and seminars for our majors. For me, however, the pedagogical choices about what I'm asking students to read, and why, and how, and what I'm asking students to write, and why, and how, work hand in hand. These interconnected choices help me to bridge disciplines in this general education course that can often feel so far apart, both for us as teachers and, in turn, for our students. My course is about the ways certain places—homes, landmarks, monuments, favorite beaches and stretches of the earth—inspire people to think about who they are and who they want to become. After these two poems about the Statue by two white women poets, the semester is dedicated to writing by people of color, mostly Black women and immigrant women. My course is also, then, about empowering students to feel authorized in surfacing, rather than hiding or erasing, their own classed, gendered, and/or raced voices—in authorizing seats at writing tables where they may have felt long unwelcome or unworthy, illegible or invisible. I connect these important dots between teaching composition and teaching poetry in my general education course through the critical-making and -annotating projects that my students compose in response to Lazarus and to Schor.

Teaching Critical Making with Lazarus and Schor

Any compositionist and any literature teacher tasked with teaching first-year writing will be quick to note how impossible it is often to balance these two parts of the work without feeling like we are watering one—or both—down. Most of our time in Composition and Literature isn't—and shouldn't be—on literature. Instead, it is—and should be—on teaching scaffolding, process, project management, time management, recursive reading and researching loops, and, perhaps above all, reflection. Poetry is the perfect way to practice these skills. Doing more with fewer poems has helped me hone better reading practices and better writing practices with my students.

Our conversations about Lazarus's "The New Colossus" (and Schor's interactive edition of it) are the foundations for that big-picture work. We unpack how Lazarus exemplifies Petrarchan conventions and expectations—but also how she remakes, rewrites, or resists them. When we encounter Mayer's shifting, remixing speaker in her "collaboration with Emma Lazarus," students are primed for one of the most important ideas of a writing class: that poetic interpretation *is* conversation, that writing *is* conversation, and, hopefully, that having a voice and a seat at the table is powerful. When we play with sonnets that resist rules—Gwendolyn Brooks's "kitchenette building" with its plural lyric "we" and its unmatched last line; Tracy K. Smith's "The United States Welcomes You" where conversation about immigration devolves to an ICE interrogation—students expect to find meaning and even beauty in irregularities, "broken"/enjambed lines and "broken"/enjambed rules. When we look at photos of the statue alongside the poems, we discuss the architectural scaffolding visible in the 1880s and the 1980s, when she was constructed and then when she was repaired. In turn, we talk about what the Statue means (or is meant to represent)—and what the US means (or is meant to represent). Inevitably, we also talk about the work we will in turn do deconstructing, reconstructing, and authorizing our identities beyond still-pervasive—and damaging—ivory-tower histories of writing studies when we join the conversation through our own projects.

Of course, I'm far from the first or only person to design this kind of critical-making assignment. Many teacher-scholars grew up watching VH1's Pop-Up Video. Today we find this annotating genre everyone from song explainers to wikis and reddits. And many professors have tried deconstructed research papers in everything from prewrite clusters or outlines to more traditional essays to full blown digital humanities and pedagogies projects that take transcription and annotation to far more sophisticated levels. My point is both the specific poem and the specific assignment and the magic they work together for students in non-major course.

When I first drafted this assignment, I was a Marion L. Brittain Post-Doctoral Fellow at Georgia Tech, with no experience in multimodal pedagogy. The logistical nuts and bolts of designing nontraditional essay assignments felt overwhelming and eye-opening at the same time—disrupting a notion I had clung to, both as an undergraduate and graduate

Figure 30.2. Early advertisement showing architectural scaffolding. *Source*: Public domain.

Figure 30.3. An example annotation that I teach students to revise for clearer/stronger interpretation; see image below for the activity I wrote to teach this stage. *Source:* Courtesy of Esther Schor. Used with permission.

student of literature, that "the research paper" was the genre I needed to learn, and then to teach, in order "to do" academic writing. I was also leery of something I didn't yet have a name for, but what M. Remi Yergeau had already termed "the rhetoric of shininess." Of course, I was wrong. My postdoc helped me shift my goals in this one assignment from teaching students to abide conventions and expectations for an invented genre ("the research paper") to helping students develop research practices—sincere curiosities and sincere inquiries, sometimes about canonical texts, genres, and forms; sometimes not. I've revised this assignment for first-year students—mostly nonmajors—and we do this as a group project in lieu of an extended, researched essay. Throughout the process, we discuss why we're making this kind of project, why in a group, why we're practicing digital writing for audiences beyond the university, how that sharpens our writing, citing, authorial, and editorial practices. It's way easier and way more fun to talk about the integrity of our sources and our citation practices when we are writing for the world, sensitive to our own public-facing identity and integrity as authors and as editors.

Figure 30.4. Interactive edition assignment sheet. *Source*: Created by the author.

Composition & Literature
ESSAY 2 PROMPT: ANNOTATED DIGITAL EDITION

ASSIGNMENT

Throughout the semester we've discussed the importance of close reading, and we've worked on drawing connections between local (specific words, phrases, lines, sentences) and global (afterlives, backgrounds, contexts, definitions, revisions, and big-picture interpretations) foci. We've also discussed the importance of active, or "distracted," reading: looking up references that have multiple meanings and that enrich our understanding of the texts at hand.

For your second project, you'll create an annotated digital edition of a text we've read so far (a single poem or a single short story). Together, you'll demonstrate how your close reading of well selected details helps you to analyze the text as a whole. For this project, you will write a critical introduction (at least 500 words); a series of annotations (at least 8); a bibliography to complement the in-text citations that appear in the critical introduction and the series of annotations; and a rationale (at least 500 words), explaining the rhetorical choices that you make in constructing this research project. By the end of the semester, I'd like us to collate these digital editions in an anthology.

Think of this assignment as a well researched, well developed, if deconstructed, analysis that extends the work of project one: in the critical introduction, you'll forward an argument which you'll support through your annotations. Your annotations will present information (facts, but also clips, definitions, images, maps, and links to useful archival materials) you've collected across your research process that shape your interpretation of this text. Your annotations will, much more importantly, present this information to develop and support the analytical line you present in your critical introduction. In this way, your annotations will work as body paragraphs that help us to understand how you locate your claims about the text in particular lines and the text and in contextual details you've sussed out.

As we'll discuss, writing, especially researched writing, is more often collaborative in professional contexts than it is individual; this is why we're extending the work of peer reviewing to composing and critical making. Moreover, writing, especially researched writing, is something we consume and produce publicly, not privately in papers that shuffle from one student to one professor at the end of a semester, and digitally, not linearly in printed pages numbered from 1 to 10. In this spirit, this assignment is designed to help you translate the skills we've been honing in our writing course to the kinds of projects you'll do in your disciplines and your careers well after English 102. The very things that may make you feel like this research project is beyond your comfort zone are also, then, what I hope will make it most useful to you and, I also hope, more enjoyable than isolated end-of-term writing.

For the last decade, on and off, interactive editions have helped me teach research practices beyond research papers—and to instill confidence in our students to understand writing, especially writing about literature, as acts that help us to claim places at tables and in conversations where they may otherwise feel they do not belong. I try to model this work with my choice of our inspiration text—"The New Colossus"—and its digital afterlives that take immigration as their explicit subject. The creative liberties many of my students take in their choices of texts, and then in their interpretations, demonstrate just how much this landmark poem *still* has to teach us about how to read other poems, song lyrics, documentaries. Students have composed beautiful projects that do anti-racist analysis. Students have also initiated conversations with me and one another about how other sequenced poems in our studies help them to reckon with the experiences of undocumented friends and peers, whose forced absences from our university community feel even scarier in the wake of the Trump administration.

My intention is for our Lazarus- and Schor-inspired projects to strengthen students' sense of belonging in academic forms, genres, and institutions—and to empower and embolden them to question, reimagine, or resist conventions within "ENGL" courses and departments that have been intimidating or even traumatizing. Students' faces light up when they see their writing as critical, creative, imaginative making with an audience beyond our individual course.

Further Reading

"The New Colossus" is Lazarus's most famous poem, and recent criticism shows how it's also an outlier. For exquisite discussions about the poem and teaching, see Cavitch, Eiselein, and Schor. For essays that contextualize "The New Colossus" within Lazarus's turn-of-the-century poetics, see Marom, Zierler, and Wolosky. It's impossible to capture all the conversations and sources about multimodal pedagogy that motivate this assignment. For an inspired and measured discussion on the ups and downs, pluses and minuses of digital writing pedagogy, see Yergeau. For discussion on the place of literature in composition courses/sequences, see Swofford and Kilgore.

Works Cited

Cavitch, Max. "Emma Lazarus and the Golem of Liberty." *The Traffic in Poems: Nineteenth Century Poetry and Transatlantic Exchange*, edited by Meredith L. McGill, Rutgers UP, 2008, pp. 97–122.

Figure 30.5. Interactive edition pre-proposal assignment sheet. *Source*: Created by the author.

Composition & Literature
ESSAY 2 PRE-PROPOSAL: CONNECTING TEXTS & CONTEXTS

THE CLASS AS A WHOLE
- Study some of the annotations in the project that inspires our work: the interactive edition of "The New Colossus" by Esther Schor and nextbook press. Let's close read this:
  - where does Schor's writing demonstrate *research* as we have been defining it? (*getting curious? running down multi-tab rabbit holes?*)
  - what details required sources? what kinds of sources (*information? interpretation? media?*)
  - where does she cite her sourses? where doesn't she?
  - where/how do you think she found stuff?—what search terms do you think she used to find the things she's writing about?
  - what do we do if we don't know what we're looking for? and/or what words, search terms etc. to help us find good rabbit holes?
- How are we transcending our inspiration? more discussion and interpretation!
  - remember that in our annotations, we're building on our work from projects 1 and 2: your goal is to pursue research that enriches your interpretation of the poem; your goal is not just to present information.
  - in each annotation, you'll want to think *first* about your *primary* text (the poem or the story) by putting pressure on what that particular word or phrase or line or sentence means for the text as a whole. how does your research (what you're learning beyond the text) enrich your understanding of the text?
- Zooming in on our inspiration
  - *good examples* from our model: "brazen giant," "sunset gates," "mighty woman," "silent lips," "wretched refuse," "tempest-tost"
  - *not-so-good examples* from our model : "greek," "fame," "torch"
  - notice complexities, even and especially when these blurbs look short or simple

GROUP CHECK IN
1. Share what y'all prepared while writing your homework. Discuss how to apply the process we just practiced together with the starting-point ideas you have assembled as a group.
2. Choose one "pressure point"—a first potential spot for annotation—and imagine how you'd start to develop an interpretation, blending discussion of primary and secondary sources and media. (*You don't need to write your notes here.*)
3. Choose another "pressure point"—a second potential spot for annotation. (*You don't need to write your notes here.*)

If y'all struggle to imagine what to do in your project, look at one of the sample projects we looked at last time, and study some of the annotations.

Next time, we'll craft/draft the proposal. For your homework paragraphs, think about the cinnamon bun metaphor we've been using: as you're writing, your big idea is shaping your discussions of the details and your discussions of the details are shaping the big idea.
1. *primary sources* (the poem or the story): what is the take-home message you're starting to circle around; what spots (details) will you want to linger over to ask/answer your overarching question?
2. *secondary sources*: what kinds of things are y'all going to need to look up? how? where?

Eiselein, Gregory. "Emma Lazarus and Jewish Poetry." *Teaching Nineteenth-Century American Poetry*, edited by Paula Bernat Bennett, Karen L. Kilcup, and Philop Schweighauser, MLA Press, 2007, pp. 151–60.

hooks, bell. *Teaching to Transgress: Education as the Practice of Freedom*. Routledge, 1994.

Lazarus, Emma. *Emma Lazarus: Selected Poems and Other Writings*. Edited by Gregory Eiselein, Broadview, 2002.

Lichtenstein, Diane. "Words and Worlds: Emma Lazarus's Conflicting Citizenships." *Woman and Nation*, special issue of *Tulsa Studies in Women's Literature*, vol. 6, no. 2, 1987, pp. 247–63. *JSTOR*, www.jstor.org/stable/464271.

Marom, Daniel. "Who Is the 'Mother of Exiles'? Jewish Aspects of Emma Lazarus's 'The New Colossus.'" *Prooftexts: A Journal of Jewish Literary History*, vol. 20, no. 3, 2000, pp. 231–61. *Project Muse*, doi.org/10.1353/ptx.2000.0020.

Miller, Cristanne. "Verse Forms." *A History of Nineteenth-Century American Women's Poetry*, edited by Jennifer Putzi and Alexandra Socarides, Cambridge UP, 2017, pp. 298–312.

Omer-Sherman, Ranen. "Emma Lazarus, Jewish American Poetics, and the Challenge of Modernity." *Legacy*, vol. 19, no. 2, 2002, pp. 170–91. *Project Muse*, doi.org/10.1353/leg.2003.0033.

Schor, Esther. *Emma Lazarus*. Schocken, 2006.

Swofford, Sarah and Robert Kilgore. "We Need to Talk: Making Writing and Literature Work for the Future." *ADE Bulletin*, vol. 158, 2020, pp. 45–58. doi.org/10.1632/ade.158.45.

Wolosky, Shira. "Emma Lazarus Transnational." *A History of Nineteenth-Century American Women's Poetry*, edited by Jennifer Putzi and Alexandra Socarides, Cambridge UP, 2017, pp. 390–405.

Yergeau, M. Remi. *Disabling Composition: Toward a 21st-Century, Synaesthetic Theory of Writing*. 2011. U of Michigan, PhD dissertation.

Zierler, Wendy. "The Making and Re-making of Jewish-American Literary History." *Shofar: An Interdisciplinary Journal of Jewish Studies*, vol. 27, no. 2, 2009, pp. 69–101. *Project Muse*, doi.org/10.1353/sho.0.0225.

31

Student Research, Digital Humanities, and Cross-Campus Collaboration

Building *Mina Loy: Navigating the Avant-Garde*

Susan Rosenbaum, Suzanne W. Churchill,
and Linda A. Kinnahan

Feminist Designs: Project Overview and Pedagogical Aims

Artist, poet, feminist, entrepreneur, inventor, and world traveler, Mina Loy consorted with nearly every European avant-garde movement, including Futurism, Dada, and Surrealism, but was contained by none. *Mina Loy: Navigating the Avant-Garde* (mina-loy.com) charts Mina Loy's avant-garde migrations through digital scholarly narratives and visualizations that contextualize and interpret her writing, visual art, and designs. The published website is the digital equivalent of a multimedia scholarly book, an open educational resource authored by students, staff, and faculty at Davidson College, Duquesne University, and the University of Georgia (UGA), and peer reviewed by an advisory board that comprises modernist scholars and digital humanists from across the US, Canada, and the UK. The website was completed in March 2020, the culmination of a five-year collaboration supported by a Digital Humanities Advancement Grant from the National Endowment for the Humanities. Its pedagogical dimensions may not be immediately visible to users because they are built into the feminist design and content of the site—an essential dimension of its experimental, collaborative ethos.

The project originated as an experiment in feminist digital humanities scholarship and pedagogy that involved undergraduate and graduate students in transforming scholarly methods and products, and in testing new processes for peer review and cross-institutional collaboration. Inspired by Mina Loy's feminist innovations, we approached this digital platform guided by principles of feminist design, which for us involves embracing style and aesthetics as crucial to the work of digital humanities, rather than dismissing them as insufficiently tech-y or rigorous. Feminist design also entails reinventing our scholarly methods in order to break down hierarchies, encourage open exchanges of expertise, reflect the diversity of human creative production, and make information accessible to a broad population.

In developing our multifaceted project, we treated students as equal partners in literary research using digital humanities (DH) methods. This approach allowed us to try out new tools together and to learn with and from our students, with librarians and instructional technologists working as essential collaborators. Students contributed not only to the site design but also developed scholarly content, including submitting their work to a process of peer review and editing. Their final work is displayed on the site on equal footing with contributions of faculty and independent scholars. In keeping with the UCLA Student Collaborators' Bill of Rights, all students earned course credit for their projects, received payment for work that did not receive course credit, and were given a choice to have their names listed on the platform or to remain anonymous.

Our aim was not to create a comprehensive digital archive or an open-source wiki but to provide a curated, multimedia, interactive platform for accessing and understanding Loy's writing, artwork, and career. The need for such a platform was clear to us as scholars and teachers of Mina Loy. Her work is difficult, especially when first encountered: her experimental writing, typified by radically new uses of language, typography, and page space, garnered attention for its bold feminism and innovative forms, often activated by encounters with visual culture. Her visual art is stylistically diverse and strikingly original, but remains largely unknown. In addition to the challenges of understanding Loy's work, Loy's career took many twists and turns, geographical as well as artistic. The difficulty of accessing her work, much of it buried in archives and private collections, compounds the challenge of tracing her career and contextualizing her artwork.

Thus, in designing our scholarly site, we wanted to teach our students close reading and research skills that could help them to analyze, contextualize, and ultimately gain a clearer understanding of Mina Loy's writing, designs, and visual art. But we also wanted to give them the opportunity to explore new ways of reading Loy's works closely on a digital platform, rendering the practice more interactive and embedded in social, material, and historical contexts. To involve students as collaborators in creating the design and content for the site, we worked with librarians and DH specialists at each of our institutions to introduce the students to the multimodal digital tools that could help them to (1) engage Loy's verbal and visual work in innovative ways, (2) narrate, contextualize, and visualize the locations and timeline of Loy's peripatetic career on the margins of the avant-garde, and (3) explore, analyze, and adopt/adapt experimental strategies used by Loy and related figures.

Student Research

Students (undergraduate and graduate) are capable of innovative, original research. Yet even in an era of flipped classrooms, the dominant model of learning remains top-down and hierarchical, perhaps even more in the production of humanities research than in the classroom. Students are invited to do interesting work, but often within a framework established by the professor. There is good reason for this scaffolding, because the professor often has knowledge, training, and experience that students lack. But what if the professor doesn't know exactly where their research will go or how they will present it? What if they are working in a new medium, one constantly shifting as technologies change? What if their project would benefit from a team of student researchers? In this regard, it is not a drawback to lack knowledge, training, and experience, because students may have skills and expertise that benefit the project at hand. To design the Mina Loy platform, we had to figure out ways to help students explore and implement DH tools we did not fully understand ourselves, collaborating with librarians and instructional technologists as intellectual partners. Our lack of expertise often enabled us to learn with and from our students.

For instance, at the start of the project, Suzanne Churchill turned the question of which platform to use for the website into a pedagogical inquiry. In June 2015, Davidson College student Andrew Rikard, supported by a Davidson College Summer Research Fellowship, created a Drupal prototype for the website. Churchill and Rikard brought the project to ILiADS, the Institute for Liberal Arts Digital Scholarship at Hamilton College, and Rikard and the team presented both Drupal and WordPress prototypes at the Modernist Studies Association's first Digital Exhibition in 2015. Rikard's research was essential to the team's choice of the WordPress platform, both for ease of use and visual design elements.

Over the years of the grant project, we designed a number of cross-institutional and individual pedagogical projects, adapting them to the subject matter of our classes and to the interests and expertise of our students. We coordinated projects across our institutions when possible, and consulted with the other team members about our students' independent research projects, which are included under a section of the website titled "New Frequencies" (mina-loy.com/new-frequencies). Students who completed research projects created maps, 3D animations, games, lexicons, galleries, and e-commerce sites to promote engagement with Loy's poetry, artwork, and designs. Inspired by digital annotations of T. S. Eliot's *The Waste Land* (1922), students created digital annotations of Loy's "Songs to Joannes" (1917) and of Loy's appearance in *View* magazine (1945). They created contextual resources for related female modernists Mabel Dodge Luhan, Frances Simpson Stevens, and Georgia Douglas Johnson. At the end of the project, Duquesne PhD students Jesse Jack and Rochel Gosson synthesized the platform's scholarly content in visual form, creating an interactive map of Loy's migrations (Jack) and timelines that correspond to the different stages and places of Loy's life and career (Gosson).

Our key cross-institutional pedagogical effort centered on researching and visualizing Loy's social and artistic network, an effort we dubbed the "Biography Project." During fall 2017, each of us taught a course relevant to mina-loy.com, giving us an opportunity to pilot the Biography Project, in collaboration with digital librarians (Emily McGinn, UGA; Sundi Richard, Davidson; Gesina Phillips, Duquesne) and research librarians (Kristin Nielsen, UGA; James Sponsel, Davidson; Gesina Phillips, Duquesne) at our respective schools. Students at Davidson, Duquesne, and UGA researched and wrote short biographies of figures associated with the historical avant-garde (chiefly Dada, Futurism, and Surrealism) who were connected to Loy in Florence, New York, and Paris. In fall 2018, Linda and Susan resumed the cross-institutional project with students in their graduate seminars on modernism and the avant-garde (mina-loy.com/bio-project-assignment).

We established and followed a shared template for the biographies that asked students to summarize each figure's career and relationship to Loy, and to evaluate that relationship with a digital humanities project in mind. Students worked with research librarians to find relevant sources and to create annotated bibliographies of their sources. In workshops conducted by digital librarians at each school, students considered the technical and conceptual particularities of gathering and "cleaning" data, writing for a digital platform, and conducting peer review through the free web app for collaborative annotation, hypothes.is (web.hypothes.is). Once the students had completed the research and writing of their figure's biography, they learned how to enter information from the biography template into a Google spreadsheet using a Data Dictionary created by Dr. Emily McGinn. An exciting outcome of this data collection was the generation of visualizations of Loy's social-artistic networks in Florence, New York, and Paris. Emily McGinn and Caleb Crumley created a final visualization of this data for mina-loy.com using a program called Cytoscape (mina-loy.com/maps/loys-social-network). This visualization concretizes how the Biography project helped our students to envision a new literary history of the modernist avant-garde with Loy at its center rather than at its margins.

A related experiment with feminist pedagogy was our effort to involve students, scholars, artists, writers and the interested public in the flash mob formation of a feminist theory of the avant-garde, or what we call the *en dehors garde*, a term we adopted from ballet ("en dehors" means "toward the outside" or "turning outward") to describe the strategies of writers and artists whose modes of experimentation do not conform to the martialized, oppositional stance associated with the historical avant-garde. Rather than assuming a militant position at the forefront of culture, women, people of color, queer, and disabled artists often came from the outside and circulated on the margins. They rarely enjoyed the power, privilege, or authority derived from membership in art institutions, or even in the countercultural, avant-garde circles that challenged those institutions. Instead, they worked and moved strategically to transform gendered, racialized literary traditions and visual cultures that excluded or objectified them (mina-loy.com/chapters/avant-garde-theory-2/the-en-dehors-garde).

Seeking to generate theory in a new, collaborative way, and building on Kathleen Fitzpatrick's recent call for "generous thinking" in the humanities, we asked contributors to "think with" us and participate in the ongoing work of reimagining the historical avant-garde as a more inclusive en dehors garde. Davidson Research Initiative (DRI) award winners Leah Mell and Mahalia Cooks helped us orchestrate a digital flash mob in summer 2018, using social media to invite scholars, students, artists, writers, and the interested public to submit digital post(card)s expressing their ideas about the en dehors garde (mina-loy.com/flashmob-invitation). We called the submissions "post(card)s" to reference the history of the picture postcard as an informal, occasional form incorporating both visual and verbal media, and to build upon the precedent of the *Postcards* forum established in 1983 by the feminist journal *How(ever)*. We invited contributors to "Compose your digital post(card) as a short break, time for reflection, gesture, speculative inquiry, or unpolished foray amidst whatever activities your summer day contains." Contributors could sign their names, adopt pseudonyms, or remain anonymous, and no prerequisites or qualifications were required (for more information, see mina-loy.com/chapters/avant-garde-theory-2/digital-flash-mob). We received many postcards from students at our institutions and farther afield, with scholars at other institutions such as Dr. Amanda Golden (NY Institute of Technology) encouraging their students to submit.

The post(card)s we received are displayed in a random grid (mina-loy.com/endehorsgarde). Users can read, select, and arrange the post(card)s to compile their own, customized theory of the en dehors garde, exporting the results as a PDF. In this way, students and the interested public can participate in the ongoing production of feminist theory, rendering it a plural, elastic, collaborative, multifaceted, and ongoing process. Although we haven't designed assignments around the post(card)s, we can imagine a number of ways to facilitate student interaction with them, including designing new post(card)s, articulating why particular cards resonated, or choosing a sequence of cards and tracing a problem, theme, or practice of theory that emerges in the sequence.

Peer Review and Website Use and Preservation

The success of student projects depended on the systems of editing and peer review that we implemented. These were essential to making sure that student work upheld high standards for scholarly accuracy, clarity, and integrity. As much as students have to offer and teach us, they may also produce work that doesn't meet scholarly standards of accuracy, citation, or accessibility. And once they've completed a course or graduated, they may have little incentive to revise or correct their work. A key question in projects like mina-loy.com is how to strike a balance between giving students the freedom to explore, invent, and design while also making sure they research thoroughly, represent accurately, cite adequately, and uphold accessibility standards, within the constraints of a summer or semester.

In designing and overseeing student research projects, we set up systems of peer review, in which undergraduates evaluated each other's work, graduate students vetted and edited undergraduate work, and the faculty PIs reviewed and commented on both undergraduate and graduate student projects. For instance, in the Biography project, we had students complete peer reviews of at least two biographies authored by students from other schools, using the open access web annotation tool hypothes.is. Students undertook revisions after each round of peer review, with the goal of producing a succinct (five hundred word), clear, and well-researched biography. These biographies also received grades and faculty feedback. Once the biographies were completed for class, three graduate students at Duquesne (John Hadlock, English PhD; Rochel Gasson, English PhD; Taylor Maldonado, English MA) undertook final editing and uploading of each figure's biography to the website's "Bios" page. For instructors interested in similar projects, we recommend having students sign release forms or agree to give editorial access, so that edits can be made to their work prior to publication.

Since completion in April 2020, the website has been hosted and maintained through the UGA libraries. We regularly use the website in our own teaching at Duquesne, Davidson, and UGA, and many faculty at other institutions report incorporating the site into their courses. On average the site receives 2500 views per month. The site has been recognized by both the American Studies Association (Honorable Mention, Garfinkel Prize 2021) and the MLA (MLA Prize for Collaborative, Bibliographical, or Archival Scholarship, 2022), indicating that the platform's innovative approach to both teaching and research has been recognized by the academy. We have shared our WordPress "DH Scholarship Theme" and site documentation in an open GitHub repository, so that scholars can use and adapt our model for other DH projects, and know of at least one project (Dr. Sophie Oliver's in-process website and exhibition of modernist women's poetry and fashion at University of Liverpool) that has taken inspiration from mina-loy.com.

Mina Loy: Navigating the Avant-Garde demonstrates both the possibilities and risks of using digital tools in humanities scholarship. On the one hand, the project demonstrates how digital tools can transform humanities scholarship and pedagogy from the traditional model of a lone scholar writing a monograph to a team of researchers, including student researchers, collaborating on a "multigraph"—an interactive, multiauthored, multimodal resource that sets UX design standards for DH scholarship. On the other hand, a risk of digital projects, which we encountered with WordPress, is the continual updating and eventual obsolescence of digital platforms, themes, and plugins. Due to this challenge, in consultation with the UGA DigiLab, we decided in fall 2022 to convert our WordPress site to HTML, resulting in a more permanent and stable digital platform to extend the longevity of the digital project, albeit with some reduced functionality (for example, the post[card] grid no longer displays randomly or generates a PDF).

While we have worked to extend the life of mina-loy.com, we have simultaneously decided to remediate the "Scholarly Baedeker" portion of the website to a more permanent print and digital form. Our DH experiment has demonstrated to us the enduring value of the book form, even as that form has been reimagined. Fortunately, alongside our efforts to rethink the book in our digital multigraph, the academic publishing industry has also adapted its understanding of the book to the digital age. We have decided to partner with Lever Press, an innovative press associated dedicated to publishing open-access monographs with print-on-demand capabilities, to publish our scholarly book on Loy's navigation of Futurism, Dada, and Surrealism under the title *Travels with Mina Loy: Navigating the Avant-Garde*, accompanied by a number of illustrations from mina-loy.com. The print companion will ideally function as a kind of handheld Baedeker or guide for students and other readers who wish to access the scholarly book in a portable, easily accessible form, while the open-access online version will house our scholarly book in a more permanent, academically supported forum. With its form adapting to changing material circumstances, much like the artist and poet it chronicles, we hope that *Mina Loy: Navigating the Avant-Garde* will inspire similar projects involving feminist poetry pedagogy.

Further Reading

An excellent introduction to DH is *Digital-Humanities* by Anne Burdick, Johanna Drucker, Peter Lunenfeld, Todd Presner, and Jeffrey Schnapp (MIT Press, 2012).

We have published a discussion of mina-loy.com in a digital handbook that provides essential steps needed to plan a digital project: Churchill, S., Kinnahan, L., and Rosenbaum, S. " 'Mina Loy: Navigating the Avant-Garde': a case study of collaborative DH design." *Visualizing Objects, Places, and Spaces: A Digital Project Handbook* (2021), doi.org/10.21428/51bee781.4a3e9679.

Feminist design inspiration from the academic arena comes from the innovative digital scholarship of Shawna Ross, Whitney Trettien, Amanda Visconti, and Lauren Klein. Marrying challenging content and disruptive visual formatting, Ross's Manifesto of Modernist Digital Humanities asks, "WHAT would a methodological modernism look like?" She visually draws attention to matters of style, insisting they are worthy of "attention and curiosity." Trettien's digital journal *Thresholds* uses split-screen architecture to embody the entanglement of texts and ideas that is the essence of critical reading and writing (openthresholds.org/home). Her Master's thesis, "Computers, Cut-ups, & Combinatory Volvelles" provided design inspiration for generating scholarly arguments and theory in nonlinear, participatory frameworks, while Lauren Klein's *Speculative Designs* informs our reader-interactive approach to the theory of the en dehors garde. Visconti's *Infinite Ulysses* offers a dynamic, engaging, intuitively navigable site that invites users to annotate and interpret James Joyce's *Ulysses*, offering a new model for interactive close reading.

Works Cited

Christie, Alex, and Andrew Pilsch, Shawna Ross, and Katie Tanagawa. "Manifesto of Modernist Digital Humanities." 11 Oct. 2016, www.shawnaross.com/manifesto.

Fitzpatrick, Kathleen. "Generous Thinking: The University and the Public Good—Planned Obsolescence." generousthinking.hcommons.org, 2018.

Klein, Lauren F. "Data by Design." 16 Aug. 2017, lklein.com/data-by-design.

———, and Catherine D'Ignazio. *Data Feminism*. MIT Press, 2020.

Trettien, Whitney. COMPUTERS, CUT-UPS, AND COMBINATORY VOLVELLES. www.whitneyannetrettien.com/thesis/#thesis.

Visconti, Amanda. "Infinite Ulysses." infiniteulysses.com.

Contributors

Reem Abbas of Jesus College, Cambridge, is a poet and literary critic currently working on classical Persian influences in the poetry of Basil Bunting. Her essay "A 'Polyphonic Score': Basil Bunting's Persian Condensations" won the 2022 Review of English Studies Essay Prize. Her poetry was shortlisted for the 2023 White Review Poet's Prize and she was a 2021 "Undertow" poet at the Poetry Translation Centre.

Mollie Barnes is Associate Professor of English at the University of South Carolina Beaufort. She's published a dozen articles and chapters on nineteenth-century women writers. Her forthcoming book—*Paper Heroines: How Women Reformers Wrote One Another's Lives in the Sea Islands, 1838–1902*—studies lowcountry women's diaries and biographies, focusing on the intersection of race and gender.

Esther G. Belin is the author of two poetry books and co-editor of *The Diné Reader*. She teaches in the Native American and Indigenous Studies department at Fort Lewis College, and the low-residency MFA in Creative Writing program at the Institute of American Indian Arts. She was raised in the Los Angeles area where she learned to transplant and strengthen her Diné worldview with the help of her parents and the resilient Indian community that remains there. She is Tłógí born for Tódích'ii'nii and lives just east of the Dibé Ntsaa mountain range on the Colorado side of the four corners.

Monique-Adelle Callahan D. is Associate Professor of English and Chair of the English Department at Emmanuel College. Her poems and translations appear in a number of journals and anthologies including *Beloit Poetry Journal, Transition Magazine, Tupelo Quarterly, Obsidian,* and *Bayou Magazine*, and her poetry collection *Anonymous* was winner of the New Voices Award. She is the author of *Between the Lines: Literary Transnationalism and African American Poetics*.

Chris Chan is Associate Director of Graduate Studies for the Department of English at the University of Pennsylvania. Prior to this role, he completed a Postdoctoral Research Fellowship at Ghent University (Belgium), and he earned his PhD in English from Penn. His scholarship has been published in *Eighteenth-Century Studies* and *Eighteenth-Century Life*.

Victoria Chang is an American poet, writer, editor, and critic. Her latest book of poems is *With My Back to the World* (2024). She has received a Guggenheim Fellowship and other awards. She is the Bourne Chair in Poetry at Georgia Tech and the Director of Poetry@Tech.

Mike Chasar is the author of *Poetry Unbound: Poems and New Media from the Magic Lantern to Instagram* (2020) and *Everyday Reading: Poetry and Popular Culture in Modern America* (2012) and the co-editor, with Heidi R. Bean, of *Poetry after Cultural Studies* (2011). A Professor of English at Willamette University in Salem, Oregon, he is currently editing *The Poetry of Bob Dylan*, a collection that will feature thirty essays by thirty poetry scholars on thirty different songs by Dylan.

Annelise Chick earned her PhD in English at the University of Georgia, where her teaching and research examined eighteenth- and nineteenth-century British literature as a site for investigating agency, materiality, and unlikely intersections of the two. She currently serves as the Scholarships and Public Relations Coordinator for the Office of University Experiential Learning at the University of Georgia.

Philippa Chun earned her PhD from the Department of Literatures in English at Cornell University in 2023. She examines representations of the dead body in nineteenth-century American literature and scientific writing. She is also interested in the utopian possibilities, and limitations, of feminism and female desire under late-stage capitalism. She has taught at Cornell, Johns Hopkins University, and Rowan University.

Suzanne W. Churchill is Professor of English at Davidson College. She is the author of *The Little Magazine* Others *& the Renovation of Modern*

American Poetry (2006); co-editor, with Adam McKible, of *Little Magazines & Modernism: new approaches* (2007); and author and illustrator of the children's book *Dinosaurs Drive Firetrucks* (2018). She has published on modernism and the Harlem Renaissance, and on periodicals, poetry, and pedagogy in various journals and collections. Founder and editor of the website *Index of Modernist Magazines* (modernistmagazines.org), she is co-creator of the award-winning, open-access, online scholarly book *Mina Loy: Navigating the Avant-Garde* (mina-loy.com) and is developing a scholarly website on Gwendolyn Bennett.

William Fogarty is Associate Professor of English at the University of Central Florida where he teaches literature of the twentieth and twenty-first centuries, focusing mostly on poetry. His book, *The Politics of Speech in Later Twentieth-Century Poetry: Local Tongues in Heaney, Brooks, Harrison, and Clifton* (2022), examines the social, political, and ethical dynamics of English-language poems made from various forms of local speech.

Caroline Gelmi is Associate Professor of English and Communication at the University of Massachusetts, Dartmouth. Her essays have appeared in *Nineteenth-Century Literature*, *J19: The Journal of Nineteenth-Century Americanists*, *The Space Between: Literature and Culture, 1914–1945*, *Journal of Modern Literature*, and *Western American Literature*. She is currently writing a history of the poetic speaker central to scholarly reading practices.

Toni Gennrich, PhD, has lectured in Education at the University of the Witwatersrand and Media Studies at Nelson Mandela University. Her interest is in literacy and teacher identity. She has developed materials for a range of media platforms. She is a member of the South African Poetry Project (ZAPP) and the Global Story Bridges Project.

Jess A. Goldberg (they/them) is Assistant Professor of English and Co-Director of Gender & Women's Studies at New Mexico Highlands University. They are the author of *Abolition Time: Grammars of Law, Poetics of Justice* and co-editor of *Queer Fire: Liberation and Abolition*, a special issue of the journal *GLQ*. Previously, they taught at Longwood University and have worked with the Penn State Restorative Justice Initiative and the Cornell Prison Education Program. Their most recent academic writing has been published in the journals *Women's Studies Quarterly*, *ASAP/Journal*, *College Literature*, *Women's Studies*, and *Public Culture*, as well as in the edited collections *Teaching Literature and Writing in Prisons*; *The Routledge Handbook of CoFuturisms*; and *Against a Sharp White Background: Infrastructures of African American Print*.

Rachel B. Griffis is an Associate Professor of English at Spring Arbor University, where she teaches literature and writing courses. She is a co-author of *Deep Reading: Practices to Subvert the Vices of Our Distracted, Hostile, and Consumeristic Age* (2024), and her writing has appeared in *Literature & Theology*, *Studies in American Indian Literatures*, *Nathaniel Hawthorne Review*, *The Cormac McCarthy Journal*, *Religions*, *Women's Studies: An Interdisciplinary Journal*, and *Teaching American Literature*.

Leah Huizar is a poet and writer. Her creative work and research centers on the cultural and historic landscape of the West Coast and the ways in which gender, religion, and colonization have shaped it. Her first book of poems, *Inland Empire*, was published in 2019. She is an Associate Professor of English at Drake University.

Erin Kappeler is an English professor turned instructional designer. Her book, *The Enclosures of Free Verse: Racializing Poetic Form in the Modernist Era*, which tells the forgotten story of how free verse was imagined as the expression of a white American race at the turn of the twentieth century, is forthcoming. As part of the Academic Innovation and Distance Education team at Bunker Hill Community College, she works with faculty members to improve student outcomes in web-based and hybrid courses.

Linda A. Kinnahan is Professor Emerita of English at Duquesne University in Pittsburgh. She is editor of the *Cambridge History of 20th Century American Women's Poetry* (2016), and the author of *Mina Loy, Photography, and Contemporary Women Poets* (2017). She has published on modernist and contemporary poetry, including *Poetics of the Feminine: Literary Tradition and Authority in William Carlos Williams, Mina Loy, Denise Levertov, and Kathleen Fraser* (1994) and *Lyric Interventions: Feminist Experimental Poetry and Contemporary Social Discourse* (2004). With Suzanne Churchill and Susan Rosenbaum, she is co-creator of the digital humanities project "Mina Loy: Navigating the Avant-Garde"; and co-author of the digital book *Mina Loy: Scholarly Book for Digital Travelers* and its forthcoming print companion, *Travels With Mina Loy*.

Michael Leong is the author of the critical study *Contested Records: The Turn to Documents in Contemporary North American Poetry* (2020) and numerous poetry books, most recently *Dear Vase Already Shattered Against the Fragile Floor* (2025). He is Robert P. Hubbard Assistant Professor of Poetry at Kenyon College.

Lizzy LeRud teaches in the Robert D. Clark Honors College at the University of Oregon. She has held the NEH Postdoctoral Fellowship in Poetics at the Bill and Carol Fox Center for Humanistic Inquiry and a Marion L. Brittain Postdoctoral Fellowship at Georgia Tech University. Her essays on American poetry appear in *Contemporary Literature, Genre, Nineteenth-Century Prose, Tulsa Studies in Women's Literature*, and *The Poetry Foundation* website.

Joe Lockard is Associate Professor of English at Arizona State University. He teaches American and African American literature and taught poetry workshops for a decade at Florence State Prison. His recent publications include *STEM Education in US Prisons* (2024, with Tsafrir Mor), *Louis Owens: Writing Land and Legacy* (2019, with A. Robert Lee), *Prison Pedagogies: Learning and Teaching with Imprisoned Writers* (2018, with Sherry Rankins-Robertson), and three volumes of the translated literature of US slavery with Shih Penglu.

James Innis McDougall received his PhD from the University of Florida and is currently serving as an Associate Professor of English at Wenzhou-Kean University in Zhejiang, China. His current research examines cultures of the transpacific with a special focus on experimentation with poetic form and ideas of cultural syncretism in early twentieth-century Chinese poetry. He has published scholarly work on poetry, modernism, food culture, higher education, and globalization.

Lukas Moe is Visiting Lecturer in the Writing Program at Wellesley College. He is writing a study of poetry in the United States from the Depression era to Civil Rights, which traces the role of poetic modernism in the emergence of a postwar multiracial avant-garde.

Sooriagandhi Naidoo is a retired educator with an Honours degree in Applied Linguistics. She has taught English at the Transvaal College of Education, Tshwane University of Technology, University of South Africa, and University of the Witwatersrand. Her interest is in border pedagogy and curriculum development. She is a member of the English Language Project (UNISA) and an ex-member of the South African Poetry Project (ZAPP).

Sarah Nance is Associate Professor in the Department of English & Fine Arts at the United States Air Force Academy. Her essays on poetry have appeared in venues such as *Arizona Quarterly*, the *Journal of Literary & Cultural Disability Studies*, and *Literature and Medicine*. She is currently working on a book about the temporality of memorialization in twentieth- and twenty-first-century poetics.

Anastasia Nikolis, PhD, is an Assistant Professor of English at St. John Fisher University. Her academic research focuses on intimacy and confession in post-1945 American poetry, with special interest in poetry and the public humanities. In her creative writing, she explores the intersections of visual art, place, and the body.

Eunice Phiri is a retired English teacher and Head of the English Department, Walmansthal High School, Soshanguve. She holds a master's degree in English Education and is currently working towards a PhD focusing on the poetry club anthology produced by learners. She is a member of the South African Poetry Project (ZAPP).

Candis Pizzetta is Professor of English and director of the Jackson State University Faculty Development Center. She serves as the general editor of *The Researcher: An Interdisciplinary Journal* and as director of the JSU Virtual Proposal Development Center, which works to train faculty grant writers at HBCUs.

Dean Rader has authored or co-authored twelve books, including *Self-Portrait as Wikipedia Entry*, *Landscape Portrait Figure Form*, named a Barnes & Noble Best Book, and *Works & Days*, which won the T. S. Eliot Prize. *Before the Borderless: Dialogues with the Art of Cy Twombly* appeared in 2023. He is a professor at the University of San Francisco and a 2019 Guggenheim Fellow in Poetry.

Susan Rosenbaum is Associate Professor of English at the University of Georgia, where she teaches courses in twentieth-century American literature, modernism, and poetry/poetics, and co-directs the Interdisciplinary Modernisms Workshop. She is the author of *Professing Sincerity: Modern*

Lyric Poetry, Commercial Culture, and the Crisis in Reading (2007), and with Linda Kinnahan and Suzanne Churchill, co-author of the digital scholarly website *Mina Loy: Navigating the Avant-Garde* (2020), and its print companion *Travels With Mina Loy*. She is collaborating on a book about Elizabeth Bishop and visual media, and is completing a monograph titled *Imaginary Museums: Surrealism, American Poetry, and the Visual Arts, 1920–1970*. Her essays have appeared in *Dada/Surrealism*, *Genre*, *Journal of Modern Literature*, and *Studies in Romanticism*.

Kenneth Sherwood has published critical articles on poetry, orality, and performance. Co-director of the Center for Digital Humanities and Culture and Professor in the Literature and Criticism graduate program at Indiana University of Pennsylvania, he edited *A Useful Art* (2003) and has published print and digital poems including *Code of Signals* (2017) and "Coal Code" (2022).

Jake Skeets is the author of *Eyes Bottle Dark with a Mouthful of Flowers*, winner of the National Poetry Series, Kate Tufts Discovery Award, American Book Award, and Whiting Award. He is from the Navajo Nation and teaches at the University of Oklahoma.

Eileen Sperry's research focuses on early modern English literature, poetics, and disability studies. Her book, *This Body of Death—Form and Decay in Early Modern Lyric*, is forthcoming. Her work has also appeared in *Cambridge Quarterly*, *Studies in English Literature 1500–1900*, *The Sixteenth Century Journal*, and *Shakespeare Bulletin*. She is currently a Visiting Assistant Professor at Skidmore College.

Ronnie K. Stephens is an Assistant Professor for a two-year college in Texas. He is presently pursuing a PhD in English with a focus on transgressive teaching and poetry as a site of activism in the twenty-first-century classroom. Stephens is also a staff reviewer for *The Poetry Question*.

Nick Sturm is the editor of *Early Works* by Alice Notley and co-editor of *Get the Money!: Collected Prose, 1961–1983* by Ted Berrigan. His work has been published at *Poetry Foundation*, *The Brooklyn Rail*, *Jacket2*, *Chicago Review*, *ASAP/J*, *Women's Studies*, and *Post45*. He is currently a Lecturer in English at Georgia State University. More information about his research, scholarship, and teaching can be found at nicksturm.com.

Anton Vander Zee teaches at the College of Charleston. His co-edited collection, *A Broken Thing: Poets on the Line*, was published in 2011. He has published widely on matters of poetry and poetics in *Modern Philology*, *Whitman Studies*, *ESQ*, *AGNI*, *Resources for American Literary Study*, and elsewhere.

Gabrielle Stecher Woodward (PhD, University of Georgia), is a Lecturer and Associate Director of Undergraduate Teaching in the Department of English at Indiana University Bloomington, where she teaches composition and intensive writing literature courses. Her research and teaching interests include the stories we tell about women artists and their creative labor, as well as the reception of antiquity and nineteenth-century British literature and visual culture.

Heather H. Yeung (楊希蒂) is Reader in Literature at the University of Dundee, and currently chairs the Literature scholarships and discipline+ catalyst for the Scottish Graduate School for Arts and Humanities. She is the author of *Spatial Engagement with Poetry* (2015) and *On Literary Plasticity* (2020), and is also an artist, book maker, and poet, and the archives of this work are held at the Scottish Poetry Library and the National Library of Scotland.

Index

Abbas, Reem, 4
abecedary, 239–42
A Country without a Post Office (Ali), 241
Adorno, Theodor, 219
Ahmed, Sara, 28
Alcheringa digital archive, 147–48, 149, 150
Alcheringa/Ethnopoetics journal, 152–53
Alexander, Elizabeth, 88
Ali, Agha Shahid, 241
alphabet (Christensen), 246–48, 249, 251
"America" (McKay), 74–75
The American Rhythm (Austin), 51–52
American Sonnets, 196–98, 199–200
American Sonnets for My Past and Future Assassin (Hayes), 75
"An Arc Still Open" (Thomas), 114, 115
Andersen, Hans Christian, 140
Andrews, Kimberly Quiogue, 195–96
Anglo-Saxons, 32
annotations, 50, 139, 232–33, 253, 257, 259, 268
anti-colonial pedagogy, 3, 16, 20, 154
anti-oppressive pedagogy: activities for, 5–6; author's overview of, 3;
further reading, 8–9, 108, 193, 200. *See also* Dinétics (Diné poetics)
anti-racist pedagogy: author's overview of, 158; enjoyment, reading poetry for, 173–77; oral poetries, 145–46; scaffolding, 255–56; slavery, teaching poetry about, 158–64; "We Real Cool," 88–91
antislavery poetry, 96–99, 99–101
Anzaldúa, Gloria, 4, 104–5, 213
apartheid, 203, 204–5
A Poet's Glossary (Hirsch), 41
architectural scaffolding, 257, 258
"Are These the Poems to Remember?," 229
Arujo, Carolina, 127
asked what has changed (Roberson), 131
"A Son's Return" (Brown), 184
assessment/grading of poetry, 14–15, 18–19, 128, 130, 204
Astrophil and Stella (Sidney), 44
Austin, Mary, 32, 49, 51–52
avant-garde, 36, 265, 267, 269–70
"A Vision of the End" (Too-qua-stee), 35–36

Baartmen, Sarah, 205, 206
banking concept of education, 204, 207

Barnes, Mollie, 6
beauty, 13, 18, 21, 139, 240, 257
Belin, Esther G., 3, 13–20
Berry, Wendell, 177
Bianca, or, the Spanish Maiden (Dutt), 56–59
Bicknell, John, 99
Biggers, John T., 115
Black poets: double consciousness, 130, 180; empathetic praxis, 131–32; Harlem Renaissance poets, 72, 180, 181, 183; lyric performance, 111–12, 113, 114, 115; paired texts of, teaching poetry with, 168–71. *See also* poets of color
Bloom, Harold, 88, 90
Borderlands (Anzaldúa), 104, 213
breaks: caesura, 39–45, 66; study of, 69, 169–70
breath, 20, 41, 42–43
The Bridge (Crane), 241
Brooks, Cleanth, 49, 113
Brooks, Gwendolyn: "In the Mecca," 241; "kitchenette building," 255, 257; "Riot," 81; "We Real Cool," 4, 87–91, 175
Brown, Hayley, 153
Brown, Jericho, 76
Brown, Kirby, 34
Brown, Sterling, 180, 184
Buffington, Paige, 15
Burch, Susan, 192

"Cabaret" (White), 139
Cabot, John, 81–82
caesura, 39–45, 66
Cain, Mary Ann, 195
Callahan D., Monique Adelle, 4–5
capital punishment, 217, 218, 223n2
Cárdenas, Brenda, 106
carpe diem poem, 175
Cecire, Natalia, 34

Chan, Chris, 4, 5
Chang, Victoria, 6, 227, 228–29, 232–33, 234–35
Charles, Jos, 83–84
Chasar, Mike, 4
Chick, Annelise, 4
Christensen, Inger, 246–47, 251
Chun, Philippa, 5
Churchill, Suzanne, 6, 267–68
Citizen (Rankine), 119, 121
"City, State, and Self," 239–40
Clark, Tiana, 168, 169–70, 171
Clifton, Lucille, 80–81
Coleman, Wanda, 196–200
collaborative projects: author's overview of, 237; digital archives, 265–72; further reading, 235, 242–43; poetry book, class, 238–42; reviews, 227, 233–35; scholarly wiki, 152, 154; team-teaching, 48–52, 135, 136–41
Collins, Billy, 24, 173
colonialism: anti-colonial pedagogy, 3, 16, 20, 154; caesura, and, 42–43; impacts of, 19–20; language, and, 15, 233; lyric I, 121; poetry, impact of on teaching, 3, 15–16, 203–4; settler colonialism, 16, 36
color. *See* poets of color; students of color; women of color
community-engaged pedagogy, 17–19
"Conceptualisms in Crisis" (Leong), 181
confessional approach, 119, 120, 122
"Conversation with Phillis Wheatley" (Clark), 168, 169–70, 171
Cowper, William, 97–98
craft: exclusionary, as, 2, 23–24, 26–27, 28, 29n1, 230; poem, of a, 196, 198; the term *craft*, 23, 232. *See also* post-craft
Craft in the Real World (Salesses), 23

Crane, Hart, 241
Crashaw, Richard, 189, 191
critical thinking, 5, 195, 207, 229. See also New Criticism
Crumley, Caleb, 269
Culler, Jonathan, 117
curricula, legislative censoring of, 16, 209–10, 212, 214

Dance Dance Revolution (Hong), 83
Dawes, Kwame, 127
Day, Meg, 190–91
Day, Thomas, 99
Deaf poets, 189–91
Death Row, 217–19, 219–20, 222, 223n3–4
Death Row poetry, 218–22, 222–23
"Declaration" (Smith), 214
The Defence of Poesy (Sidney), 41
Deleuze, Gilles, 238
Derrida, Jacques, 238, 241–42
devices. *See* poetic devices
De Villiers, Phillippa Yaa, 205–6, 208
Dewey, 237–38
DH. *See* digital humanities (DH)
Dickinson, Emily, 33–34, 112, 113, 175, 212
diction, 79–84, 84–85
digital archives, 8, 147–48, 214, 266. *See also Mina Loy: Navigating the Avant-Garde* (mina-loy.com)
digital humanities (DH), 265–66, 267, 269, 271–72, 272–73
digital pedagogy, 253, 257, 261, 265–67, 268–70, 271–72
Dinétics (Diné poetics): assessment/grading of poetry, 14–15, 19; author's overview of, 13–14, 15, 17–18; community-engaged pedagogy, as, 17–19; further reading, 21; land as a device, 14, 18; sounds, 15, 19–20; teaching of, 19–20; unsettling of pedagogy by, 15–17
Dismantling Racism Works, 173
Disney, 140
Doja, Shehzar, 43
Donne, John, 63, 65
Dos Passos, John, 183
double consciousness, 130, 180
D'où venons-nous? Que sommes-nous? Où allons-nous? (Gauguin), 28
Dove, Rita, 131, 229
dual-credit courses, 210–11, 213, 214
DuBois, W. E. B., 130, 180
Dunbar, Paul Laurence, 33, 34, 111–12, 113–14, 115
Duncan, Dennis, 246
Dutt, Toru, 56–59
The Dying Negro (Bicknell and Day), 99

Eagleton, Terry, 80
ecopoetics, 18, 246, 248
EDWI (Emerging Diné Writers Institute), 17
EFAL (English First Additional) teachers/learners, 203–7
Eliot, T. S., 35, 175, 230, 268
"Elms" (Glück), 80
Emerging Diné Writers Institute (EDWI), 17
empathetic praxis, 127–32
empathy, 4–5, 56, 127, 130, 132, 160
Empathy Exams (Jamison), 127
en dehors garde, 269–70
English First Additional (EFAL) teachers/learners, 203–7
"Enter the New Negro" (Locke), 180
erasure poetry, 213–14
Erkkila, Betsy, 88, 90
ethnopoetics, 146–47, 148–49, 150, 152, 156n1

"Eulogy for a Pair of Kicks" (Kearney), 230–31
"Explode the Poem" (Minnen), 139

feeld (Charles), 83–84
feminist design, 266
feminist pedagogy, 255–56, 265–66, 269
Filreis, Al, 115
Fitzpatrick, Kathleen, 176, 269
Florence Poetry Collective, 219–22, 223n3
Florence State Prison, 218
Fogarty, William, 4
Forms of Contention (Robbins), 71
For the Confederate Dead (Young), 168
found poetry, 5, 179, 180–82, 184–85
free verse poetry, 3, 31–37
Freire, Paulo, 204, 237
full-service sex work (FSSW), 137–38
further reading: anti-oppressive pedagogy, 8–9, 108, 193, 200; antislavery poetry, 99–101; avant garde, 36; caesura, 45; collaborative projects, 235, 242–43; confessional poetry, 123; Deaf poetics/pedagogy, 192; Death Row poetry, 222–23; De Villiers, Phillippa Yaa, 208; diction, 84–85; digital humanities (DH), 272–73; digital writing pedagogy, 261; Dinétics, 21; empathy, 132–33; found poetry, 185–86; historical poetics, 53; imitation exercises, 200; indexes, 251–52; Indigenous literature, 36–37, 154–56; learning, teaching of, 53; lyric, 59–60, 116, 123; "The New Colossus," 261; oral poetry, 154–56; slavery, 165; sonnets, 76–77; stanzas (rooms), 69–70; SWer poetry, 142; versiprose, 59–60; "We Real Cool," 91; Wheatley Peters, Phillis, 172; white supremacy culture, 177–78, 214–15
Fussell, Paul, 41
"The Future of Poetry Studies" (Wang), 79

Gan, Wanyu, 239–40
Gauguin, Paul, 28
Gelmi, Caroline, 4
generous thinking, 269–70
Gennrich, Toni, 5–6
Gen Z, 113–14
Gerwitz, Julian, 190, 192
Gill-Peterson, Jules, 32
Glenn, Jeremy, 210
The Gloria Anzaldúa Reader, 104
Glück, Louise, 80, 119, 120
Goldberg, Jess, 5
Gosson, Rochel, 268
grading/assessment of poetry, 14–15, 18–19, 128, 130, 204
Graff, Gerald, 195
Greene, Roland, 188, 190
Gregory, Jamie, 210
Gregson v. Gilbert, 157–58, 164
Griffis, Rachel B., 5
griots, 111, 114–15
group work. *See* collaborative projects; team-teaching
Guattari, Felix, 238

Hadi-Tabassum, Samina, 184
Harjo, Joy, 233
Harlem Renaissance poets, 72, 180, 181, 183
Hartman, Saidiya, 159, 160
Hayes, Terrance, 75–76, 233
Hayot, Eric, 117
Henderson, Alice Corbin, 32
Hirsch, Edward, 41
historical poetics, 4, 47, 52, 53, 112

Hmong people, 213–14
Hobbs, Katie, 218
Hobsbaum, Philip, 41
"Homage to Phillis Wheatley" (Young), 168, 169, 170
Hong, Cathy Park, 83
Hood, Jamie, 137
hooks, bell, 174, 176, 209, 255
Hughes, Langston, 27, 34
Huizar, Leah, 4

I. See lyric I
I Can't Talk About Trees Without the Blood (Clark), 168
"If I were a pony" (boarding school student), 17
"If We Must Die" (McKay), 115
"Ignorance" (Collins), 24
imitation, 170, 174–75, 195–200
"I'm Nobody! Who Are You?" (Dickinson), 112, 113
imperialism, 24, 36, 41–42, 64–65, 66, 95–96, 99
"In Bondage" (McKay), 74
Index, A History of the (Duncan), 246
indexes, 245–51
Indigenous cultures: erasure of, 3; language, use of, 15; sounds, 15, 19–20
Indigenous Nations Poets (In-Na-Po), 17
Indigenous pedagogy, 13, 15. See also Dinétics (Diné poetics)
Indigenous poets, 14, 16–17, 32, 34–36, 229–30
Indigenous sound studies, 15
In Memoriam A.H.H. (Tennyson), 56–57, 59
In-Na-Po (Indigenous Nations Poets), 17
"In the Mecca" (Brooks), 241

introductory poetry courses, 47–52, 67, 159
"Invocation" (McKay), 73
"Is Hip Hop Poetry?" (Pinsky), 24

Jack, Jesse, 268
Jackson, Virginia, 112, 117
Jamieson, John, 99
Jamison, Leslie, 127, 130
Jeffers, Fanonne, 167, 172n1
Just Us (Rankine), 132

Kalish, Jon, 147
Kappeler, Erin, 3, 48
Karatani, Kojin, 64
Kaul, Suvir, 95
Kearney, Douglas, 25, 230–31, 233
Keats, John, 44, 74, 75–76
Kendi, Ibram X., 130–31
King, Martin Luther, 81
Kinnahan, Linda, 6, 268
Kinsella, John, 29n1
"kitchenette building" (Brooks), 255, 257
Kolb, Rachel, 189–90, 192

land as a device, 14, 18
Lavery, Daniel, 175
Lazarus, Emma, 253, 254, 255, 257, 260, 261
legislation, curriculum-censoring, 16, 209–10, 212, 214
Lennard, John, 41
Leong, Michael, 3, 181
LeRud, Lizzy, 5
"Let Us" (Doja), 43
Levin, Janina, 128
Levine, Caroline, 215
Lewis, Robin Coste, 25–26, 27, 28–29
LGBTQIA+ community, 79, 136, 209, 210, 211, 214
Life on Mars (Smith), 131

listening, 139, 149–52, 156n1
literary imperialism, 24
"The Little Mermaid" (Andersen), 140
Lockard, Joe, 6
Locke, Alain, 180
logic of abstraction, 24
"The Love Song of J. Alfred Prufrock" (Eliot), 175–76
Lowell, Robert, 119
Loy, Mina, 183, 265, 266–67, 267–70
lyric: antislavery poetry to teach, 96–99; assumptions of, challenging, 4; author's overview of, 95, 103–4; critics and, 117; griots, 111, 114–15; imperialism and, 95–96; little drama of, 111, 112–13; lyric *I*, 105–6, 107, 117–22; New Lyric Studies, 7; reading aloud, 190–91; subjectivity, and, 104, 105, 107, 117–20, 122, 190; *you*, 119, 120, 121
lyric *I*, 105–6, 107, 117–22
lyricization, 112, 117

Martin, Trayvon, 131
Marvell, Andrew, 175–76
McDougall, James, 6
McGinn, Emily, 269
McKay, Claude, 34, 72–75, 76, 115
memorization, 58, 59, 60
Meter, Rhythm, and Verse Form (Hobsbaum), 41
Methuselah sentences, 223n4
Milton, John, 44
Mina Loy: Navigating the Avant-Garde (mina-loy.com), 265, 267–70, 270–72
Minnen, Jennifer, 139
modernism: rupture, narrative of, 31, 33–34; teaching of, 179–85; unsettling of, 34–36

Moe, Lukas, 4
Mohawk, John, 174, 177
Monroe, Harriet, 32
More, Hannah, 99
Moretti, Franco, 245
Morris, Tracie, 25
Moten, Fred, 44
"Mother | Line" (Saxena), 43
Muench, Simone, 234
myths of teaching poetry, 203–5, 207–8

Naidoo, Sooriagandhi, 5–6
Nance, Sarah, 5
Native American and Indigenous Studies (NAIS), 34, 36
Native American poets, 32, 34–36
Navajo people, 13, 17–18, 20. *See also* Dinétics (Diné poetics)
"The Negro's Complaint" (Cowper), 97–98
"Negro Spiritual" (McKay), 73
"The New Colossus" (Lazarus), 253, 254, 255, 257, 260, 261
New Criticism: author's overview of, 7; craft and, 26; creativity, and, 195–96; lyric, 111; lyric *I*, 119–20, 121–22; privilege, and, 24; speaker, on the, 188; timeliness of pedagogy, 2–3
New Lyric Studies, 7. *See also* lyric
new mestiza, 4, 104–5
Nezhukumatathil, Aimee, 120–21
Nikolis, Anastasia, 4
Norton Anthology of American Literature, 33, 34
Norton Introduction to Literature, 48, 51
novels, poems in. *See* versiprose

O'Donohue, John, 18
Okun, Tema, 173, 174

"On being brought from Africa to America" (Wheatley Peters), 97, 167, 169, 170, 171
"On First Looking into Chapman's Homer" (Keats), 44
"On Listening to Your Teacher Take Attendance" (Nezhukumatathil), 120–21
"On the Wounds of Our Crucified Lord" (Crashaw), 189
oral poetry: anti-racist pedagogy, 145–46; author's overview of, 145; listening, 149–52, 156n1; teaching of, 146, 147–49, 149–52, 152–54
order, desire for, 159, 161
Oxford Dictionary of Literary Terms, 103

pairing of poems, 35–36, 80, 112–13, 122, 167–72, 184, 212
Palgrave, Frances Turner, 58
Paradise Lost (Milton), 44
The Path on the Rainbow, 32–33
pedagogies: anti-colonial pedagogy, 3, 16, 20, 154; author's overview of, 15; community-engaged pedagogy, 17–19; feminist pedagogy, 255–56, 265–66, 269; Indigenous pedagogy, 13, 15. *See also* anti-oppressive pedagogy; anti-racist pedagogy; digital pedagogy; unsettling the curriculum
peer reviews, 266, 269, 270–71
performance of poetry, 57–58, 145, 146, 149–50, 163, 182, 188–89, 192
Philip, M. NourbeSe, 5, 157–59, 161, 162, 163–64
Phiri, Eunice, 5–6, 204
Pinsky, Robert, 24, 25
Pizzetta, Candis, 5
"Plastic Beauty Floats through Frustrated Days" (Liulu), 240

plasticity, 32
Plath, Sylvia, 119
Plato, 127
Playlist for the Apocalypse (Dove), 131
"The Poem as a Field of Action" (Williams), 184
Poems, Poets, Poetry (Vendler), 103
Poems on the Slave Trade (Southey), 97–98
Poems on Various Subjects (Wheatley Peters), 97, 167
Poem Talk, 115
poetic abecedary, 239–42
poetic devices: Dinétics, 13, 14, 18, 19; land as, 14, 18; lyric subject, 120, 122; myths of, 205; unsettling of, 98–99
poetic diction, 79–84
Poetic Meter and Poetic Form (Fussell), 41
poetry: antislavery poetry, 96–99, 99–101; Death Row poetry, 218–22, 222–23; empathetic praxis, as, 127–32; enjoyment, reading for, 173–77; erasure poetry, 213–14; found poetry, 5, 179, 180–82, 184–85; free verse poetry, 3, 31–37; grading/assessment of, 14–15, 18–19, 128, 130, 204; myths of teaching, 203–5, 207–8; order, desire for, 159, 161; peer reviews, 266, 269, 270–71; reading aloud, 187–92; reviews of, 227–35; SWer poetry, 135–41; transcriptions of oral, 150–52; translations, 20, 83, 153–54, 175, 191. *See also* Dinétics (Diné poetics); lyric; oral poetry; pairing of poems; performance of poetry; sonnets; teaching poetry; unsettling the curriculum
The Poetry Handbook (Lennard), 41

poetry readings. *See* oral poetry; reading aloud
poetry reviews, 227–35
poets: Deaf poets, 189–91; definitions of, 188; Harlem Renaissance poets, 72, 180, 181, 183; white poets, 32, 34. *See also* black poets; Indigenous poets; poetry; poets of color
poets of color: double consciousness, 130, 180; empathetic praxis, 131–32; Harlem Renaissance poets, 72, 180, 181, 183; lyric performance, 111–12, 113, 114, 115; paired texts of, teaching poetry with, 168–71; reviews of, 229–30; sonnets, and, 71–76, 212; teaching poems by, 26, 27
Pope, Alexander, 246
Porn Carnival (White), 139
post-craft, 3, 23–24, 29n1
"Praises of Bantu Kings," 153
Prendergast, Monica, 182
The Princess (Tennyson), 56
Princeton Encyclopedia of Poetry and Poetics, 188
Prins, Yopie, 117
prisons. *See* Death Row; Death Row poetry
privileging, 24, 42, 65, 66, 107, 152, 189, 233
Prose, Francine, 232

Quick, Catherine, 148

racialization, 31–32, 33, 36
Rader, Dean, 6, 227–28, 229–32, 233–34, 235
Rankine, Claudia, 119, 120, 121, 132, 247
reading aloud, 187–92
readings. *See* further reading; supplemental readings

recitation, 58, 59, 60
Reeves, Tate, 210
reviews, 227–35. *See also* peer reviews
Reyes, Barbara Jane, 63, 65
Rhys, Jean, 183
Riding, Laura, 26–27
Rikard, Andrew, 267–68
"Riot" (Brooks), 81
Robbins, Hollis, 71–72
Roberson, Ed, 131
Robinson, Dylan, 148
Romantics, 60, 72–73, 74, 188
rooms, 63–67, 67–69
Rosenbaum, Susan, 6, 268
Rothenberg, Jerome, 146, 147
Rukeyser, Muriel, 27
Ryan, James, 196

Saʼąh Naagháí Bikʼeh Hózhó (SNBH), 19, 20
Salesses, Matthew, 23–24
Salt Marsh (Biggers), 115
"Samson" (McKay), 73
Saussure, Ferdinand de, 45
Saxena, Ankita, 43
scaffolding, 159, 241, 255–56, 256–57, 258, 267
Schor, Esther, 253, 257, 261
Schramm, Wilbur, 26
Schuller, Kyla, 32
self-assessments, 14, 19
"Self Portrait as Scallop" (Nezhukumatathil), 120–21
self-reflection, 19, 206–8
settler colonialism, 16, 36
Sexton, Anne, 119
sex workers, 135–38, 140–41, 142n1
Sharpe, Christina, 159
Sherwood, Kenneth, 5
Sho (Kearney), 230
Sidney, Philip, 41, 42, 44
Skeets, Jake, 3, 13–20

"Skinhead" (Smith), 131
slavery, 5, 74, 96–99, 157–59, 167
Slavery (More), 99
Smith, Gary, 89
Smith, Patricia, 131
Smith, Tracy K., 131, 214, 255, 257
SNBH (Saʼąh Naagháí Bikʼeh Hózhó), 19, 20
sonnets, 65, 67–69, 71–76, 76–77, 97–98, 196–98, 234, 255
The Sorrows of Slavery (Jamieson), 99
sounds: centering of, 190–91; hierarchies of, 19; Indigenous sounds, 15, 19–20; thoughts and, 45
The Sounds of Poetry (Pinsky), 25
sound studies, 15
South Africa, 203–4
South African Poetry Project (ZAPP), 203–8
Southey, Robert, 97–98
Spaide, Christopher, 87, 88
Sperry, Eileen, 5
Spillers, Hortense, 88
spoken word. *See* oral poetry
stanzas, 64–67, 67–69, 98, 205
Stecher Woodward, Gabrielle, 4
Stephens, Ronnie, 6
Stewart, Susan, 188
Stommel, Jesse, 18–19
Stout, Cathryn, 210
strophes, 65, 66–67
students of color, 3, 118, 121, 180–81, 190
Sturm, Nick, 6
subjectivity, 104, 105, 107, 117–20, 122, 190
Sudjic, Olivia, 70
Sullivan, James D., 88
supplemental readings, 211–12, 213
["surely i am able to write poems"] (Clifton), 80–81
Suture (Muench and Rader), 234

SWer poetry, 135–41

Taboada, Javier, 147
talisman poems, 69–70
teaching habitus, 204
teaching poetry: antislavery poetry, 96–99; caesura, 39–45, 66; Death Row poetry, 218–22; diction, 79–84; digital archives, 266–67, 267–70, 270–72; dual-credit courses, 210–14; empathetic praxis, 127–32; enjoyment, reading for, 173–77; ethnopoetics, 147–49, 149–52, 152–54; found poetry, 179, 180–82, 184–85; free verse poetry, 31–37; imitation poems, 170, 174–75, 195–200; indexing poetry, 245–51; introductory courses, 47–52, 67; lyric, 96–99, 104–7, 111–16; lyric *I*, 117–22; modernism, 179–85; myths of, debunking, 203–8; pairing of poems, 167–72; poetry books, collaborative, 238–42; reviews, poetry, 227–35; scaffolding, 159, 241, 255–56, 256–57, 258, 267; sonnets, 73–76, 234; stanzas (rooms), 63–67, 67–69; supplemental readings, 211–12, 213; SWer poetry, 135–41; versiprose, 55–59; voices/reading aloud, 187–92. *See also* anti-racist pedagogy; collaborative projects; Dinétics (Diné poetics); team-teaching; unsettling the curriculum
Teaching to Transgress, 174
team-teaching, 48–52, 135, 136–41
Tedlock, Dennis, 146, 149
Tennyson, Alfred, 56–58, 188
Texts from Jane Eyre (Lavery), 175
The Waste Land (Eliot), 35, 36, 268
"This is Just to Say" (Vick), 174–75
Thomas, Lorenzo, 111, 114–15

"Three Ripples in the Tuckaseigee River" (Williams), 241
"To His Coy Mistress" (Marvell), 175–76
Tongues of their Mothers (Xaba), 205
toolbox courses. *See* introductory poetry courses
Too-qua-stee, 35–36
traditional teaching frameworks, rethinking of, 3, 4
transcriptions, 150–52
translations, 20, 83, 153–54, 175, 191
Trethewey, Natasha, 71–72
Troyan, Cassandra, 137, 140–41
Tucker, Herbert, 25
"Two Roads," 227, 233

Understanding Poetry (Brooks and Warren), 49, 113
ungrading, 18–19, 20
"The United States Welcomes You" (Smith), 255, 257
unsettling the curriculum: curriculum-censoring legislation, 16, 209–10, 212, 214; Dinétics (Diné poetics), 15–17; ethnopoetics, 147–48, 152; free verse poetry, 33–36; poetic devices, 98–99; supplemental readings, 211–12, 213; white supremacy, 173–74, 177

Vander Zee, Anton, 4
Vang, Mai Der, 213–14
Vendler, Helen, 80, 88, 103, 113, 146, 229
versiprose, 55–59, 59–60
Vick, 174
voices: of incarcerated writers, 221; inclusion of, intentional, 17, 18; of poems, 25; privileging of, 24; reading aloud, 187–92; of reviewers, 228

"Voyage of the Sable Venus" (Lewis), 25–26, 27, 28–29
Voyage of the Sable Venus and Other Poems (Lewis), 25

Wang, Dorothy, 79
Warner, Marina, 67
Warner, Michael, 24
Warren, Robert Penn, 49, 113
Weatley Peters, Phillis, 5, 96–97, 167, 168–71, 172n1
"We Real Cool" (Brooks), 4, 87–91, 175
Werner, Craig Hansen, 88
Westbrook, Steve, 196
"We Wear the Mask" (Dunbar), 111–12, 113
White, Rachel Rabbit, 139–41
"The White House" (McKay), 73–74
White Mainstream English (WME), 212–13, 215
whiteness: of free verse poetry, 31, 32–33; of student populations, 117–18
white poets, 32, 34
white supremacy, 5, 48, 52, 72, 173–74, 177, 210, 232
Whitman, Walt, 33–34, 159, 212
Wilburn, Thomas, 210
Williams, Jonathan, 241
Williams, William Carlos, 174–75, 183, 184
Willison, Judith, 185
WME (White Mainstream English), 212–13, 215
women of color, 15–16, 26
Wood, Joseph, 217
word choices, 4, 79–80, 83, 84
Writers & Books, 118
Writing and Difference (Derrida), 241–42

Xaba, Makhosazana, 205

Yarbrough, Wynn, 88
Yellow Rain (Vang), 213
Yergeau, M. Remi, 259
Yeung, Heather, 3, 4
you, 119, 120, 121

Young, Kevin, 168, 169, 170

"Zacuanpapalotls" (Cárdenas), 106
ZAPP *(South African Poetry Project),* 203–8
Zong! (Philip), 157, 158–60, 161–64
Zong Massacre, 157, 159, 161

www.ingramcontent.com/pod-product-compliance
Lightning Source LLC
Chambersburg PA
CBHW021956220426
43663CB00007B/840